The fantasy fiction formula

Deborah Chester

Manchester University Press

Published by Manchester University Press
Altrincham Street, Manchester M1 7JA, UK
www.manchesteruniversitypress.co.uk

British Library Cataloguing-in-Publication Data is available

ISBN 978 1 7849 9288 0 hardback
ISBN 978 0 7190 9706 5 paperback

First published 2016

Typeset by Carnegie Book Production, Lancaster

The fantasy fiction formula

Contents

Foreword by Jim Butcher

When I was twenty-five years old, I knew everything about writing.

Oh, I was taking Professional Writing courses from Debbie Chester at OU at that time, and she kept talking about things I'd never encountered before, but since I already had a Bachelor's Degree in English Literature, with an emphasis in Creative Writing, I clearly didn't need any of what she was trying to teach me. After all, I had been reading fantasy all my life, and had a degree and everything.

Debbie had merely published forty novels.

Yet she persisted in trying to teach me her nonsense. And so I determined that I would prove to her, irrefutably, that she was flat wrong. My chosen method for doing so was ingenious in its simplicity—I planned to do absolutely everything that Debbie told me to do.

I would fill out her worksheets. I would build structured outlines. I would create my characters with her wooden caricature-building methods, utilize all her little tags and traits, break my stories into scenes and sequels, and even use her stupidly predictable story climax structure.

So I did it. I did everything Debbie told me to do.

And I wrote *Storm front,* the first book of the *New York Times* #1 Best-Selling Dresden Files.

Which, you know, showed her.

I remember being that kid in her class. I remember how many times I mentally rolled my eyes at concepts she was trying to teach me. And I spent two years doing everything

I possibly could to sabotage my own chances of success as a writer while ignoring her sound, professional, practical advice.

So, aspiring writer, let me do you the favor I wish someone had done me. Let me tell you what you need to hear.

Shut up and do what Debbie tells you to do.

Let me repeat that, in all capital letters, so you'll know how serious I am.

SHUT UP AND DO WHAT DEBBIE TELLS YOU TO DO.

Who am I to tell you that?

I'm the guy who took the principles of story structure which she taught me and built a career on them. As I type this, I have published twenty-four novels, the last five of them #1 *New York Times* best-sellers. The highest-paid actor in Hollywood narrates the audiobooks. The Dresden Files has been made into a television series and an award-winning roleplaying game. My books have been translated into a score of languages, and there are copies of my work on every continent, including Antarctica. The graphic novel adaptations of the series have been nominated for a Hugo Award.

And to this day, I still occasionally refer to my notes, taken in her classroom at the University of Oklahoma, back when I knew everything.

Listen carefully to what Debbie has to say about telling stories, aspiring writer.

She knows exactly what she's talking about.

Author preface

So you want to write fantasy, and guide readers to places where wishes matter more than facts. Does that mean your imagination is teeming with exotic places, heroic people, strange creatures, and the mysterious forces of magic? Have you been building a wondrous, unique, and special world in your imagination? Has the day now come to write a novel set in that world? Are you thinking large scope, with a plot that spans several volumes and a cast of hundreds?

Perhaps you love fantasy but you don't feel ready as yet to tackle a novel and would rather focus on short stories as you hone your craft. Tackling a few thousand words at a time—instead of a thousand pages—is a very sensible way to start your writing apprenticeship. Although this book will be focusing primarily on novel writing, short story writers will find the chapters on plotting, viewpoint, character design, scene and sequel construction, and climax helpful as well.

How do you begin your urban fantasy or epic quest? What do you do first? How do you organize your ideas, develop a plot, create characters that last from start to finish without crumbling, and move the story all the way to its conclusion? What's involved in writing a rollicking good story, one that others will enjoy reading?

My training and experience as a novelist—with over forty books published—has taught me answers to such questions. I began writing fiction when very young, and I stubbornly struggled with knotty plot dilemmas, characters that didn't always say or do what I wanted, and stories that hit dead ends, until I finally found the Professional Writing program at the University of Oklahoma and learned not only what writing craft is but how to trust it.

As a novelist, I've experienced the sublime pleasure of writing a story where everything goes well. I've suffered through the misery of stories where nothing seems to work. I've written my heart and guts into some of my novels, and I've written books during personal situations so distracting that only my formal training in the writing craft kept me on course. I know what it's like to ache to put my characters onto the page. I understand the frustration of being stuck and baffled, with no idea of how to fix the problem in front of me. And I am grateful for having done the time, and sweated through the drills and exercises, and paid my dues in order to become published.

Writing is not easy. It takes thought, commitment, and hard work to learn what you're doing. And after your first publication—or your twentieth—those same qualities remain necessary in putting together a short story or a novel. Each new plot and set of characters brings some unique challenge—and that's one reason I continue to find writing exciting and fun, year after year.

In my teaching career, I've coached numerous students who were adept at pouring their creative, imaginative abilities into world-building, yet enrolled in my classes with only the vaguest notion of how to plot, write cohesive scenes, or design dimensional characters. I firmly believe that there should not be a veil of mystery draped over the creation of viable stories.

Therefore, this book is all about my parting the veil and explaining to you what is often a simple—although not always easy—process in crafting fantasy fiction.

The rules, writing principles, formulas, tips, and suggestions that I've included are based on an archetypal pattern of story that's existed in Western civilization since antiquity. I call it elemental story design, and its appeal has touched readers across time and generations. Its foundations draw from myths, legends, folklore, definitions of good and evil, and both the shortcomings of human nature and its capacity for heroism.

Fantasy is the mystic of fiction. It requires readers to believe in magic and the supernatural, to accept the unexplainable as a normal part of the setting. And although fantasy expects readers to believe these things "just because" and offers no rational basis for them, fantasy is not illogical.

All fantasy stories—whether ranging from clock punk to Jasper Fforde's Thursday Next novels to Neil Gaiman's yarns—operate within parameters set by their authors. And although those boundaries may be fantastical, or possibly bizarre, they are the rules of that story world. Fantasy itself is an enormous, elastic genre that carries its share of beloved traditions, stereotypes, and dear old writing masters. Yet it's adaptive enough to span what's hip and edgy, deconstructed fairy tales, Goth, punk, and alternate history. New writers are shaking up old concepts all the time, keeping fantasy alive and fresh.

In exchange for their willingness to "believe," readers expect fantasy writers to lead them to wondrous places never imagined before. Willing to disconnect from rationality in order to step onto train platform nine and three-quarters, they seek to explore concepts that have no basis in reality as the actual world knows it. They anticipate visiting places where wondrous things can happen with the wave of a wand or the chanting of a spell.

Despite the many subgenres within fantasy, I separate it into two large, basic divisions: urban fantasy and traditional fantasy. Not because of their settings, but because of their mindset.

Urban fantasy began as a variant of dark fantasy and horror, and since the 1990s it has become the dominant preference of modern readers. It blends the supernatural with thriller or mystery plots served up in *film noir* atmosphere. It stems from a modern, contemporary mindset. Although Good remains distinct from Evil, and Light separate from Dark, writers tend to shade those distinctions in the best *noir* tradition.

Readers—eager to escape mundane jobs and over-scheduled, high-pressured lifestyles—walk the edge in the pages of urban fantasy. They experience danger and the risk of death safely at home while vicariously seducing sexy vampires, outwitting evil fairies, and generally kicking supernatural butt. No matter how intense the story grows, in the end, predators and monsters will not prevail against the protagonist.

Traditional fantasy centers on power/political struggles or straightforward action-adventure. It operates from a medieval or historical mindset, and its roots stretch all the way back to the dawn of storytelling, to Homer and earlier, to the origin of myth itself. Traditional fantasy's primary appeal lies in the transformation of the protagonist from ordinary to heroic.

An apparently ordinary protagonist leaves home, or finds a large blue dragon's egg in the forest, or is apprenticed to a mysterious man called the Spook, and in consequence becomes a larger-than-life hero, able to meet challenges and survive danger. The evolution of the character—whether through training or dangerous experiences—prepares him or her for the big showdown against some force of evil at the end.

Readers of traditional fantasy vicariously experience the chance to leave home for exciting adventure, to be trained in heroic combat and/or in magical powers, to become larger than life, to grow from ordinary into someone with an extraordinary Destiny.

Whether you prefer dragons, vampires, or elves that drive tanks, there's room in all types of fantasy for everyone and everything both imaginable and unimaginable.

For the duration of this book, you and I are going to be a collaborative team. Your job is to bring the talent and story premise. Mine is to supply the nuts and bolts—or magic formula, if you will—of how stories are built.

Although some examples have been invented to illustrate points of technique, many are excerpts drawn from my own published fiction under my real name and various pseudonyms such as Jay D. Blakeney, Sean Dalton, and C. Aubrey Hall.

The latter have been selected only because they demonstrate whatever technique I'm discussing. When other authors or novels are mentioned or recommended, they have been chosen in particular because I feel they illustrate story design clearly enough for you to observe and study. Also, I will be referring to film examples at times—not because I'm veering into screenplay writing but because I feel the visual imagery of movies can spark a prose writer's imagination.

I've organized *The fantasy fiction formula* to assist both beginners and intermediate writers. If you're in the former camp, I suggest that you read the chapters in order from start to finish. I've arranged them in the way I personally approach a book's design—from the basic conception of an idea, to the development of a plot outline, to the writing itself through beginning, middle, and ending. If you're in the latter group of writers, somewhat experienced in creating fiction, then by all means feel free to read the chapters in any order that appeals to you.

Now, let's get started.

1

Formulating a story plan

Although we creative types sometimes dream of writing unfettered by restrictions or boundaries as Lady Muse pours inspiration through us, the reality is quite different. Any writer serious about working steadily in the fiction arena sooner or later realizes that relying on dreams and inspiration alone won't get the job done. Therefore, when writing fiction you need a plan. That plan should contain—among other things—specifics about your story premise, its intended length, how it will start and where it will end. Otherwise, you'll remain a lost sojourner, unlikely to make much progress with your story skills.

Structural form

Just how long is a novel supposed to be anyway? Generally, books run from about 60,000 words to 100,000 words. However, authors such as George R. R. Martin or Robert Jordan produce tomes that run as long as 150,000–200,000 words.

Even if you're an eager Martin or Jordan fan, please remember that the father of epic fantasy—J. R. R. Tolkien—did not write excessively long, sprawling, hefty, over-populated books, and unproven beginners who have not yet published their first novel are advised to keep their manuscripts below 100,000 words.

Does this edict seem arbitrary and unfair? Does the very thought of it make you howl with frustration, especially since you're possibly planning at least twenty-eight massive volumes for your epic? No matter how vast and ambitious your premise is, authors these days must abide within the realities of publishing economies—meaning the costs of paper, ink, and shipping. Simply put, manuscript lengths beyond 100,000 words cost more to produce. Higher costs make publishers less likely to gamble on completely unknown authors.

Of course, there are always exceptions, such as Hugh Howey's *Wool* (2011). If your first book is a 250,000-word masterpiece, if you publish it yourself digitally, and if it proves to be a mega-hit, publishers will probably clamor for you.

Otherwise, as long as you intend to stay within the traditional arena of paper publishing, draw a deep breath and accept whatever length restrictions your desired publisher sets. If you plan to write urban fantasy, aim for an approximate manuscript length of 70,000–85,000 words. If you want to write traditional high fantasy featuring battles of Good versus Evil, then stay under 95,000 words. Once you've broken in and once you're famous, then you can—perhaps—nudge your manuscripts above the 100,000-word barrier.

Forcing yourself to write shorter means your plot will be lean and tight. That's good! Packing it with fiction muscle means fewer flabby, rambling passages that don't do much for your story.

As a general reference, here are additional fictional forms and lengths:

- Novellas: roughly 35,000–50,000 words.
- Novelettes: 15,000–30,000 words.
- Short stories: 2,000–10,000 words.
- Short shorts: 1,500 words or less.

If you're mathematically alert, you will notice there are gaps between these categories. That's because these lengths aren't precise. (Neither are stories written strictly by arbitrary rules, no matter how many formulas and principles we have.)

A story is built with a beginning, middle, and an ending. (If you choose to adopt the screenwriter's terminology for any form longer than a short story, you may refer to these three parts as act one, act two, and act three.)

Whatever lingo you use, each of these three components contains specialized elements necessary to the delivery of a good story. These elements include: grabbing reader interest; sustaining reader interest; steadily increasing tension and suspense regarding the outcome; guiding readers through an emotional catharsis; providing a satisfying resolution of events; answering the story question; and delivering poetic justice.

They are designed to capture readers, and move them from start to finish while keeping them enthralled.

A tall order? Yes. But it's a manageable one. I will be explaining them individually to help you understand the writing principles that support each of them.

How long should the beginning be? That depends on the scope and complexity of your plot, but a loose guide is approximately one to three chapters of a short novel (up to five chapters in a really long book) and maybe the first four or five pages of a short story.

The climax, by the way, can take up roughly the same number of pages. Everything else falls in the middle section.

Does this mean the middle could be longer than the beginning and ending combined?

Yes, indeed.

Who said these three structural parts must be of equal length? Certainly they're not of equal intensity. The middle of a book, by the way, is the toughest part to write. It's where an unwary writer can drown in a swamp or wander forevermore within a maze of muddle, never to emerge. However, I'll deal with how to navigate such pitfalls safely later on.

Beginning tasks

One of the worst mistakes I see among inexperienced fantasy writers is the desire to teach their readers. This impulse manifests as the dreaded fifty-page explanation, background summary, and info-dump opening whereby said writer informs his readers of his world's terrain, climate, history for the past nine thousand years, mythology, and magic system.

Snore.

"But my readers *must* know all of this at the start," Wally Writer wails. "Otherwise, they won't understand what's going on when my characters are attacked by the leaping swamp-lizards of Malfrasia."

I assure you that if you start your book with a lecture, no reader will ever reach page seventy-two, when your protagonist finally shows up to fend off the swamp-lizards.

Granted, the fantasy genre requires a fantastical world—one generally very strange and bizarre to readers. Because of this, more description and information is needed for this genre (and its sister, science fiction) than any other type of fiction. But *more* does not equate to *a lot*.

Write the history if you must. Write the explanation. Describe the mythology and magic in loving detail. Get that all keyed into your computer.

Then set that file aside and don't insert it into your manuscript.

You do need to know it. You should work it out ahead of time so that you understand it thoroughly. That knowledge will help you write your action scenes with clarity, specific detail, and authority. But your needs as a writer are not the same as what readers require to follow your plot.

When you succumb to the temptation to fill your opening with explanation, what you're really communicating is a lack of confidence in your story. You're betraying to your readers that you haven't fully as yet worked out this information for yourself. Worst of all, you're signaling that you don't believe your readers are intelligent enough to piece together a general idea of the situation from a couple of hints, an emotional reaction, and a little dialogue.

Instead of lecturing, get your protagonist into trouble in the opening sentence, and keep her there. We'll worry about the evolutionary origin of the swamp-lizards later, after Princess Shequ has fought them, been wounded by them, seen her royal bodyguard slain by them, and been stranded alone in the wilderness hundreds of leagues from her father's castle.

Exciting opening action should result in bigger trouble for the protagonist, so why bog things down with a rambling back story? Use an ambush instead to hook readers. Then they will want to see what Princess Shequ does next. Can she make it out of the wilderness and find help before she dies of the venom festering in her wound?

As you hook readers—drawing them in via exciting action and plenty of trouble for your characters—you will make them curious to learn more. Small snippets of background can be woven in from time to time —not too much, mind! Use just a little, here and there. A sentence or two of explanation is fine. At first, raise questions in a reader's mind and pique his curiosity. Think of the film *E.T. the Extra-Terrestrial* (1982) and how the boy Elliot entices the alien from the dog house by placing pieces of candy on the ground. He spaces each one so that E.T. has to venture from hiding in order to pick them up.

In a similar way, lure your readers into wanting to know the history or the background. Promise to explain later. Don't bludgeon your audience at the start with what they're not yet interested in receiving.

You cannot create sympathy for your characters by explaining things. Instead, strive to establish a sympathetic bond between protagonist and reader. You accomplish this by showing your character in trouble and depicting in action or dialogue how she's coping with it.

It's not until readers care about or sympathize with your characters that they'll want to know more. When the excitement of the novel's beginning is over, and readers are well and truly hooked, then—out there in the middle of the plot, when the pacing permits a brief lull in the story action—you can share a few paragraphs of what you've invented.

Returning to my example ... after the opening ambush, Princess Shequ totters out of the wilderness—starving, in rags, and delirious—and finally collapses at a castle moat. However, she's too feverish to realize that she's mistakenly arrived at the stronghold of her father's worst enemy. While she tosses and turns in the care of the local crone, you can now—at long last—insert a page of back story explaining why her father is such bitter enemies with her host.

Okay, I've made my point and hammered it home. So now, are you thinking ...

If I don't *open my book with a plodding treatise on the origins of the Wobbly Wizards of Viddle Valley and how they prophesied the coming of a young hero who would be born able to converse with animals and river spirits, and who would be raised on a farm by his dullard uncle who thought his nephew was weird, and how said young hero would then leave the farm and seek his Destiny,* what am I to use instead?

Your story's opening should contain several elements, including a hook in the first sentence; introduction of the protagonist and story goal; introduction of the central story question; a clearly established viewpoint; a set up of the story situation as it's happening right now in story time; the location and time of day; introduction of an immediate antagonist; scene action and conflict; hints planted for later developments; numerous small hooks to grab reader curiosity and sustain reader involvement; and the first complications.

Whew! That's a lot to do, isn't it?

As you consider these tasks and responsibilities, you may find them overwhelming. Don't let the number of them intimidate you. They will fit within the first thirty or so pages of your book just fine. An experienced novelist can combine maybe a third or more of these elements within a few paragraphs.

Everything else then happens in scene structure and character introduction during chapters one, two, and three.

The first sentence is possibly the most important one you'll write in the entire manuscript. Those twenty-five words or less often determine whether a reader will buy your story or toss it back on the store shelf.

Today's commercial fiction market—of any genre—is tough and crowded. Readers have plenty of other leisure/entertainment options at their fingertips besides reading. Your story will be competing with everything from movies, television, gaming, Internet shopping, and hanging out with friends, to books by established, big-name authors.

This is not to discourage you or to make you feel as though you'll never succeed, but to introduce you to the challenge of being sharp, fast off the mark, and inventive.

Fantasy fans possess more patience than many readers, but even they want compelling involvement immediately.

Let's look at some invented examples of opening lines:

1: Robard the assassin lurked in the shadows, ready to climb the castle wall as soon as the sentry on the battlements turned his back. That's when someone up there dropped a screaming girl into the moat.

2: It seemed like just another ordinary trip to the grocery store when I turned down the cat food aisle and came face-to-face with a vampire sucking the shelf stocker's throat.

3: Surrounded by his snarling pack of werewolves, the Wolf King bared his teeth at me. One signal from him, and I would be lunch.

Do you see how each of these openings is short, designed to grab reader curiosity, and indicates trouble for the viewpoint character? Readers may not know the character well enough yet to care much, but curiosity will compel them to read the next paragraph, and the next, until they turn the page.

Different types of hook

	Type of hook	Explanation	Where used
#1	Raising a question	This serves to provoke reader curiosity.	Story opening or any scene or chapter opening.
#2	Introducing a vivid character	A compelling or extreme character can entice readers forward. Just don't add too many characters at the same time to avoid reader confusion.	Story opening or any chapter opening. Can launch a new scene.
#3	Using unpredictability	The unexpected is always interesting.	Story opening or the start of any scene.
#4	Changing the existing circumstances	Change upsets and threatens whatever status quo is familiar to your characters. Even positive change can cause stress, which is terrific for story purposes.	Story opening, possibly the type of hook used most frequently in this application.
#5	Creating immediate danger	Putting the protagonist in trouble and establishing worry, threat, or physical risk is very effective. A short prologue showing the villain executing a bad deed will work well.	Story or chapter opening. Also effective when changing viewpoint. Danger makes a strong cliffhanger for ending scenes or chapters.
#6	Utilizing a sinister atmosphere	An ominous setting or mood can imply threat or danger about to happen.	Story opening. Chapter opening or ending.
#7	Leaping into action	The old tactic of in media res remains effective. It brings excitement and movement to the story.	Story opening. Chapter opening or ending. Scene opening.

If you can entice readers to turn to page two and keep going, then you're on your way.

Types of hooks

A variety of hooks exist, and while they can be used as plot twists and chapter endings, they're also useful for story openings. The chart opposite lists some of the most useful hooks.

Often novelists combine more than one hook together to achieve a unique effect.

Whatever hook you employ on page one to engage reader attention – sympathy, curiosity, etc. – please remember that a novel's opening should be simple no matter how complicated the plot may turn out.

Be clear and easy to follow. Provide no barriers or hardship for readers to suspend disbelief and enter your story world.

Above all, remember that you don't need to throw everything you've got at readers all at once.

Introducing the protagonist

You have a reader and a leading character. They need to meet as soon as possible. (Please refer to Chapter 2 for additional information because how you construct your protagonist will affect which method of character introduction you'll use in your story's opening.)

From the opening line, readers are trying to identify which character is the protagonist. The protagonist/viewpoint character is a reader's guide through the story events. Readers are going to pretend they're this character. They're going to experience the story through the protagonist's eyes and heart. That's why readers want the protagonist's introduction to occur as soon as possible.

If readers dislike your main character, they won't stick with the story. So they're searching for a chance to imprint and bond with a character they'll appreciate or sympathize with.

If you introduce too many characters simultaneously, you run the risk of confusing your reader. Instead, begin with your protagonist, then add a second character, then another ... one at a time. You don't have to space each entrance pages apart, but give readers a chance to assimilate them.

Readers assume the first character to appear in the story is the protagonist.

That doesn't mean you can't open with your villain doing something nefarious, but make it clear this individual isn't the star player.

Now, consider the following four questions:

What first or lasting impression should my protagonist make on readers?

How should I bring my protagonist into the story simply, quickly, and efficiently?

How can I demonstrate what kind of person the protagonist is without stopping to dump in his back story?

How do I make my protagonist sympathetic and likeable?

The answers to these questions lie partially in the lead's design and partially in which method of characterization introduction you select. (Information on various types of introduction can be found in Chapter 2.)

Planning the plot

Reading copious amounts of fiction will help you instinctively understand how stories are shaped in a general way. Reading will help hone your story sense. However, you should also—if you haven't already—explore myths of all kinds, including studies of them. I suggest you examine Vladimir Propp's *Morphology of the fairy tale* (1968), Joseph Campbell's *The hero of a thousand faces* (2008) and *The power of myth* (2011), and Chris Vogler's *The writer's journey* (2007), which adapts

Campbell's work to a plot template. Depending on how deeply you want to dig into these topics, Adele Berlin's *Enmerkar and Ensuhkesdanna: a Sumerian narrative poem* (1979) and *Poetics and interpretation of biblical narrative* (1993), and Heda Jason's *Patterns in oral literature* (1977) may be worth a look as well.

At the most basic level, stories—whether short or novel length—require at least two characters, conflict generated between those two characters, and a test at the end. Granted, a lot more goes into a plot, but without these fundamental elements, your idea will crumble.

Since I've already explained why any story needs a protagonist, antagonist, and conflict between them, let's look at the test. It's the whole point of any story. Plot exists to test the protagonist.

The protagonist's objective and how he or she goes about achieving it gives your story its framework and direction. The test begins in the story opening, when your protagonist is faced with a substantial problem that can't be ignored. The test continues throughout the course of the story, as the protagonist tries, fails, tries harder, fails again, tries really hard, almost succeeds but then fails, and then pushes to the utmost for victory or defeat.

The test is completed at the story's end.

Not before.

Is there anything worse than reading a novel where the solution occurs too early, leaving the rest of the story to meander aimlessly? What if Saul Stridefinder reaches the Secret Cave, successfully solves the riddle that forces its monstrous guardian to allow him entrance, unlocks the innermost gate with the magic key presented to him ten pages earlier by a helpful old crone, and emerges with the Holy Grail in his rucksack? He immediately hands over the Grail to pay his debts, and is freed from the curse that's plagued him for the past seventeen years. What if this happens on page 107, leaving more than two hundred additional manuscript pages to fill?

Oops.

And, no, sending Saul Stridefinder retracing his steps homeward, only to encounter a series of random demons, rainstorms, man-eating goats residing under rickety old bridges, shape-changing young maidens wandering through the forest to cross his path, etc.—plus spending three chapters on how he kindly rebuilds the rotted sheep pens for an attractive widow living alone in a meadow—none of this constitutes a good second half. Reading such a "plot" is much like eating the so-called soup created by your roommate tossing every leftover from the refrigerator into the saucepan. Such swill might be edible, but chances are that parts of it are going to be decidedly peculiar and less than satisfying.

In contrast, is there anything better than flipping pages rapidly, reading faster and faster, intent on the nail-biting suspense of wondering how Thor Hammerblow will escape the dragon's lair alive when the potion that drugged the dragon wears off too early, leaving Thor face to face with an irate, venom-spitting creature?

And after Thor fights the battle of his life, drawing on every bit of strength and cunning he possesses, perhaps he does escape, but only after suffering a serious wound and the death of his best friend. Even worse, the dragon is so incensed that Thor has dared raid his treasury that now the malevolent creature is following Thor, pursuing him home with the intention of destroying Thor's village and everything he holds dear.

Saul checks off a list of tasks, but he's never challenged the way Thor is. Pit your protagonist against a bigger problem than she's ever faced before, and don't rush the process. Don't hand out the solution too early. Don't protect your protagonist from harm, consequences, ramifications, emotional upheavals, perilous situations, agonizing decisions, or ethical quagmires.

After all, is an easy test really a test? Think about what the word "challenge" means. How can you stretch your characters to meet one?

For your protagonist to be well and truly tried, the opponent must be slightly stronger or possess the advantage. When you work out in the gym by using weights that are too light, your muscles don't become stronger. In the same way, your protagonist can't grow or change unless she meets problems bigger and tougher than expectation.

Test your premise

Your concept may be terrific—at least in your imagination. But will it hold up to examination? Is it really strong enough to sustain 75,000 words of story? Is it good? Or is it fragile, delicate, full of plot holes, and insufficient?

Well, you've created it or been inspired by it. Chances are you're emotionally attached to your idea. And you should be!

But you can't protect it or shield it. You must be sure it's strong so it doesn't let you down partway through. Testing your premise is the sensible thing to do, just as I hope you would test the ropes and equipment before climbing a rock face.

Welcome to the SPOOC. I strongly suggest that you check every plot you invent against the SPOOC elements of plot before you write your rough draft. SPOOCs are tricky to master at first, and you may think the exercise is silly or a waste of time. However, if you don't discipline yourself enough to test your plots in the planning stages, you'll find that having to throw away a hundred pages or more of manuscript will be an even bigger waste of time.

The SPOOC is an acronym for a two-sentence plot equation as follows: Situation, Protagonist, Objective, Opponent, Climax.

Situation means the backdrop of trouble, the threatening change in circumstances that will force your protagonist to take action.

Protagonist is the central character in your story, the person your story is centered on. This individual is most affected by the situation and must drive the story to its climax.

Objective means the protagonist's goal. It can be the solution the protagonist is seeking in order to rectify the story problem or situation. It can be an object or talent the protagonist wants to possess very much. It can be a person the protagonist wants to frolic with more than life itself.

Opponent is the antagonist of the story, the person directly preventing the protagonist from reaching his or her objective. The opponent may even endanger the protagonist. A weak or passive opponent will undermine any plot's effectiveness. It's best, therefore, if the opponent is strong, resourceful, wily, unpredictable, and dangerous.

Climax is the ending of the story, the most intense and dangerous portion of your plot, where the protagonist and antagonist should have a showdown that resolves the situation. Even better, the climax is where the protagonist will be tested so hard that all seems lost before she's let off the hook.

Whenever I'm planning a novel, I approach my premise from several different ways. As soon as possible, I use the SPOOC to help me pull essential elements of plot together. The SPOOC's two plot-planning sentences seem like nothing, too simple to bother with, but they actually aren't easy to do. If I become impatient and skip them, I always regret it. Even worse, I end up having to throw manuscript pages away and rewrite.

I suggest you use the SPOOC as a testing template to measure your idea and check it for holes and weaknesses, but it shouldn't be approached in a paint-by-numbers fashion. Let your creativity flow first as you think about your characters, their backdrop, their problem, etc. If what you've come up with can't fit into the SPOOC template, you'll know you've overlooked something critical to the success of your story.

To repeat, a SPOOC should be formulated into a two-sentence plot equation. The first three elements form sentence one. The last two elements form sentence two and are phrased as a question. It should look like this:

Situation: When his young daughter is kidnapped,

Protagonist: King Faldain

Objective: vows to do anything to get her back.

But can he bring her safely home when

Opponent: the evil wizard Tulvak Sahm

Climax: demands Faldain's soul as the child's ransom?

Let's examine this example taken from my novel, *The king betrayed* (2003) a bit more closely. You might think that it's too simple to support an entire novel. It seems so on the surface, but the SPOOC isn't intended to encompass all the motivations, subplots, and details a book requires. The SPOOC is simply about establishing the central story question that spans beginning to end. This is the spine of your story. The rest of its skeleton can then be connected to it.

So cut down to the most essential details. Who is your protagonist? What is his immediate, most important, most urgent problem?

I don't need, at this stage, to worry about Faldain's marital problems or the intrigue within his court or the neighboring realm that's threatening war against him. Those difficulties can supply subplots and even a motivation behind the abduction. Developing them will come later after I have the central SPOOC figured out.

Try not to get sidetracked by all the additional details your story will eventually require. Take things one step at a time.

Returning to my example: If a man's child is taken, he'll do everything he can to get her back, won't he?

The opponent needs to be the central, primary antagonist—the character most intent on wreaking havoc on the protagonist's life and happiness. You need to understand your antagonist's motivations and you need to be sure that these two characters really are in direct opposition to each other.

The climax should be a calamity, a crisis. It should not be an easy problem for the protagonist to solve. Yes, a father naturally wants his child back. She's his little darling. He adores her. He'd do anything for her … he thinks. Until he's told the ransom price.

Your soul isn't so easy to give up, is it? Not if you have strong religious beliefs, which Faldain has.

Now, had I wanted to take the novel in a slightly different direction, I could have changed the test by altering the ransom demand to something else that Faldain might most fear or dread.

That's how flexible this plotting device is. Once you've put your idea through the SPOOC test, perhaps you aren't satisfied with it. In that case, play the "what if" game and plug in alternatives.

For example, Faldain has more than one child. And perhaps he's not a guy of much faith. So as a writer, I have to probe inside my protagonist to find his weakest, most vulnerable spot. Perhaps what he loves most are his two children, and he loves them equally. What if the wizard demands his son for the return of his daughter?

Can you see the quandary that would put Faldain in? What a quagmire of trouble. What a terrible choice for a parent to make. How will this affect him as a father? What will it do to his marriage? What about his realm? If his son is his heir, then the political stakes go up.

How can he possibly choose?

(Incidentally, I wish now I'd plotted the book this way instead of the direction I chose at the time.)

SPOOC examples

The following SPOOC is done incorrectly. See if you can spot the errors.

Example 1–A

Situation: When her unicorn escapes its pen and runs away,

Protagonist: Ala

Objective: searches for her beloved pet.

But can she find the unicorn when

Opponent: a huge, violent storm drenches her and

Climax: forces her to seek shelter for the night in a cave?

What's missing? The problem and objective are clear, but there's no antagonist. Forces of nature are random. They may create hardship and they can generate excitement, but they're not an opponent. They're merely adversity. They don't actually put conflict into the story. As a result, there's no climax either. Nor do we learn if Ala finds her pet.

Example 1–B (corrected)

Situation: When her unicorn escapes its pen and runs away,

Protagonist: Ala

Objective: searches for her beloved pet.

But can she regain the unicorn when

Opponent: her envious cousin Melie

Climax: steals the animal and hides it in a dangerous cave?

Unlike in the first example, Ala now has an opponent, a cousin who doesn't like her for some reason. Melie doesn't want Ala to retrieve her unicorn, so she hides it.

Why would Melie do such a wicked thing?

The answer lies in Melie's motivation, which can be plotted in due course.

Example 2–A

Situation: When his village is cursed and the crops start failing,

Protagonist: a teenage wizard named Jue Mandrake

Objective: wants to lift the curse and save the fields.

But can he break the spell when

Opponent: Drugo, the evil wizard that cast it,

Climax: dies of old age?

What's the problem here? There's an antagonist, isn't there? Yes, but now the climax is missing. How convenient that the old dude collapses and dies just as Jue starts to confront him.

The ending is too convenient for reader belief, and much too easy. There's no showdown. The village is saved without Jue having to tackle anything dangerous. The premise falls flat. There's no suspense as to the outcome, and readers will feel cheated by the whole thing.

Example 2–B (corrected)

Situation: When his village is cursed and crops start failing,

Protagonist: teenage wizard-in-training Jue Mandrake

Objective: wants to lift the curse.

But can he break the evil spell when

Opponent: Drugo, the evil wizard,

Climax: insists that Jue fight him in a sorcery duel to the death?

See how I raised the stakes? See how I have set up the scenario so that Drugo goes right for Jue's most vulnerable point, his inexperience?

Drill exercise 1:

Choose your favorite fantasy novel, one you've re-read numerous times. If you can't choose among your favorites, the first Harry Potter book will do.

Answer the following questions:

- Who is the protagonist of the story?
- Who is the primary villain?
- What does the protagonist want above all else? (in this book; not across an entire series)
- What does the primary antagonist want? (in this book; not across the entire series)
- Who wins at the story's conclusion and how?

Drill exercise 2:

From your answers to exercise 1, write a SPOOC plot equation. Make sure you confine it to two sentences. Don't skip any of the elements. You may have to try more than once to whittle a complicated story down to its basic plot essentials. Ignore the subplots and focus on the main storyline.

Drill exercise 3:

Now repeat this exercise for your story idea. You can't harm your premise, but you may find holes in it. If so, be glad. You now have the opportunity to fix them.

2

Character design

When I first began learning the writer's craft, I struggled with characters. If they occurred to me already fully formed, I was fine. But if I had to create a character from scratch, I muddled along and often ended up with pieced-together creatures that were illogically motivated, contrived, or stereotypes. Eventually I learned how to manage better character design.

In this chapter we'll look at story roles and functions; character construction; character introduction; character complexity; magic; and setting.

Story roles

Characters fall into one of three general groupings: primary, secondary, and minor.

It's best if you have one protagonist. This is the star of the story. This individual is the most important. Think of actors being cast for a major motion picture. There may be several prominent actors hired, and everyone will be negotiating for top billing. Who gets the lead credit in your novel or short story?

- Who has the most at stake?
- Who has the most to lose?
- Who can most often be at the center of all the important story action?
- Who has the most to learn or discover?

Story roles

Protagonist: the central character, the most important role.	Primary story roles
Antagonist: the central opponent to the protagonist, the second most important role.	

Sidekick: the companion and helper, provides skills, information, and assistance as needed.	Secondary story roles Secondary characters can be on the protagonist's side, or serve the antagonist.
Mentor/confidant: the adviser, the listener, the sounding board, the teacher. Someone trusted enough to be confided in.	
Love interest: the romantic figure.	

Background: crowds or individuals standing or moving as part of the setting. Often appearing as villagers, the army, courtiers, etc.	Minor story roles
Service: individuals with or without dialogue as they wait tables, drive wagons, groom horses, polish swords and armor, feed dragons, fetch candles, etc.	
Information: individuals sought for their knowledge and assistance.	

Think long and hard about who you choose for your protagonist. If you've chosen the wrong character for that role, your story may split in focus as a more goal-oriented, active secondary character steals the scenes.

George R. R. Martin's popularity notwithstanding, it's best if you avoid tackling an ensemble cast of multiple protagonists until you're an extremely skilled and experienced writer.

Instead, keep your characters manageable by establishing a hierarchy of importance. Let's consider the Harry Potter series (1998–2007) as an example.

Harry is the star. Without question, he's the central character. He stands out as the protagonist, the most special of all the inhabitants in J. K. Rowling's special world.

Ron is one of Harry's sidekicks. While he's Harry's closest friend and is extremely important to the stories, he remains a buddy and helper. Hermione is another of Harry's sidekicks. She's appealing, interesting, helpful, and intriguing, but she comes in second after Ron in terms of importance to Harry.

Hagrid is occasionally a sidekick, and sometimes a mentor to Harry.

Dumbledore is a mentor.

The amount of pages devoted to each character indicates his or her ranking of importance. Readers adore Rowling's secondary characters, and Harry couldn't succeed without them. But the hierarchy is clear. There aren't multiple protagonists.

In any story, both the protagonist and antagonist can each have his or her own set of secondary friends or minions. Therefore, an antagonist can have sidekicks, a confidant, and a lover just as the protagonist can.

Often you'll find stories where the protagonist and antagonist are in love with the same individual. In such triangles, winning a relationship with the love interest may serve as the goal and story question. Certainly the conflict will be focused and directly oppositional.

If the protagonist and antagonist each share the same confidant, something weird is going on. Very likely the confidant is a double—or even triple—agent, working one side against the other. This can lead to wonderful plot twists.

Another variation of story function is that a secondary character can play more than one role within the story. For example, Squire Pember is both a sidekick and confidant to Sir Wilfrid. Or Trina, the demon killer who lives in the apartment next door, is John Shapeshifter's sidekick, confidant, and lover.

Character construction

Myriad details make up character design, but let's separate them into two major divisions—physical and psychological. Some authors tackle the physical aspect first and then burrow into heart and mind. Others take the opposite approach. Would you rather zigzag back and forth? Do so, if that's what works for you.

With physical construction, it's obvious that you should decide whether this will be a human, animal, or supernatural creature. You also need to determine whether this character will be mortal or immortal.

Then consider the following:

Appearance

Physically, what does this individual look like? I'm talking hair and eye color (or pelt color, if necessary), height, weight, body type, degree of athleticism if any, general state of health, and taste in clothing.

Not important, you say? Oh, but it is. Whether you describe any of this for your readers, you should know every detail specifically.

It's helpful to make yourself a dossier sheet and print out

copies so you can fill in this information for each member of your cast.

I always have students who leap eagerly at this task, willing to give it a try. And then I encounter the doubters and resisters. If you're the latter type, I urge you to adopt any method you wish as long as you create the specific details I've mentioned.

Why?

Because a vague character—one that's basically an undescribed entity walking across the story pages while spewing dialogue—is an inconsistent character that will never come to life. Vague characters don't carry their weight in fiction.

Appearance feeds into a character's psychology, both personally and culturally. Like it or not, we're affected by what we look like and by how we feel.

For example, a healthy athletic individual sees a flight of stairs and thinks, *Great! A chance to work my glutes.* But a weak or ill person sees the staircase as a difficult obstacle.

"Don't be so lazy!" Healthy Hal yelled down the stairwell. "Come on!"

"Haunted houses are no place for asthmatics," Wheezing Wilma replied. "I'm staying right here."

Name

What will you call your characters? My grandmother—no fantasy reader—once asked why I couldn't use simple names. I shrugged off her question at the time because I love exotic, fantastical monikers. However, author Jim Butcher has created a charming character in Bob, the spirit that lives in a skull in wizard Harry Dresden's basement.

I have Tobeszijian. Jim has Bob.

Neither name is better or worse than the other although I've learned it does help readers if you devise pronounceable names. Tobeszijian is a minor character in a traditional fantasy where long, complicated names distinguish the elves from humans. Bob, on the other hand, is a player in a very modern urban fantasy series. His real name is much longer and more formal, but the protagonist calls him Bob, which is indicative of the casual, contemporary setting.

Character names should fit the individual's personality, setting, story role, and background. Pay attention to the connotations of any name you want to use. Like Charles Dickens, John D. MacDonald, and J. K. Rowling, let your names shape reader perception.

For example, would you trust Dickens's Mr. Squeers?

Would you eat dinner with MacDonald's Foster Goss?

Would you enroll in a class taught by Rowling's Professor Snape?

Whether you've ever met these characters in the pages of a book, what does each name convey to you?

If you want readers to like a character, give that story person an appealing name. If you want readers to dislike or distrust a character, see the examples above. There's nothing subtle about this technique, and there shouldn't be.

While you don't have to reach for the extreme of naming your hero something like Tank Brawnarm, it's certainly more vivid and evocative than John R. Beige.

In fantasy fiction, if you use an ordinary name, you'll be forced to describe more in putting that character across to readers. Your character will have to say more and do more to become vivid in reader imagination. But if you assign the name Ermentrude Flibber to a female character, reader imaginations will already be conjuring up comical notions of what she's like before she ever opens her mouth or walks across the room.

As for psychological character design, it deals chiefly with personality, motivation, complexity, and background. It's by far the more interesting and challenging aspect of characterization. Let's consider the elements necessary to create it:

Personality

Usually I suggest starting with about six traits of personality for a protagonist or antagonist. Think about the qualities in people that you admire or dislike very much.

For example, I admire intelligence, honesty, integrity, honor, loyalty, reliability, determination, and competence.

I dislike dishonesty, sneakiness, cheating, vagueness, indecision, betrayal, insincerity, tardiness, irresponsibility, cruelty, and timidity.

No character should be one-hundred percent good or completely evil. Modern readers are too sophisticated for such simplistic characters. So design a judicious mix of the good and bad.

For your protagonist, select four or five positive traits—ones that will enable this individual to be likeable, active, and appealing—and then mix in at least a couple of flaws.

For your antagonist, reverse the process. Select a majority of negative traits, but mitigate them with a few good qualities. Let readers see that the villain has the capacity for good, but is choosing not to use it.

If you're creating an anti-hero, say someone as dour as the central character in Stephen Donaldson's *The chronicles of Thomas Covenant* (1977–2013), keep in mind that this character is still a protagonist, is still a mix of good qualities along with the bad, and is probably hiding many of his or her best qualities on purpose.

Pattern of speech

A character's dialogue should reflect her personality, temperament, education or background, dominant impression, and pre-occupations through vocabulary and voice patterns. Doing so helps individualize your characters so they don't all seem alike. Therefore, give one member of your cast a hesitant or jerky way of speaking.

"Well, now, I don't know ... I mean, it's just not quite ... well, right, is it? What do you think?"

Let another be gruff and impatient, speaking in short sentences or fragments:

"Get on with it, man! Stop dithering. Just make a decision and be done."

A character may be fond of using slang—although if it's modern it will date your manuscript quickly—or certain old-fashioned expressions, such as

"Weak as water!"

You may want to give someone in your cast a stammer, although I don't recommend it because it's a chore to punctuate t-that k-kind of thing consistently through, ah, ah, ah, through an entire m-manuscript.

Personality or a dominant pre-occupation influencing vocabulary and rhythm of speech is more effective than stammers, grunts, dialect and all its horrors of spelling, tics, and—*quel horreur!*—foreign accents.

Avoid the gimmicks, and focus instead on letting your character's chief concern shine through. For example:

"Sir, I don't think we ought to be venturing too deep into the forest tonight. I hear tell there's BRs in there."

"BRs? What are you going on about?"

"Big Rodents. Fearsome hostile, I'm told. I don't want to be a snack, that's all."

"Steady. We aren't going to be eaten."

"That's what you say, sir. But it's dark in them woods. Dark and nasty and full of creatures all hungry and wanting us for dinner."

See the difference? The first character is chattering nervously as he conveys his concern about hostile creatures roaming the forest. No matter how calmly the other character dismisses this concern, Character 1 can't let his fears go.

Other differences are added in through Character 1 addressing Character 2 as sir and using slightly incorrect grammar. Even without attributions—such as John said—it's possible to tell the two speakers apart.

Motivation

This addresses the reasons why a character does what he or she does, why this individual is making certain choices and decisions, why this person is pursuing a particular goal, and why this person won't quit.

Motivation springs from a combination of factors, including the personality of the character, some event or condition in the character's past that's driving him now, and what advantage the character hopes to gain by achieving his objective.

The motivations of the antagonist should be complex and intriguing. The motivations of the protagonist can be complex or fairly straightforward. The motivations of secondary characters can be simple. What's important is that you know the reasons why in each and every character you create.

Complexity

It took me a long time to figure out character complexity. At first, I went at it from the wrong direction, thinking I needed to add more background, more traits, more and more and more details. I didn't understand that complexity—sometimes known as dimension—is created inside a character.

It is achieved when a character's inner problem or flaw is in conflict with that character's external situation or behavior. This sets up a tension within an individual that intensifies as the story stakes rise.

The most intriguing characters are like onions, made of layer upon layer, to be peeled away in scenes and story complications.

A flat or one-dimensional character is someone whose surface and inside match exactly. There's nothing more to discover, no secret to reveal, no vulnerability to test in the story climax. Such a character may work in a minor role, but, if given a larger part, will read as boring.

Let's consider a character I'll call Jessika.

Her family's leopard bloodlines are long and famous among the were-clans. Her father is renowned for his fighting prowess and leadership. Her mother is a fearless hunter and master strategist. Jessika has been reared in luxury. Her home is a stronghold responsible for guarding the northern border. She's tall and lean. She walks with sinuous grace. Her hair is tawny and long, and her eyes are golden and slanted at the tips. Jessika is temperamental and impatient, imperious, arrogant, intelligent, poised, and extremely sure of herself. Her privileged status has given her considerable self-confidence. Her first shape changing goes smoothly. As a were-leopard, she's gorgeous and quick, as adept a hunter as her mother. Her second changing goes equally well—perhaps even better—than the first. When Jessika is put in charge of a guard patrol, she proves to be a competent leader.

Are you snoring yet? Perhaps when you began reading the above paragraph, you felt intrigued by Jessika. By the time you reached the end, however, were you feeling bored or impatient?

Were you wondering, *what's going to happen to her home and family? When will she be in trouble? When is it going to get good?*

That's because your story instincts were telling you that if Jessika doesn't encounter a problem very soon, she can be as accomplished and beautiful as any were-leopard out there, and ***readers won't care***.

Let's start over.

Jessika is a beautiful young were-leopard from a prominent family. She's grown up privileged and pampered. Her parents have high expectations of her. As soon as she undergoes her first shape changing, she's scheduled to be put in command of a guard patrol.

But although Jessika knows how to conduct herself in the complicated etiquette of her parents' court, she is dreading the rapidly approaching time of her changing. The indications are absent. Her night vision hasn't improved. Her appetite isn't increasing. When she ventures outside the stronghold walls to run alone through the forest, she feels clumsy and slow. Her hands and feet experience none of the tingling that indicates claw development. She's been taught to notice any signs of restlessness, violent temper, or wide fluctuations of body temperature, but such signs are absent. Her temper is ragged, but that's due to nerves.

She feels the awful certainty that she will not be able to shape shift when the time comes. She will disgrace herself and her parents. She will live in the stronghold as a despised and pitied failure, a throwback never allowed to take her rightful place at court, never allowed to mate, never to be the heir. Among the commoners, throwbacks are killed. Jessika knows her parents will show her mercy, but they'll be ashamed of her. They'll permit her to live in the stronghold and provide her with shelter and food, but she'll be forever banished to the shadows of the lower levels. Her name will no longer spoken, and her future will be over.

There's no one she can confide in or express her doubts to. She dares betray no sign of weakness, no uncertainty. She lives every day as a lie, pretending to have self-assurance. Inside, she's a tense knot of fear.

See the difference in these two versions of the same character? The second Jessika hasn't a lot of depth yet, but she has much more than the first Jessika. She has the potential to make readers sympathetic and curious about what will happen to her.

At key points in a story's unfolding, events or antagonists will pressure a character into removing the mask and revealing some aspect of the true nature inside.

There should always be a contrast between a character's inner self and outer appearance or behavior. This contrast also adds to dimension.

Therefore, Jessika 2 strides around and acts confident, but inside she's a nervous wreck.

A villain may act like a friend through the first half of a story, but at some moment the mask will slip. These glimpses of true nature are exciting to readers, especially when the mask is put back on.

Sometimes, an unpleasant adversary may actually be an ally in disguise.

Rowling's Professor Snape is probably her most complex and intriguing character in the entire Harry Potter series. I recall the intense debate that raged when the books were first published: was Snape a good guy or the villain he appeared to be?

His psychological design is masterful. His true nature and outer behavior are in constant conflict, creating the dimension and depth that make him work so well. He truly does hate Harry's father, and he despises Harry, yet he's willing to protect Harry from harm again and again. Inwardly he's in a vise of torment. The chance that he might surrender to his emotions and join Voldemort's side keeps reader anticipation high.

The arc of change

Complexity from the contradiction of surface characteristics and true nature, personality traits, self-concept, self-doubt, guilt, and inner conflict all provide writers with material to create a gradual transformation within the protagonist and possibly an important secondary character or two.

Stories are about change. Besides the basic plot problem to be solved, plots exist to push protagonists into taking risks and meeting challenges. Every turning point in the story serves to make protagonists grow a little—or diminish, should the story happen to be about a central character's devolvement.

If there are no flaws within your protagonist at the story's beginning, how can you expect this character to improve or grow by the story's end?

Introduction methods

You should introduce each member of your story cast in a memorable way. You want to make a strong first impression on readers—a lasting impression. To accomplish this, writers have several methods at their disposal. All of them will work just fine for any character, whether major, secondary, or minor. Some are more effective than others, but all can be useful, depending on the type of story and characters you're dealing with.

Method 1: out-of-viewpoint description

This approach is fast and easy. It involves pausing the story to provide readers with a physical or personality description. The author tells readers the information. Breaking viewpoint, the author intrudes into the story to share detailed description and pertinent background quickly.

Although a skilled writer can make this method work, it's not one that I usually recommend. For one thing, readers are disinclined to believe what they're told. They would much rather be shown a character in action so they can make up their own minds. Generally, in the first few pages, readers aren't really concerned with knowing how tall the protagonist is or that he's inherited the Grivaldi nose. Instead, readers want to know if they can care about him.

Method 2: introduction through dialogue

This one works best for secondary characters rather than the protagonist because it requires at least two cast members already established in the story. If used for the protagonist, it means her entry will be delayed.

The two conversant characters—who must be clearly identified as not being the protagonist—are on the page, discussing the individual who's about to appear. What they say can be true or it can be lies. Either way, they're influencing readers who must decide for themselves who they'll believe.

Example:

The informer scuttled up to the cop in the shadowy alley. He looked over his shoulder and up at the building walls towering above them. He looked at the pavement. He looked at his shoes. He looked everywhere and anywhere except at the cop's face.

"Well?" the cop demanded. "What have you got?"

"Heard the vamps are getting a new master. 'Sposed to be comin' in tonight to take over."

"Yeah? We figured it was just a matter of time."

"You shouldna took out Old Master," the informant muttered. "He was scary, all right, but we knew where we stood with him."

"He was insane, unstable," the cop said without apology. "What can you tell me about the new one?"

"Bad, real bad. If you think Old Master wouldn't follow the rules, you ain't seen nothin' yet. This one's Etruscan."

"Etru—*what?* Is that up near Boston?"

"No, no. Etruscan. Pre-Roman." Seeing the blank look on the cop's face, the informant flapped his hands. "Italian."

"Oh. Right. From New Jersey, huh?"

"*No!* From Italy. He's one of the *old ones*. He's a predator, first and last. Not some smooth-voiced Frenchman who'll run a cover-operation nightclub and keep the vamps legal. With Grivaldi around, they'll come out huntin'. I'm tellin' ya, it's gonna be bad."

"Grivaldi, huh? I'll make a note of that name."

Although, as I've mentioned, this introduction method delays the protagonist's entrance, the appeal is that readers have the fun of comparing or contrasting the character's actual appearance and behavior to what's been said about him. If readers like or believe the informant, they'll be inclined to believe what he's saying about Grivaldi. But readers may choose to wait and see for themselves.

Consider how J. K. Rowling's characters talk about Voldemort, and how no one but Harry seems willing to even speak his name. Through the course of a book, that builds a powerful image and expectation in readers' minds. When he does appear, Voldemort is every bit as bad as we've been led to believe.

Introduction through dialogue is a useful means of planting for later developments, hinting at back story, and bringing in complications.

Method 3: introduction through environment

Your protagonist's personal space can indicate personality, habits, preferences, taste, and activities.

In this method, the character has not yet entered the story. Instead, first the author describes the protagonist's home, dungeon, turret, forge, stable, or belongings—whatever will display some of the protagonist's true nature or the masks she wears.

The surroundings of a character, the possessions, or the home all betray who and what she is.

Here's an example:

The apartment looked like someone had bought a storage unit at auction and dumped everything in the middle of the living room. It was a rat's nest of scruffy, mismatched furniture; tattered, discarded curtains piled in heaps on the floor; rusting iron candlesticks encrusted with candle wax; broken dolls; old store mannequins with blank, staring eyes—all overlaid with the flotsam of pages torn from books, vellum documents, and maps. At first glance it could have been mistaken for a hoarder's den, except for the table under the window.

Covered with a dingy remnant of lace that dragged the floor, the table held five items all precisely placed in a diagonal line: a skull, a burning candle, a tiny iron bowl of salt, a Christian cross carved from olive wood, and a Sig-Sauer handgun.

What do these details tell you about the woman who leases this apartment? Maybe a little or a lot, depending on whether this description is presented in the book's opening pages or later, when there's more context for readers to piece together.

Introduction through surroundings works best for villains and secondary characters, less so sometimes for the protagonist. It provides an intriguing contrast with the actual appearance and demeanor of the character the habitat belongs to.

Method 4: introduction through action

Although mentioned last, this method is nearly always the most effective and efficient way to bring a character into your story. It's showing the reader your protagonist (or any character) in action, doing or saying something typical of that individual's personality. This creates that vivid first impression we want to make on our readers. It's active, not static. It can also serve to show the protagonist already in trouble or coping with a problem—which means you're setting a hook, creating change in the existing circumstances, raising questions to make readers curious, and pitting the protagonist against conflict—all in the space of a few paragraphs.

Introduction through action can be used for any and every character—important and minor—in your story. Because it's adaptable and tailored to demonstrate the unique personality of each member of your cast, it's never going to be repetitious or predictable to readers. The only way you can botch introduction through action is if you give each character an identical entry action.

Example from *The king imperiled* (2005) by Deborah Chester:

Naked to the waist, daubed with paint, and screaming at the top of his lungs, Anoc ran through the smoke and confusion of the battlefield. The war drum he was supposed to be beating had been torn from him and smashed, and so he plunged through the melee of fighting warriors and knights, clubbing anyone who attacked him with his carved beater stick.

He was searching for a sword, any real weapon he could snatch from the hands of a dead man. He'd forgotten that it was forbidden for him to be on the actual battlefield. Barely twelve seasons old, small and scrawny, he had not yet been proclaimed warrior age, had not yet passed the rituals. No matter how many growth spells he attempted to work on himself, his efforts to hasten manhood remained futile. Nevertheless, he knew he was destined to be a warrior. He was, after all, the Deliverer as born and proclaimed. The song of war throbbed in his bones and ran so hot in his blood he could not obey orders. Instead of fleeing to the caves as he'd been told, he screamed the war cries of his elders and ran toward danger.

Although I can't think of any drawbacks to using introduction through action, there are a couple of pitfalls to avoid.

The first is to make sure the action entry actually fits the character's personality. In other words, don't have your protagonist crash through a window in a shower of breaking glass while shooting wizard fire to every corner of the room if this character is truly a meek, unassuming guy without an ounce of actual magical power.

The second pitfall happens if you lose your nerve and write an entrance that's too low key. Remember this is no time for you to be timid or cautious. You need to cultivate your inner flair for the dramatic, and push yourself past your comfort zone. Readers aren't going to laugh at a vivid, boldly drawn character. Instead, they might just sit up and think, *This person's interesting.*

Magic

Magic should be so integral to the story, whether it's desirable or feared, that its absence would diminish the plot. Accordingly, magic is considered to be a "character," one that helps set fantasy apart from other genres. It should never be a tacked-on afterthought.

Consider its source. Does it come from nature, from the gods, from within certain creatures? How is it summoned? Through rituals or potions? Through incantations? Through an internal focusing of mind and will? Through emotions?

Does every individual in your story possess magic, or do only certain individuals have it? Must a character attend a school to be trained in the magic arts, like Harry Potter and his friends, or does it just come naturally?

Will your protagonist be superlative at it—like Harry Potter—or a bit wonky, like Neville?

Is your protagonist the only member of her family to possess magic? How do they feel about that? Are they proud, or uncomfortable? Harry Potter's aunt and uncle keep him in the closet under the staircase and give him toothpicks for birthday gifts. Tom—in Joseph Delaney's *The last apprentice* (2005)—is the seventh son of a seventh son and when he leaves the farm to start his apprenticeship in binding bogarts and trapping witches, his brothers are much relieved to be rid of him.

In my fantasy novel, *The sword* (2000), one kingdom is beset with all sorts of horrific demons and supernatural predators, requiring constant vigilance from the populace. The adjacent kingdom—bordered by a river the creatures can't cross—is safe. Its people have a much different mindset and can't relate to the fears or customs across that river.

The other important aspect of magic sometimes overlooked by inexperienced writers is that it should come at a cost. If magic is free, if it's easy to have and easy to use, then what will keep the protagonist from winning the first encounter against a villain sorcerer? How can you hope to sustain the story question to the end? One snap of the hero's fingers, and the bad guy is vanquished ... *poof!*

On the other hand, if only the antagonist possesses magic, and doesn't have to pay for it either, then the protagonist has no way at all to survive. Once again, the story will end in the first scene when the protagonist is zapped to ashes.

In Jim Hines's delightful romp of a novel, *Libriomancer* (2013), the protagonist can reach into books and draw out guns or objects that will help him fight the evil forces. But he can only use a book so many times before the magic starts to char and destroy the story.

In Tim Powers's novel, *The Anubis gates* (1997), every time Romany (or Romanelli) casts a spell, he has to cut himself for the blood. As the situation grows more dire, and his strength diminishes, he starts to bleed from the nostrils as a result from using magic. He's diminishing himself, bit by bit. This builds anticipation and suspense toward the eventual outcome by raising the question, can he hold out until the end?

When you read, do you observe how authors handle magic in their characters? Do they turn the price of magic into part of the protagonist's inner problem? Do they make it integral to the protagonist's arc of change?

When you read a story where the writer has cheated and contrived the magic, or used it inconsistently, do you feel as though you've been shortchanged? Are you disappointed? What would you do differently?

Special world

A wondrous setting is required in fantasy, even if it's the gritty, dirty back alleys of modern-day Singapore. So what exactly will make it special? Or unusual, or peculiar, or fascinating, or intriguing?

The name of the game is research, extrapolation, consistency, specificity of detail, and creative license. If you're writing urban fantasy, what city will you choose? London? Paris? Bangkok? Dallas? You will need to look at maps and familiarize yourself with whatever is distinctive about the place. It's best if you've visited your choice and know it well enough to capture its flavor. When Jim Butcher was planning his book *Storm front* (2000), we discussed which city he would use for the setting. Jim knew he wanted his books to take place in a large metropolis. He chose Chicago because it hadn't been done to death by other authors and because he'd been there and felt comfortable with it.

Suzanne Collins uses the tunnels beneath New York City as a setting for her book, *Gregor the overlander* (2004). Rosemary Clement-Moore uses a high school for her novel, *Prom dates from hell* (2008).

In other words, the most mundane setting can be rendered extraordinary by how you present it. Look in your own backyard and see how you can imaginatively render it into something special. If Collins can transform cockroaches into kindly characters, fantasy truly is capable of magic.

However, if you're writing traditional fantasy, you can't visit medieval Germany or medieval anything, unless you tour standing castles and fortresses. You must then research and extrapolate. There are plentiful sources of information about historical clothing, food, dwellings, customs, recreation, weaponry, combat, etc.

Draw whatever details appeal to you and tweak them to fit your characters' circumstances. As long as you use common sense and extrapolate or combine plausibly, you can have an enjoyable time world-building. Remember that the more specific you are, the more believable your setting will be.

Drill exercise:

In designing your protagonist and antagonist, complete the following checklist. Don't worry if you can't find all the answers quickly. You shouldn't be able to. Take your time and think through each question or point. The more of them you complete, the more complex your characters will be. The fewer questions you bother with, the weaker your character design will be.

For some secondary characters, work through only the necessary portion. However, important secondary roles—especially those that will carry a viewpoint and a resulting subplot—should address the majority of the list.

Make sure you actually write down the answers. Don't just think them. Create a dossier file for each of your important characters.

Character design checklist

1. What is the character's story role?
2. State your character's full name.
3. What portion of this name is used by the character or others?
4. State any nicknames for this character. Used by whom?
5. State the character's age.
6. Physically describe the character.
7. List the character's primary personality traits.
8. What personality tags (or behaviors) demonstrate these traits?

9. Besides tags of name and personality, what other prominent tags will be displayed by this character?
10. How will these tags be shown to readers?
11. How often will these tags be demonstrated?
12. Describe/explain the character's background.
13. What is the character's primary story goal?
14. Why?
15. What is the character's personal objective or dream?
16. Why?
17. What personally is the most important thing or person in this character's life?
18. Why?
19. When opposed or thwarted by someone, how does this character typically react?
20. Why should a reader like this character, or want this character to succeed?
21. If this character is a villain, why should a reader dislike this character, or want this individual to fail?
22. Describe this character's belief system or personal code.
23. State how it developed.
24. If this character were to state what he or she really believes in or cares about, in his or her own words, what would this character say?
25. If this character's worst enemy were to state what's wrong with this character, what would he or she say?

26. How are this character's goals essential to his or her sense of self-worth, self-concept, or ideal of happiness?
27. Describe this character's habitat or favorite surroundings.
28. What is this character's most prized possession?
29. Why?
30. What skills does this character possess?
31. If this character can perform magic, describe his or her powers.
32. At what age and in what circumstances did these powers first manifest?
33. Describe this character's training in magic, if any.
34. How has magic affected this character's personal life?
35. If this character does not have magical powers, is that common or extraordinary?
36. Describe any familiars or spirits that serve this character.
37. What are the terms of such service? (Willing or coerced?)
38. Write a short, vivid introduction through action for this character.
39. Who in the story will serve as a foil to this character?
40. How? (Be specific.)
41. Describe this character's childhood.
42. Describe this character's parents.

43. How did this character's parents treat him or her?
44. Who was the most important individual in this character's early life?
45. Why?
46. What was the most significant achievement in this character's childhood or past?
47. What was the biggest disappointment or tragedy in this character's childhood or past?
48. How is this character like you?
49. How is this character unlike you?
50. What makes this character unique?
51. What is this character currently proudest of?
52. What are this character's flaws?
53. Do these flaws drive this character?
54. How?
55. What are this character's secrets?
56. What hidden guilt does this character carry?
57. What inner sadness does this character conceal?
58. What mood is typical for this character?
59. How does this mood affect the tone of the story?
60. What is this character most afraid of?
61. What makes this character cry?
62. What makes this character laugh?
63. If the character were asked to complete the statement: "I am ________________" what would the character say?

64. Describe how the surface appearance or behavior of this character contrasts with his or her true nature.
65. Under what circumstances does this character's true nature reveal itself?
66. Is this character a loner?
67. Can this character trust and/or work with others?
68. Does this character ever confide in anyone, or seek advice?
69. If so, when and why?
70. Who is the confidant?
71. What about this character needs to change?
72. What does this character need to learn?
73. Does this character have the capacity to change or learn?
74. Would you trust this character with your life?
75. Why or why not?

If you answer all of these questions for your protagonist, the dossier you'll generate will be very long. You need to know your character thoroughly, of course, but beware the temptation to fill your entire writing time with cast dossiers.

I often tackle this questionnaire in sections. I begin by answering the easiest questions, meaning those I already know when beginning the exercise. Then I make sure I focus on a few key items, such as those dealing with motivation and what the character most fears. ➡

By then I want to put the character into a scene and see how she behaves under stress. So I'll write a scene featuring plenty of conflict. It's a sketch that may or may not make its way into the final draft of my manuscript. But I like to see my characters in action, moving around and speaking dialogue. If I'm not happy with the result, I look over the dossier or questionnaire and tweak it.

On the other hand, if I'm satisfied, I may go ahead and put the character into my story and write chapters until I hit a problem. Then I'll look at the questionnaire again and see if I can now answer the questions I've skipped. Sometimes I will be halfway through my novel before things click and I fully understand the true nature of my protagonist and how I need to set up his arc of change across the full span of the story.

With practice, you will find your own approach to character design, one that works optimally for you.

3

Viewpoint

Viewpoint is the reader's guide through your story. It provides insight and perspective. It can make the difference in whether your reader bonds with your protagonist. It's both a filter of perception and a camera angle into the plot. It's a conduit from your imagination to your reader's. It's a direct connection into the heart and soul of any viewpoint character. You can use it to bring your story alive.

It is one of the largest differences in how a prose story versus a filmed (or televised) story is presented to audiences.

Although motion pictures can provide a marvelous source of stories, worlds, characters, and imagery, if you've been feeding your imagination from television and film in recent years more than from reading, you may find the task of handling viewpoint to be a challenge. The solution? Read all the fiction you can get your hands on. Do it *now*.

Presenting viewpoint

How do you know when you're writing in viewpoint or not? How do you know when you've shifted viewpoint? How is it done?

Viewpoint is subjective and internal. It's written from the inside of a character looking outward at the world around him. It's perception, intelligence, observation, attitude, belief, emotion, perspective, bias, and personality—all rolled into one.

When you write *in* viewpoint, you're inside the selected character. The story is shown to readers through that character's eyes, through what that character experiences as the action unfolds. The viewpoint character isn't a reporter, isn't a bystander, isn't neutral, and isn't objective.

The viewpoint character has a stake in the story's outcome. The viewpoint character is at risk. The viewpoint character is *involved.*

Because of the subjectivity, we have three primary ways in which we establish, present, and maintain viewpoint.

Emotions

If you share a character's emotions with readers, you are writing in that character's viewpoint.

Example from *The queen's gambit* (2002) by Deborah Chester:

The chancellor thrust a parchment at Talmor. "Then sign your accusation of treason, damne!"

Talmor did not think his knees would support him if he stepped forward to take the paper, but they did somehow. He stared at the writing, and for a moment the words blurred and ran together. There was thunder in his ears and from a long distance away, he heard Sir Kedrien say, "Sign at the mark, if you can write."

Another insult. Talmor looked up sharply, some of his fear forgotten. "I am educated, sir."

Thoughts

A character's internalized thoughts, either indirect or direct, also indicate viewpoint.

Example from *The queen's gambit*:

"Oh, come!" Lervan said heartily, holding out his hand. "What good comes of black looks and resentful hearts? I want money. I care not whence it comes."

"Very well," Theloi said. "I shall authorize a fund for your grace."

Going to his desk, he wrote hurriedly, splattering ink, and signed his name with an angular loop. Tossing down his pen, he turned to Lervan with the paper in his hand. "Take care, your grace," he said in a cold, hostile voice. "Remember who your true friends are and how unwise it would be to make enemies when you are in most need of allies."

Lervan eyed the paper avidly. Already his head was swirling with plans of how to spend his new largess. Hedrina would look magnificent in sapphires. He would commission a necklace, a stunning necklace, to adorn her lovely throat. Aye, and there would be other jewels to lavish on her, for she must be rewarded for making him so happy. He supposed he would have to give Pheresa a trinket as well and buy a cup of the finest eldin silver for the baby's gift. But first there was a new horse he wanted, and he must have new clothes, for surely Pheresa would not wish her consort to look shabby. His style would now lead the court, so he would have to employ the very best tailors.

Theloi cleared his throat, and Lervan hastily pulled himself from his daydreams.

Physical senses

When you share a character's sensory input, you are writing in viewpoint as well. Use of the physical senses is most effective in engaging reader imagination.

Examples from *The queen's gambit*:

Sight

Talmor broke his oath and let the fire go.

The hurlhound should have exploded in a huge puff of ash. It should have been torched, set on fire, and destroyed by the force Talmor unleashed. Instead, he saw the flames engulf the monster, blaze up with such intensity that everyone stumbled back, raising their hands to shield their faces. He saw the hurlhound crouch low as though it meant to topple over, then it jumped to its feet, restored and whole again. It absorbed the fire into itself until the flames vanished completely.

Hearing

"Filthy, just as I said," the steward announced. "Bide a moment while I light a lamp."

It seemed to take him forever to find one, but at last she heard the unmistakable rasping scrape of a strikebox.

Touch

The soultaker latched onto her fingers. She felt its slimy surface, the clammy, half-rotted texture of its hide. The evil of it seemed to flow straight into the marrow of her bones as it started up her arm.

Taste

A cup was pressed to Talmor's lips, and his head gently lifted so that he could gulp down a few swallows. The water was fresh and cool, and eased him greatly.

Smell

Squaring his heavy shoulders, Lervan strolled to the door and put his hand on the latch.

No one stopped him. He let himself out and stood a moment on the filthy little street, drawing in great lungfuls of fetid air. The sewers in this part of town were disgraceful, he thought, wrinkling his nostrils. Something, no doubt an animal such as a rat or a dog, had obviously died close by. He glanced about but did not see a putrid, swollen corpse. Nor did he remember such a ripe stink when he arrived.

Magic

Sighing, Talmor clenched his fist and felt the heat coiling there inside his palm. He could feel the violence building, both anger and shock entwined and ready to strike out. The air felt hotter than ever, as though the room were on fire. It was oppressive heat, the kind that was painful to breathe. But he knew he could get much, much hotter.

When he glanced up at Pears, he saw a glimmer of fear in the older man's eyes, fear swiftly hidden. But he could read the thoughts inside Pears's mind as plainly as though they were written on a scroll. If he chose, he could read deeper ... every wish, every fear, every emotion. Swiftly Talmor averted his eyes. It was wrong to soulgaze, *wrong*. He had sworn he would never do it again.

A shudder passed through him. Gritting his teeth against the forces he could no longer reliably control, he said, "Quick! Fetch some water."

Pears hurried to bring a wooden pail of water. He lifted the drinking dipper, but Talmor glared at him. "Get back!"

Dropping the dipper, Pears stumbled back just as Talmor felt the violence inside him escape. It spewed from him, a blazing heat that shot down his arm with such power he cried out. A ball of fire burst into flames in mid-air, the force of it pulling him nearly upright. With all the willpower he possessed, he threw the flames at the water pail.

The fireball extinguished with a sharp crack of sound, and the bucket rocked back and forth. Steam rose from the wood. As Pears crept forward cautiously to peer into the pail, Talmor already knew it was bone-dry.

The air in the sick room cooled at once. The violence in him was gone, spent. Exhausted, he dropped down on his cot and flung his arm across his stinging eyes. He hadn't lost control like that in years, not since the day he lost his temper with his half-brother Etyne and burned him.

Pain

The hurlhound snapped at his throat, missed, and closed its jaws on his arm instead.

He felt a searing pain, so immense, so horrible, that he cried out. The creature shook him the way a dog shakes a rat, and he heard—and felt—the crunching snap of bone beneath the hurlhound's teeth. Agony poured through him, and he screamed again.

As is evident even in these examples chosen to illustrate a particular viewpoint signal, indicators are seldom isolated. Instead, they're often used in combinations. Blended together, they appear again and again in a variety of ways, never letting readers forget whose viewpoint they're in.

As long as you're sharing the thoughts, emotions, and/ or feelings of a character, you're in that viewpoint. But if you establish viewpoint as belonging to Princess Extrema, for example, but inadvertently share the thoughts of Lady Kluliss while the two women are talking, you've committed a viewpoint slip.

Does it matter?

Yes!

An occasional slip jars readers and annoys them, but frequent slips create a jumbled mess that I call floating viewpoint. It's hard to read and unnecessarily confusing. While a careless writer may think she's conveying nuance and texture by not controlling viewpoint, the reality is that she's creating chaos.

Even if you're planning to feature more than a single viewpoint in your book, stick to one viewpoint per scene.

As you plan a scene, decide from whose viewpoint it will be presented, establish viewpoint by sharing that character's emotions, thoughts, or feelings, and don't veer into any other character's subjective perspective until the scene is completed.

> *Drill exercise 1:*
>
> Read the following example of jumbled, floating viewpoint. Mark each viewpoint indicator used. How many viewpoints are used? To what effect?

Jada hurried into the nightclub, eager to start the evening. Although twenty minutes early, she'd heard that Paul's mother valued promptness nearly as much as a witch's bloodlines. *I can't afford mistakes tonight,* Jada thought.

But the dance floor was crowded with guests, many of them clutching glasses of blood or steaming green cocktails. Their tipsy laughter and loud voices told Jada the party had been in full swing for a long time.

In a cage above the music pit, Gina stopped shimmying to the beat and shifted back into human form to catch her breath. Curling her hands around the oiled steel bars, so cool against her heated skin, she crouched to hide her nudity and watched poor, clueless Jada stumbling through the crowd. *What a twit.* Gina would have felt sorry for the girl, but sympathy was something she'd sold a long time ago, along with her soul.

Pushing through the dancers, Jada struggled toward the back where a long table was set up. A male vampire clutched her arm with vise-grip fingers and twirled her until she staggered. He couldn't believe the flood of emotions choking this girl. Why did she want to cry? Breaking free of him, Jada kept going. She'd glimpsed the guests of honor still sitting at the table, including Lady Francesca.

Jada felt as though she'd missed a step and was about to fall down a long staircase. What had gone wrong? Why was everyone already here? How could she be so late? Gina had stressed the time several times when she called yesterday. Jada had even written it down.

Paul was sitting next to his mother. Waving, Jada sent him a look of appeal. "I'm sorry," she mouthed.

He rose to his feet, his face stony. In the throne-like chair, his mother watched this girl her son had chosen, watched her buffeted this way and that by the revelers. Anger coiled through Lady Francesca. This bedraggled, timid creature was no fit wife for Paul. He required a consort worthy of the Jekylli name, a woman who carried herself like a queen and could part the unruly crowd with a wordless look of command.

"Don't, Mother," Paul murmured. He knew his mother's temper, knew her mood was already black enough without Jada insulting her this way. "Something must have happened." *But Jada,* he thought, disappointment sour in his mouth, *why did you fail this first and easiest test?*

Drill exercise 2:

Read this revised passage written from one viewpoint. Mark how many times viewpoint is indicated. Note which details have been omitted. To what effect?

Jada hurried into the nightclub, eager to start the evening. Although twenty minutes early, she'd heard that Paul's mother valued promptness nearly as much as a witch's bloodlines. *I can't afford mistakes tonight*, Jada thought.

But the dance floor was crowded with guests, many of them clutching glasses of blood or steaming green cocktails. Their tipsy laughter and loud voices told Jada the party had been in full swing for a long time.

Dismayed, Jada looked past the crowd to the back where the guests of honor were sitting at a long table. Her gaze shifted quickly away from the imposing figure of Lady Francesca to a cage swinging high above the music pit. Gina was dancing there, her leopard spots as dark as the shadows themselves.

As Jada stared, Gina abruptly stopped her leonine

movements and shifted to human form. She was nude, her taut body glistening with sweat.

Look at me, Jada commanded.

Gina crouched low, hiding her body in the shadows darkening the bottom half of her cage. Her gaze met Jada's, and she bared her teeth in a grin that was both taunt and confession.

Jada rocked back on her heels, forcing herself to break eye contact. She heard Gina's throaty laugh, and her anger burned red at the edges of her vision. *Gina did this*, she thought. *All that fake concern on my behalf. How many times did she tell me the party would start at eight o'clock? She wanted me to fail!*

It was tempting to spin around and run, but Jada refused to give Gina that satisfaction. Determined to face Lady Francesca and do what she could to smooth over this disaster of etiquette, Jada pushed through the crowd. Dodging a drunken warlock, she found herself in the vise-grip of a male vampire who twirled her around, trying to make her dizzy so he could mesmerize her.

No! Jada blocked his attempt to read her mind. His handsome face twisted in an expression of what might have been pity, and he let her go. Although certain he'd read her emotions, even if she hadn't let him into her thoughts, Jada fought the desire to throw a temper spell that would crash down the ceiling.

Stay calm, she told herself.

As she approached, Paul rose to his feet. His face was stony, which betrayed his disappointment in her. Jada saw his mother's expression of glacial contempt. Although Paul bent and murmured in his mother's ear, Lady Francesca's anger remained visible.

Jada gathered her willpower like a cloak. *If I have to fight her to prove myself worthy of Paul's love, so be it.*

The two passages aren't identical, are they? What have we lost in example two? A few internalizations, but little else. We still know that Jada was sabotaged by Gina, and the potential mother-in-law is on the warpath.

What have we gained with example two? A stronger, smarter, better-motivated protagonist who shares her reasons (with readers) for why she doesn't confront Gina immediately or why she still intends to face Lady Francesca. Jada is now much more appealing and someone with whom readers can sympathize.

It's also important to remember that viewpoint isn't established only once and never mentioned again. Entwine it through your story. Make it a vital component of the story.

After all, it can be less a matter of *what* readers experience in your novel than *how* they experience it. Viewpoint is your means of channeling emotion, feelings, magic, logic, and plausibility into the plotline.

Now, in handling viewpoint, you have several decisions to make right away.

Viewpoint decision 1

Which type of viewpoint will you use? From a practical standpoint, you have two options: first-person or third-person. Let's examine them in more detail, along with the impractical forms of viewpoint that are too experimental, artsy, or weird for use in commercial fiction.

First-person viewpoint

To write from this perspective means using the pronouns "I, me, my."

Advantages: It's a very intimate viewpoint. Readers become the viewpoint character's confidant. This character will be sharing thoughts and feelings that otherwise would be secret and never known.

The tight focus—sometimes known as limited point of view—means that you'll be less likely to slip out of viewpoint or make mistakes with it. For that reason, it's considered one of the easiest types of viewpoint to manage.

Plot twists in first-person stories can be dynamite because they're very surprising and seldom predictable.

Disadvantages: First-person is a very intimate viewpoint. Readers aren't always comfortable being so close, so *internal* with the viewpoint character. This closeness means that emotions have to be conveyed vividly without being overwritten. Go too far or exhibit flamboyant emotions and internalizations in first person, and your character will seem egotistical and vain. Underwrite, and your character will seem to be a cold, unfeeling robot.

The tight focus also means that plotting sometimes can be tricky—especially if you plan to use only one viewpoint through the entire story. You will be limited solely to what your protagonist knows, guesses, or can find out.

A few years ago, the rule was that if you wrote a story in first-person, you didn't change viewpoint for any reason. Today, writers may shift viewpoint among several first-person perspectives if they wish.

The last disadvantage worth noting is that if you're writing a suspenseful story or one where the protagonist is physically endangered, it's harder to get readers to suspend disbelief, enter the bubble of the story world, and *worry* about the safety of the protagonist since obviously the narrator survived the adventure to tell about it.

Second-person viewpoint

To write from this perspective means addressing the reader directly by using the "you" pronoun. It appears occasionally in artsy mainstream fiction, but 99.9 percent of the time it is not used in commercial fiction.

Advantages: I know of none, unless you want to try something very experimental in a short story.

Disadvantages: It breaks the "fourth wall" and destroys reader suspension of disbelief.

Third-person viewpoint

To write from this perspective means using the pronouns "he, she, or it."

Advantages: This is the most commonly used perspective, the one that's most comfortable and familiar to readers. It can be limited to a single character's point of view, or it's easily adaptable to multiple viewpoints. It allows you to use your protagonist's name as an identifier. And you have the flexibility of deciding how intimately or distantly you'll connect your character to your readers.

Disadvantages: Because of its flexibility, third-person viewpoint is the hardest to control. If you're not careful, you can shift unintentionally from one viewpoint to another. This can make your book confusing to read.

Omniscient viewpoint

To write from this perspective is to allow for direct author intrusion, to float from the mind of one character to another only to share what each of them is thinking, and to provide what is sometimes known as the "god perspective." It is the hardest viewpoint to write well and seldom is used in commercial fiction.

Advantages: In the hands of a skilled writer the omniscient point of view can provide lightning-quick insight into the emotions and motivations of several characters. Such insight enriches the nuances of dialogue and scene subtext.

Disadvantages: Almost no one does it well. Let me repeat that. *Almost no one does it well.* At its best, the general effect comes across as old-fashioned and out of date. At its worst, viewpoint floats from character to character, often shifting from sentence to sentence. The result is a muddle of chaotic thoughts. Readers find it difficult to bond with any particular character or settle into the story. Like second-person viewpoint, omniscient is not recommended.

Viewpoint decision 2

Another critical choice for you is whether you'll write your story in a single viewpoint or from multiple perspectives.

My recommendation is that you use a single viewpoint when writing short stories. This approach is focused, efficient, and cohesive—elements that work well in a story only a few thousand words long.

But if you're attempting a novel, your choice of one viewpoint versus several should be guided by three factors—the subgenre of fantasy, the scope of your plot, and your skill level.

Trends come and go in the fiction market. Writers push the boundaries and break the rules all the time. And no matter what point I make, someone can always find an exception to it. However, in a general sense, urban fantasy tends to favor single viewpoint—often first-person. Traditional fantasy, especially epic-sized, requires multiple viewpoint—usually third-person.

With that said, not all traditional fantasy is on an epic scale, requiring a dozen doorstop-sized volumes and a thousand characters. There's adventure fantasy, sword-and-sorcery fantasy, coming-of-age fantasy, deconstructed fairy tales, romantic fantasy, etc. Any of these can be written from a single perspective if desired.

The protagonist, antagonist, story goal, and what's at stake determine a plot's scope. If only one viewpoint is used, that will of course belong to the protagonist.

Can your star character be at the center of all the important story action from start to finish? If so, you need only one viewpoint. If not, you'll require perhaps a second viewpoint.

I suggest that you consider your current skill level with honesty. For instance, if you've written several novel-length manuscripts and feel ready to tackle an epic tale that's been building in your mind since you were eleven years old, then perhaps it's time to select how many viewpoints your masterpiece requires and give them a try. We writers should stretch our abilities and meet new challenges in order to grow creatively.

However, if you're writing your first or second novel and you still feel very unsure of what you're doing, or if your previous efforts collapsed partway through and you couldn't finish them, then you're better off using a single viewpoint. At this stage in your development, it's wise to shelve your ambitious epic until your writing skills can do it justice. Practice on simpler plots first.

Viewpoint decision 3

Let's say that you've decided to utilize multiple viewpoints for your next fiction project.

Okay! How many?

Maybe you're thinking you don't know yet and you intend to just switch viewpoint as needed.

Stop!

Writing by the seat of your pants is loose and fun and wild and free-wheeling. It feels great, creatively, until you're partway into your novel and get stuck.

Before you become too enamored with the notion of using several perspectives, consider the fiction principle that each viewpoint should drive a story line.

In other words, each viewpoint besides the protagonist's should be developed into a subplot. That means the viewpoint character will then become the protagonist of his or her own storyline, with a goal, an antagonist, a story question, and a climax of its own, yet subsidiary to the main plot and star protagonist.

How many such subplots can you juggle? Give the answer some thought.

Ideally, a book of large scope needs no more than four viewpoints. A book of huge scale might stretch to encompass six.

I can hear some of you sputtering protests now: "But I don't want six subplots! I just want to shift viewpoint to show what my mage is thinking when he climbs into the cave."

Why is it so important for readers to know what the mage is thinking? Is his internalization going to advance the story? Or will it give away what could otherwise be a terrific and surprising plot twist?

Changing viewpoint

If you're sure that your book really needs multiple viewpoints and you're determined to tackle the challenge, then you need to know why, when, and how to change viewpoint.

There are three valid reasons for why the viewpoint should be changed. Let's consider them individually.

To follow the story is the most valid reason for multiple viewpoints. Say that your plot is a fairly simple, straightforward adventure. Yet in the last third of the story, when the conflict is becoming intense and the characters have split up—perhaps the protagonist is battling werewolves while the sidekick goes for help—there may be the need to cut from the protagonist's perspective to the sidekick's and back again.

Such cross-cutting action, when written well, boosts the suspense level and heightens dramatic intensity.

Another example of shifting viewpoint to follow the story is whenever the protagonist has been sidelined and is now incapacitated, or tied up, or in some other passive mode. Because nothing is happening in such situations, the story either has to skip ahead in time until the protagonist wakes up or cuts the ropes, *or* the viewpoint can change to another character who's busy in story action.

To convey motivation is the second reason for why you might change viewpoint. Doing so explains a character's actions in order to sustain reader sympathy.

Let's say that you're teaming up a man and woman on a quest. The woman is the protagonist. She's in a strange town, about to undertake a long and hazardous journey. She needs protection, so she ventures into a tavern to hire muscle. The only promising candidate—brawny and tall, with a capable sword strapped to his belt—is semi-drunk, disagreeable, and nasty. He insults her so horribly she storms out, determined to attempt the journey alone.

Now, because the man is a character who will become heroic as the story progresses, you don't want readers to think he's a foul-mouthed jerk. So when the heroine leaves, viewpoint is shifted to the man. Through his internalization, we learn why he's drunk. (His best friend was buried that morning.) He's been turned out of the king's army on a trumped-up charge. He's out of money, and he can't pay his landlord. He thinks the woman is a fool—too beautiful to survive long on her own without coming to harm—but he needs to be practical about earning a living. He couldn't care less about her quest, but he requires work. So he stumbles out of the tavern and goes after her.

The third reason to change viewpoint is to let readers know that harm is about to befall the protagonist or someone the protagonist cares about. By shifting to the viewpoint of the villain, we allow readers to see the approaching threat as it's being planned and implemented. If readers care enough about the protagonist, they will read faster, wishing they had some means of warning the protagonist about what's going to happen.

Done skillfully, this heightens suspense. Used too often, however, it will destroy any hope of plot twists.

When should viewpoint be changed? The optimum place is at the start of a new chapter. There's already been a break in the flow of the narrative. Shifting perspective there is the least jarring and disruptive. Next best is at the end of a scene.

Never shift viewpoint within a scene.

Never shift viewpoint within a scene.

Never shift viewpoint within a scene.

I'm repeating this point for emphasis. There are valid reasons for this rule of writing, which I'll address in Chapter 5.

Always complete a scene from one perspective. Then you can insert a space break between the paragraphs for emphasis and shift.

In considering how to shift viewpoint, think of it in terms of driving a car. When you want to switch lanes, you don't (I hope!) abruptly jerk your vehicle over without warning the other drivers. Instead, you check your mirrors, use your turn signal, and smoothly angle your auto into an adjacent lane.

Use a similar procedure for shifting viewpoint. Signal to readers what you're doing. Use the chapter or space break between scenes as a physical signal. Use the new viewpoint's name in the first sentence. Don't rely on pronouns for this.

For example, if you're leaving Lord Justin's viewpoint for Bobkin's and you refer to Bobkin as "he," readers will assume you're still in Lord Justin's perspective.

"Don't follow me again," Lord Justin said. He glared at the boy, hoping the little pest finally understood he wasn't welcome.

He waited a while, watching him stride away. He wished he had food, yet before he could steal more he had to make sure he wasn't under surveillance. Bobkin knew stealing was wrong, but survival mattered more than honor.

Are you confused yet? Compare it with this version:

"Don't follow me again," Lord Justin said. He glared at

the boy, hoping the little pest finally understood he wasn't welcome.

Bobkin waited a while, feeling lonely as he watched the wizard stride away. He wished he had food, yet before he could steal more he had to make sure he wasn't under surveillance. Bobkin knew stealing was wrong, but survival mattered more than honor.

Two simple changes make all the difference. This viewpoint shift has employed all the signals: a physical break, a name, and an immediate internalization indicator. The shift is clear and plainly marked. There's no reason for readers to be confused.

If you're using multiple viewpoints from the first-person perspective, you'll have to signal even more obviously.

My suggestion is that you shift at the start of a new chapter rather than at the start of a new scene, and that you use the new perspective's name as a chapter subheading.

Example:

Chapter 2

Bobkin

Sadly, I watched the wizard Lord Justin striding away from me. I was hungry and lonely, but he'd made his dislike of my company clear. Since I couldn't be with him, there was no chance of him providing me with food. I would have to steal again, provided the constables weren't still keeping an eye on me. I didn't want to rob a shopkeeper, but survival mattered more than honor.

Drill exercise:

For additional practice in understanding viewpoint, choose one of your favorite books written from a single viewpoint and select a chapter. Using three colored markers—e.g. green for emotions, blue for thoughts whether direct or indirect, and red for feelings such as physical senses, magic, pain, etc.—mark the viewpoint indicators in the appropriate colors.

When you've finished, observe the proportion of colors. Has the author relied primarily on emotions, meaning most of your marks are green? Is the passage mostly marked in red? All blue? Or is there a balanced blend from start to finish? Notice how often viewpoint is indicated.

Next print out a chapter from your manuscript. Mark it in the same way. Are your colors disproportionate or balanced? Or are there paragraphs lacking any color at all? What does that mean? How might you revise your viewpoint indicators to rectify these problems?

4

Dialogue

Dialogue isn't characters merely sharing a conversation. Instead, it's a device of characterization, plot advancement, and setting reinforcement. If you examine genre novels of today written for mass-market audiences, you may find the majority of them feature scenes that are about ninety-five percent dialogue. Scene dialogue—that snappy, give-and-take exchange of verbal conflict—keeps the story pacing brisk. And in the aftermath of scenes, dialogue can be a method of supplying information and motivation to readers without putting the story on pause.

When I was a teenager writing my first, fumbling efforts at fiction, I enrolled in a correspondence course for writers. Each month a large manila envelope of instructions and a writing assignment arrived by mail for me to complete and return for evaluation. One of those lessons instructed me to listen to real-life conversation in order to develop an ear for dialogue.

After eavesdropping as much as I could, I mistakenly thought I was supposed to duplicate what I overheard. Not the content, of course, but the delivery.

The trouble is that most real-life conversation is meaningless, aimless social chatter. It seldom gets to the point. It's frequently boring, especially to listeners who aren't participating. Real-life talk is filled with pauses, fumbling for words, fragments, gaps supplemented with gestures, and slang.

When you try to copy any of that too closely in your fiction, you may find yourself stalled. Aimless dialogue keeps scenes from developing properly. Plots can't move forward. The pacing lags.

Eventually I realized that character speech in fiction is only a replication of conversation. It's nothing more than a simulacrum, representative of conversation while it works hard to carry the storyline forward. Good story dialogue gets to the point quickly and stays focused. It's goal-oriented. It's streamlined and designed to facilitate scene conflict.

Story dialogue has a job to do. Every word coming out of a character's mouth should serve a valid purpose.

Characterization through diction

In Chapter 2, I addressed so-called speech tags—distinctive and habitual phrases or expressions that make a character stand out from the others. ("Zounds, man! Are you mad?")

Characters can be individualized through their diction—i.e. which words they choose, their vocabulary level, and their rhythm or style of speaking. Their background, geographical location, socio-economic status, and education also factor in.

In other words, each character should speak in a way that reflects personality and background. And the most vivid, memorable characters will exhibit dialogue that tags them distinctively from each other.

Example from *Crystal bones* (2012) by C. Aubrey Hall:

> Diello approached the sentry. "We've come to see the steward, please. We've brought a banquet cloth from the weaver Lwyneth."
>
> The sentry wasn't interested. "Be off. Your kind can't come peddling here."
>
> "We aren't peddling!" Diello said indignantly. "It's commissioned. We're delivering it."
>
> "So you say, but as to the truth of your prattle, I know not." The sentry made a shooing motion.
>
> Diello stood his ground. "Ask the steward if you don't believe us."

The man grinned, showing the gaps of missing teeth. "Hark at you!" he said in false admiration. "Standing up to me like someone important and demanding I bother Master Timmons on a day like this, when he's so busy he don't remember his own name. Get on!"

"Ask him," Diello insisted. "Or I reckon you can explain to his lordship why there's no cloth spread for his banquet tonight."

The type of fantasy you're writing should also affect character diction. Some authors of high-fantasy epics tend to go too far in seeking archaic speech patterns:

"My lords," quoth he, "have a care, I beseech thee. Thou wilt be in mortal danger if thy borders are breached."

Besides the obvious pitfalls in trying to use thee and thou correctly, the antiquated attribution of "quoth", combined with stilted diction and old-fashioned vocabulary, will quickly become too much for most modern readers. You want to supply the flavor of days of yore without sounding like a stereotypical pirate. Try this:

"My lords," he said, "have a care. You're in mortal danger should your borders be overrun."

The dialogue is still formal and stilted, but it's less archaic now. The key is to choose one old-fashioned element but keep everything else more modern.

On the other hand, even if you're writing urban fantasy, you don't want to go too contemporary.

"Watch your back, dudes," he said. "If your border falls, *whoa!* You're in, like, majorly serious danger."

A secondary character, playing the role of comic relief, could speak this way, but you probably don't want your protagonist to come across as a stereotypical young urban American slacker.

Let's tweak it again:

John eyed the creatures with misgivings. Were they elves? He thought so, but he didn't want to goof this up.

"My, uh, lords," he said, hoping that was the correct way to address them. "If your border's protection goes down, you're in serious danger."

You can see how each of these examples is conveying the same message, yet indicating differences in personality and time period. The more extreme versions create inadvertent, campy humor. The dialed-back versions are offering flavor without overkill.

Dialogue that advances plot

Have you ever participated in a conversation where the other person kept hinting at something without openly discussing it? Did you feel some hidden agenda was going on, but you couldn't guess what it might be? And when the chat was over, were you left feeling puzzled or irritated by the encounter?

Psychologists might slap a fancy label on such behavior, calling it passive-aggressive game playing.

Perhaps you initiate a conversation with someone because you have a question to ask or a request to make, but you're unsure and timid. You keep circling the matter without being able to make yourself come out with it. After maybe fifteen minutes of aimless chitchat and belabored small-talk, your baffled companion demands that you "get to the point!" and you blurt out your request.

If you're annoyed by these situations in reality, imagine how impatient readers will be with characters that waffle, dither, and blather.

The majority of the time, at any given point in your story, readers want you to just get on with it.

Accordingly, in scene dialogue, hesitant characters will delay only for a sentence or less before plunging into what they want to discuss.

More importantly, characters will not waste time with idle chatter. They enter the scene with an objective, and they use dialogue as a means of persuading their opponent to surrender that objective to them.

So dialogue advances plot by stating the scene goal. It advances plot by serving as a verbal weapon in scene conflict. And it advances plot by keeping scenes focused and germane to what the story is about.

Dialogue and setting

Please do not halt your characters on their quest to recapture the Glorious Goblet of Gilhallow so they can discuss how prettily yon stream trickles beside yon road.

Nor do I recommend that two characters stand in front of a castle fortress, telling each other that it's built of white stone quarried in the Welsh mountains, that the stairs are hewn from stout oak felled from the Forest of Nottingham, and that it takes six stout men to turn the portcullis wheel. By this point, should Sir Notsomuch be asking for the name of Lord Bragberry's castle architect?

When characters tell each other things that they both already know, simply for the benefit of readers, that's an offense known as dialogue of information.

You'll find it in some of the old genre classics. It also tends to crop up in the sloppiest modern fantasy fiction. It's pernicious and undesirable. Please eradicate it from your manuscripts.

While fantasy writers must always juggle with the problem of how to convey information and explanation to readers, this is not the way.

As for how dialogue suitably reinforces setting, it's a subtle effect that results naturally from discussions about solving the plot problems.

Example from *Mage fire* (2013) by C. Aubrey Hall:

> "Let's stop," Cynthe said at last, sinking down. Her chest was heaving, her face red.
>
> Diello knelt, wishing the air wasn't so thin. The shadows were lengthening under the trees. He heard an eagle cry in the distance but paid it no heed.
>
> "Have ... to keep ... going," he panted.
>
> "I—I don't know if I can," Cynthe said. "The wind's getting too strong."
>
> "Vassou," Diello, asked, "how much farther?"
>
> "Untie me, and I'll scout."
>
> Cynthe unfastened the rope from Vassou's harness, and the wolf shook himself.
>
> "Wait here," he said, and headed into the snowy brush. His pale coat blended in with the surroundings, making it impossible to watch where he went.
>
> Diello pulled his hands farther inside his sleeves and turned his back to the icy blast.
>
> "How's Scree doing?" he asked.
>
> Cynthe finished tucking a corner of Scree's blanket around him. "I can't tell. Stand over here beside me, and we'll block some of the wind from him."

Diello and Cynthe aren't telling each other that there's a blizzard or that their friend Scree is hurt. They're talking naturally about the problems they're facing as they move him through worsening weather conditions.

Let's look at another excerpt from the same novel:

By midafternoon, the ground leveled off.

We must be at the top, Diello thought. He ducked through a narrow fissure between two leaning slabs of rock and came out into the open. *Is this Qod's meadow?* Diello wondered. A gust of wind made him stagger. Turning around, Diello saw dizzying views in all directions.

"It's beautiful," Cynthe said in wonder.

"Yes," Vassou agreed. "Very beautiful."

Scree moaned and sank down, clutching his head. "I cannot look. I am dizzy. I am going to fall."

Cynthe laughed. "You can't fall. You're on solid ground."

"There is a spell on me," Scree insisted. "Everything is spinning."

"Not everyone can manage the great heights," Reeshwin said.

"Put your head between your knees," Cynthe instructed Scree. "Keep your eyes closed and rest a moment."

Again, the characters are discussing the setting but in a natural way that supports description. Scree's vertigo on the mountaintop supplies a moment of humor. Anyone who's felt the same way about heights can sympathize.

Dialogue pitfalls

Besides dialogue of information, there are other errors to avoid in writing dialogue.

One is to avoid long, rambling speeches. When you let a character pontificate—even if it's to relate his special destiny to the young, untried hero—you run the very real risk of reader boredom.

If someone's lecturing, no story action is happening. You must remember to keep your story moving forward. If there's no quick, back-and-forth exchange of dialogue, the pacing bogs down to a standstill.

Remember how you feel when one individual monopolizes the talk at a party.

Remember also how difficult it can be to sit through long, stultifying classroom lectures. Wasn't it Henry II who ordered his bishop never to deliver a sermon longer than ten minutes? That was all the king could endure.

So if you find yourself with a character—we'll call him Sir Oswald, just for fun—who talks his way through a long paragraph, then through a second paragraph, and maybe even a third, with no response from another character, please rethink this scene and conversation. Perhaps Sir Oswald is a stuffy old wart with a pompous manner and too much self-conceit. Perhaps Sir Oswald is the kind of guy that causes other characters to moan and scatter when they see him coming because no one wants to be cornered by the old windbag.

Fine!

Just be sure that when he starts one of his tirades, another character quickly interrupts him. Or someone asks a question, then another, and another. (Much as mischievous students sometimes do to keep a professor flustered and off-track when lecturing.)

The viewpoint character also can tune out Sir Oswald and muse her way through an internalization, planning her next course of action, and fail to hear any of the speech until Sir Oswald clears his throat and demands, "Well? What do you have to say about my proposal?"

Again, remember that dialogue is merely a simulation. We only have to provide the semblance, the appearance, of talking. We don't have to make readers slog through every boring word.

An additional problem with the rambling character comes from long paragraphs of big words. Do people really speak this way? Or do they interrupt each other, utter fragments, and so on? Check your copy by reading your characters' dialogue aloud. It will become obvious quickly if your characters sound stilted or unnatural.

Another pitfall comes from the temptation to use dialect

and/or foreign languages. We're not in the magical land of film and television. We don't have actors to depict accents and inflections for us. Our medium is prose. Putting so-called special effects across to readers can be a challenge, one that's often not worth the extra bother of description and explanation.

The trouble with dialect is twofold: how to spell it and will readers understand it? A judicious drop or two of dialect, used as a speech tag, can be charming. Too much can become fatiguing—or even incomprehensible—to read.

Examine the novels of Brian Jacques for dialect. Every type of animal in his charming *Redwall* series (2009) speaks in a distinctive way. The hares use a brisk stereotypical British military "Right-o! What?" lingo. The moles use a broad county accent. The sparrows speak in terse, quick bursts of pidgin English. If readers can grasp imaginatively the rhythm and sound of these accents and dialects, Jacques's books are tremendous fun. But at some point, especially for adult readers, the charm may wear off. I remember trying to read one of his later books and struggling to get into the story until I finally realized that the badgers were speaking with a Swedish rhythm. At that point, the dialogue finally began to make sense.

Now, nineteenth-century literature can provide us with numerous examples of dialect used in novels. But in that era, with no way to record accents or unique dialects, some novelists did labor meticulously to depict them for readers who had never traveled. In the classic *Huckleberry Finn* (1885) by Mark Twain, dialect found along the Mississippi River delta was utilized for the benefit of readers who would otherwise have no idea of how people in that region spoke.

As inventions such as recording devices, radio, and television became commonplace, dialects were better served by such media and became less commonplace in prose fiction.

However, to some degree, writers of fantasy fiction face the same dilemma as the nineteenth-century authors. If your story world has been invented entirely by you, how will your readers know anything about the characters' accents and unique colloquialisms if you don't include them?

Nevertheless, how necessary is dialect to your plot? Will your setting be less vivid or believable if you avoid it? Be honest. Chances are you need much less of it than you suppose. Err on the conservative side because a little of it goes a long way.

In my own traditional fantasy work, I've tended to follow the model of Hollywood filmmakers in the 1950s—where the ancient Romans were always played by actors with the most Shakespearean, aristocratic British voices and the slaves were always played by American thespians. It was an easy, vivid way to put class distinction across to movie audiences. Accordingly, I write dialogue for my characters where the more important roles speak correctly and the lesser types of servants and squires use ungrammatical, rougher language.

Compare Harry Potter's dialogue to Hagrid's. The giant is allowed a touch of dialect in his speech to contrast with the more erudite teachers and students at Hogwarts.

As for slang, it works best in urban fantasy, especially if the characters are going for snarky humor. Slang in traditional pseudo-medieval fantasy has to be invented—although it's delightful how modern and current many of Shakespeare's Renaissance expressions remain. Even so, if you use too many "modern" expressions in pseudo-medieval dialogue, you run the risk of appearing anachronistic. If you use invented or authentic historical slang, chances are you'll have to supply their meanings to baffled readers. That can be cumbersome to the plot.

Don't even think of adding a glossary at the end of your manuscript. You are not Mr. Tolkien and do not rate his privileges.

The trouble with modern slang in urban fantasy is that slang is so darned trendy. It's designed to be transitory. Therefore, it dates quickly. And out-of-date slang becomes, like, majorly lame, right? Boom!

Publishing is a slow business. Unless you're going to write exclusively for the e-book market, you have to think roughly three years ahead. By then, your cutting-edge slang may have been left in the dust, especially if you're writing urban fantasy for teens.

Use slang if it's appropriate and will add color to a character's dialogue, but make sure it's long-lived rather than super-trendy.

The next dialogue pitfall worth mentioning is inconsistency of speech. As mentioned earlier in this chapter, you want a character's dialogue to reflect her personality and background. That means whatever vocabulary, favorite expressions, or slang, and speech pattern you select for said character should remain consistent throughout the book.

In other words, you don't want a character speaking in this effusive way in chapter 1:

"Bartholomew, my dear, *dear* old friend! How have you been? Come inside and warm yourself by my fire. I'm certain I can offer you a little sherry. No? Some tea then. Oh, forgive me. I'm not letting you get a word in, am I? I do tend to natter on. But then, I'm so terribly delighted to have a visitor. It's been, what, goodness me ... has it really been twelve years since I last saw you?"

And then, in chapter 4, the same character now speaks like this:

"It's all over for me, mate. I'm done for. That swine Bartholomew, I should have known he was an agent for the rogue-wizards. All that smiling ... a damned cutthroat, tricking me that way."

Or,

"Come in. Good to see you. I've got plenty to say about that scoundrel Bartholomew."

Unless our speaker has been wearing disguises and playing several roles, and readers clearly understand who he truly is, these different samples of dialogue will come across as inconsistent. Muddling a reader's image of the character means the character no longer stands out distinctively.

Inconsistency usually happens because of writer carelessness, forgetfulness, or fatigue. And, in the case of long book manuscripts, the effort to remember each important character's speech patterns and idiosyncrasies can become difficult. But it's worth the effort. I find it helpful to list my characters, with notations about certain expressions or diction beside each name, and keep it posted near my computer.

The last pitfall I'll mention is speech attribution. In other words, how do you identify who's saying what?

Please have consideration for your readers by breaking to a new paragraph for each different speaker. Don't jam multiple speakers together in the same paragraph. It may all be clear in your head, but your readers may not be able always to keep everyone straight.

Example:

John smiled at Tanya, baring his teeth. "Don't eat with the goblins, my dear. It's a nasty habit." "Stop telling me what to do. You don't boss Kerry around. Why do you pick on me?" "Because," Kerry spoke up, cleaning his nails with a dagger tip, "I like to live on the edge, little one, and you're going to fall into the ravine."

Can you follow the dialogue? Maybe. But the following approach is much more readable:

John smiled at Tanya, baring his teeth. "Don't eat with the goblins, my dear. It's a nasty habit."

"Stop telling me what to do. You don't boss Kerry around. Why do you pick on me?"

"Because," Kerry spoke up, cleaning his nails with a dagger tip, "I like to live on the edge, little one, and you're going to fall into the ravine."

Attributions also cause problems when writers try to be too inventive with synonyms. "Said" and "asked" are such plain little words they may make you worry about their overuse.

Said is simply a punctuation word. The reader's eye goes right over it as readily as over a comma or period.

But strive too hard for substitutions, and you get in the way of your own story.

Consider this:

"Oh, it was horrible. Horrible!" she quavered.

"Try to stay calm," he reassured her. "Tell me what you saw."

"That f-face at the window," she stammered. "The claws raking the glass to get inside."

"You're safe now," he soothed. "Go on."

"It scratched and scratched," she whispered. "I could hear the wood splintering."

"When did the demon break inside?" he probed. "Can you remember the exact time?"

"No," she shuddered. "It was too awful! I keep seeing those red eyes. And it was laughing at me."

"My God!" he exclaimed.

Unbearable, isn't it? This kind of writing may be centered on a horrific event intended to be frightening, but the clumsy attributions are creating a campy effect.

There are several problems with this example. The first is that the worst attributions here aren't actually verbs of speaking. A person doesn't "quaver" words or "shudder" words. Careless readers sufficiently caught up by the story may accept the sloppy imagery. But what we actually want to express is that this character is speaking in a voice that quavers. Or this character shudders—a variant of trembling—before she replies.

Another error comes from the attributions such as "reassured," "soothed," "stammered," and "exclaimed", which echo what's already been expressed by the dialogue itself. In each of these instances, the dialogue alone has expressed the manner in which it was spoken. There's no need to hammer readers with a description as well.

As for "probed," in connection with everything else, it becomes too much. The man isn't interrogating this frightened woman. He isn't digging all that deeply into her account. Therefore, he isn't actually probing for answers. The misuse of meaning serves to compound a general effect of implausibility.

Perhaps you've noticed that I haven't criticized the attribution "whispered." That's because it conveys useful information about the volume level of her voice. Choosing to whisper when she describes the demon raking the glass with its claws hints at her emotional state as she remembers that detail. And unless supplied with that precise attribution, readers would not otherwise know she's speaking softly.

The final problem with this example is that there are only two people speaking. Once it's established what's happened to whom there's no need to attach an attribution to each exchange. The paragraph breaks and the dialogue content are sufficient for readers to follow what's being said without misunderstanding. Were there more than two characters present, however, names and attributions would be used for clarity.

Let's look at it again:

"Oh, it was horrible! Horrible." Her voice was quavering.

"Try to stay calm," he said. "Tell me what you saw."

"That f-face at the window. The claws raking the glass to get inside."

"You're safe now. Go on."

"It scratched and scratched," she whispered. "I could hear the wood splintering."

"When did the demon break inside? Can you remember the exact time?"

She shuddered, burying her face in her hands. "No! I keep seeing those red eyes. And it was laughing at me."

"My God!"

See the difference? Yes, this example may be melodramatic and silly, but it's much more readable than before.

Character action or description of movement and reaction can also serve to identify the speaker without the necessity of an attribution. This allows you to vary your usage in several ways, keeping the process from becoming monotonous and predictable.

Drill exercise:

Think about the attitude and image you want your character to project. If, for example, you want to achieve an urban, snarky tone, choose two novels that feature such dialogue.

As a suggestion, you might try Jim Butcher's *Storm front* and Rosemary Clement-Moore's *Prom dates from hell.*

Select a page of dialogue from each book and type it out. Print the samples on separate pages of paper. Lay each page beside a page of your manuscript's dialogue.

Among the three samples, compare how the exchanges flow. Look at the attributions, particularly where and when they're used. Besides the author's choice of diction, how does each line of dialogue advance the plot?

This should give you some ideas of how to edit and tighten your dialogue.

5

Scene structure

You have your cast of characters in mind. You know their names and personalities. You've been imagining your setting since you were thirteen. You know every leaf and blade of grass in your story world. You also intend to write a coming-of-age quest in the grand Tolkien tradition, and at the end your hero will fight an evil dragon to the death. You've planned a big event to open your story—let's say a tragic accident happens at the castle and your young hero is unjustly blamed for it. All he can do now is run away, and prove his honesty, merit, and honor by performing a heroic act. After a blistering confrontation and public humiliation, Hero sneaks out of the castle, swims the moat, and sets forth to find the magical Gleaming Goblet of Galsworth.

By this point, perhaps you're thirty-five pages into your great epic, but the moment Hero's foot hits the road, your momentum slows down. You fill a few more pages with description and character angst, and then you scare up an encounter with a Medusa-headed gorgon guarding the only road through the Dreadful Forest. Then what? You know Hero's destination, but how will you get him there? It's a long way from his grandfather's castle to the evil dragon guarding the Gleaming Goblet of Galsworth.

If you're very determined and highly imaginative, no doubt you will think up numerous other encounters of random dangers and hazards on the road. You will attach new companions and friends to Hero with glue. Once he acquires some traveling buddies, you can fill more pages with everyone sitting around the campfire, eating the bread that they've somehow managed to bake without an oven or a day off from walking to let the yeasty dough rise. And while they're munching toast made over the fire, they're listening to some ancient mentor droning on about the entire history of their planet, realm, and mythological system. That will certainly fill up more pages of your so-called novel, but readers will have long since yawned and tossed your epic aside.

Too clichéd, too boring, too slow. Nothing, despite all the character dialogue, is happening. Or—despite all the random crises which Hero always solves successfully—nothing is advancing the story except when you contrive another event.

Trying to write a book this way becomes a wearisome slog. It's exhausting, bewildering, and discouraging. Many a would-be writer gives up partway through or else limps on and on and on, producing a vast, unreadable lump of manuscript that interests no one except its creator.

Until you understand scenes and their structure, you're doomed to trudge through the Bog of Puzzlement. I know, because I used to write that way, too.

A combination of narrative, description, scenes, and sequels goes into prose fiction, especially novels. While experimental short stories sometimes may be confined to a single one of these elements, they're seldom much good. Readers of genre fiction generally aren't interested in avant-garde experimentation. They don't want to be bored.

Instead, they want a rousing good story. They want to be engrossed in your setting, enthralled by your characters, and entwined with nail-biting suspense as to how the story will turn out.

Novels need narrative passages and deft touches of description, but, most importantly of all, novels need scenes.

Scenes are dramatic units that form a vital part of a plot's construction. They're the basic building blocks of fiction. So what, exactly, does any of that mean?

Scenes and their aftermath, which I'll discuss later in

Chapters 9 and 10, comprise your plot. Scenes can be defined as confrontations between at least two characters in disagreement over a specific objective. These confrontations, when written correctly, push the story forward, reveal character, intensify story suspense, and raise the stakes.

If you watch more films than you read books, you may find yourself confused when trying to determine what is and is not a scene. That's because a cinematic scene is not quite the same thing as a scene in written prose.

The former refers to whatever transpires in a particular location. Let's say two characters argue about whether to enter a dragon's cave. If you were writing a screenplay, the argument outside the cave would be a scene and the exploration inside the cave would be another scene. The location has changed. The camera, if you will, has been moved.

But in prose, we can write several scenes in the same setting or room. We're not concerned with where a camera is. We're focused on what the characters are actually doing and how they achieve a resolution to what they're in conflict about.

If you haven't been reading much lately, I urge you to resume your acquaintanceship with novels.

The scenes in a book or short story organize the plot and keep it moving from start to finish. When constructed well, scenes prevent your plot from bogging down. You will not run dry of material.

Poorly written scenes, conversely, drop you into plot holes, leave you stranded at dead ends, let you split focus between two or more characters, confuse readers, lessen the suspense level until readers simply don't care what happens next, muddle the story question, and eventually cause the entire book to fail.

As structural components that carry the drama, scenes present confrontations between characters, with later consequences.

Instead of just scribbling descriptions and aimless conversations, train yourself to think beyond having your characters talking and moving around. Think of every important situation in your story plan in terms of actual scene structure and how each scene will begin, how the conflict will be developed, and how the scene will end.

Scenes create a dramatic structure that mimics real life to some extent. They help readers suspend disbelief to vicariously experience the story action in a compelling, believable way.

Think about your personal life for a moment. Ever wish you could fast-forward through some segments of your day? Or do you long to replay an hour that was so enjoyable you wish you could repeat it?

Ah, but you can't. You have to live through each moment.

In a similar way, scenes simulate "real life" by avoiding summary. There should be no narrative in a scene.

Are you telepathic? No? You have only your perspective, your powers of observation, your memories, your perceptions to draw on as you go about your day. You can't know what another individual is thinking, can you? Oh, you can guess. You may be so well acquainted with him or her that your guess will be accurate. But even so, you're trapped inside your own skull.

Scenes also simulate "real life" by being written from a single viewpoint. From start to finish, a scene should belong to only one perspective. If you're writing multiple viewpoints, switch before or after a scene, but never during it.

Can you travel through time? Can you step from one dimension to another, shift forward into the future or wander in the dim halls of the past? Not in real life, alas. You have your memories of the past. You have your expectations of the future, but you remain always in the *now* of time.

Scenes simulate "real life" by taking place in the now of your characters' lives. Flashbacks can transport readers to the story's past, but even flashbacks—once entered—are written as though they're happening now.

As you walk to work, perhaps you see a child playing dangerously near a busy road. You run to push the child to safety, then continue on your way. The child grows up to be a surgeon who marries your daughter and later performs a life-saving procedure on your wife. Or the child grows up instead to become a meth addict and thief. He steals your identity, and once you see him caught and jailed you wonder why you saved his grubby neck when he was little.

Scenes simulate "real life" when their outcome shows effects and consequences later in the story.

The goal of each scene should relate clearly to the central story question. When there's no relationship, the scene seems like a random event. Too many random scenes causes readers to lose the connection ... and lose interest.

The conflict within each scene should be focused on that scene's goal. If you allow the conflict to ramble off course, the scene will crumble.

Conflict within scenes should be between people or sentient entities. In other words, an event centered on your protagonist arguing with a lifeless, mindless rock isn't conflict and it isn't a scene. (Mind you, an argument with a sentient rock is a different matter. In my C. Aubrey Hall young adult fantasy, *Mage fire*, there's a creature that appears to be a rock but is, in fact, a shape- shifter named Qod. Qod is intelligent, clever, kind, and focused on a goal of its own.)

As for internal conflict, that's basically prolonged introspection as the viewpoint character attempts to process some disaster that's befallen her. There's certainly a valuable use for internal conflict in fiction, but it doesn't belong within scenes. Scene conflict should be external.

The best-planned scenes end in ways that make things worse for the protagonist, and they eliminate solutions and options that the protagonist hopes will rectify his story problem. If designed effectively, a scene should increase the protagonist's trouble and raise the stakes.

Midway through your plot, your protagonist should be in worse trouble than at the start. And the last section of your story should feature a culmination of trouble, worry, and hardship that tops everything else.

Every scene, from a writer's perspective, is designed to remove the protagonist's options, one by one, until the protagonist has no choice but to face the villain in the story's climax. The worse things are for your protagonist, the better your story. But if things are going smoothly for your protagonist, your story is in a lot of trouble. The pacing will slow down, and readers will grow bored. Not because they're cruel or want to see your protagonist struggle and suffer, but because they want to see your protagonist tested hard then win.

Every scene you write should have a valid reason for being in the story. If a scene doesn't change the protagonist's situation, however slightly, or if it has no impact on later story development, cut it.

Now let's examine more closely what goes into a scene and how it's constructed.

Structural parts

Successful scenes, good scenes, well-written scenes are built in a particular way which enables them to do their job. Such scenes contain a goal, conflict, and a resolution. Conflict and resolution are discussed in the following two chapters.

Scene goals

The scene goal is a target that provides the scene with direction and organization. What—in this place, at this moment—is your protagonist trying to do? If you're not sure, then figure out the answer or ask yourself if you have sufficient material to write a scene.

Scenes should be reserved for the high points of your drama. These turning points should matter to the outcome of the story and propel it forward.

Trivial issues, with vague goals, low stakes, and little motivation, do not deserve to be written as scenes. They can be summarized. Above all, don't waste your time—or the reader's—on some long, dull passage where characters in perfect agreement stand around and chat with each other.

Everything in a scene revolves around the goal. The protagonist (or scene's viewpoint character) wants to achieve this goal. The antagonist opposes it.

The scene doesn't start until the protagonist thinks, states, or acts on a scene goal. It needs to be specific and obtainable now. Make it clear because there's no need to conceal it from readers. It should relate to either the central story goal or to a subplot's goal.

For example, let's say we have a protagonist, Princess Iphegenia. Her problem is that her small realm controls a magical gateway of critical importance to the rest of the world. Powerful merchant cartels want to use it to shorten their trade routes, but they don't want to pay Iphegenia a tariff for the convenience. Each cartel wants to control the gate so it can levy tariffs on its competitors.

So, given that background motivation, Iphegenia's central story goal is to keep her throne. To do that, she must fend off invaders who are out to depose her and annex her realm (and the gate). As I've explained in Chapter 1, story goals are inverted into questions that are answered in the climax. Therefore, will Iphegenia save her throne and keep control of the magical gate?

If we're writing a short story, with two or three scenes and a climax, we'd open the story with Iphegenia on the eve of battle, beseeching her old-fashioned generals to accept the strategy of the mercenaries she's hired. Then there would be the battle scene, and a denouement.

But if we're writing a novel, with many scenes to plan, we have to consider what Iphegenia would do first to accomplish her primary story goal. And each of those actions—the important ones—should be dramatized into individual scenes. Scene goals are smaller objectives designed to achieve the main story goal. And, in turn, each scene goal becomes its own scene question which must be answered at the scene's conclusion.

Iphegenia wants to save her realm. What should she do first? Consult with her chancellor and ministers? Perhaps they don't agree about the danger. Send for her general and raise an army? Will the stiff-necked old geezer agree with her, or is he in the pocket of her most adversarial adviser? And if she can't gain support for raising an army, what will she do next?

Can you see how each scene will be leading to those that follow?

Generally, when you look at published fiction to isolate and examine scenes, you may experience some initial difficulty locating the start of a scene. That's because authors do a bit of what I call scene positioning. It sets up for the scene to come, either through description or narrative. But the scene actually begins with the protagonist's goal. It can be delivered through dialogue, an internalized intention, or implied through the character's actions.

Example from *The pearls* (2007) by Deborah Chester:

> Eager shouts rose among the company. Someone produced a rope, and ex-Centruin Fomo—instead of putting a halt to their purpose—slung it over a rafter for them.
>
> In moments they had the dog out of the sack, tied by its hind legs, and hoisted it upside down by the rope. Small and white with a brown head, the dog snarled and snapped, twisting and struggling all the while, as the men danced around it, teasing it and laughing.
>
> Wilbis pulled a knife. "Let's dance for his eyes, eh?"
>
> "Aye! Aye! I'll wager four —"
>
> Shadrael stepped into the taproom. "Let the dog go."

Do you see the positioning in the above sample? It lasts for four paragraphs, setting up the players, the locale, the mood, and what's going on. The last paragraph, where Shadrael appears and orders them to release the dog, is a statement of his scene goal.

Next, let's see a goal implied through character action:

Example from *The pearls*:

> In New Imperia, Bronzidaec hurried along the broad loggia of the inner palace courtyard, keeping well away from the hot sunlight that could betray him, keeping so close to the shadows that his shoulder brushed the wall stones. He pattered along, hurrying, hurrying so fast he panted. His heart thudded rapidly.
>
> Never before had he taken such a risk, not at noontime, not in the bright daylight, not among so many people.

Character action runs the risk of not being as clear as a spoken goal, but it can be combined with an intention, as follows:

> Even under the loggia's shade [Bronzidaec] felt exposed. His enchanted disguise was thin at best, and he feared the sun might shine straight through him. The old palace, he thought wrathfully, had been full of crannies and deep shadows, but the new palace was filled with sunlight all day and blazed with candles at night. He loathed it here. He told himself that perhaps Master would be so pleased with his news that Master would release him.
>
> *You are a fool to believe it*, he thought. A century of bondage stretched before him like an eternity.
>
> But perhaps Master would be pleased. Master *must* be pleased. Bronzidaec had great hopes of being rewarded with more food and permission to sleep on a fine cushion in Master's quarters.
>
> But Master would *not* be pleased if news came to him slowly. Time to hurry, hurry, hurry.

In the above sample, intention is mingled with the character Bronzidaec's motivations, explaining why he's taking a risk in seeking his Master during daylight hours. When using this approach, take care that an implied goal is always supported by the context of what's happened previously.

Drill exercise:

Select a chapter of action and/or dialogue from one of the following fantasy novels: *Storm front* by Jim Butcher; *The alloy of law* (2011) by Brandon Sanderson; or *Harry Potter and the sorcerer's stone* (1998) by J. K. Rowling. Within that chapter, locate and underline the protagonist's scene goals. Are they delivered through an internalized intention, stated through dialogue, or implied through the character's actions? To what effect?

6

Scene conflict

It's important to know the difference between scene conflict and adversity, and the effect each has on your story.

Scene conflict can be defined as two characters in opposition over a clear, specific goal.

Adversity is random bad luck.

Scene conflict advances the story, creates more change in the protagonist's situation, raises the stakes, makes the story outcome less certain, and heightens suspense.

Adversity may be shocking and unpredictable when used once. Too much of it, however, drops story tension, lessens plausibility, decreases reader sympathy for the protagonist, and destroys reader interest in the story's outcome. After all, if the protagonist only encounters random bad luck, again and again, he'll be perceived as a loser. Unfair? Perhaps, but reader sympathy will still fall away. Too much random bad luck will also convince readers there's no point in the protagonist continuing to try. He'll appear to be an idiot if he doesn't surrender his story goal and go home.

The conflict in a scene should be about its goal. The scene protagonist wants to achieve the goal. The scene antagonist wants to stop her from doing that.

For example, if Princess Iphegenia asks her general to raise an army, he should throw up objections and do his best to dissuade her from the idea.

Because as soon as a scene goal is formed, stated, or acted upon, an opponent should oppose it.

Why? How mean is that? Isn't that setting up a protagonist to fail?

No, it's delaying the resolution of a novel until its climax. It's keeping the story going to the end. It's providing readers with a good time by making them worry about how things will turn out.

Novels open with an event of change and then deal with a progression of more change. There can be no progression of events unless the protagonist hits opposition. The stronger the opposition, the better the story.

When things are going well for your protagonist, your story is in trouble.

When your protagonist is in trouble, your story is going well.

As you plan a scene, ask yourself what's at stake in it. You need to know because the stakes connect to your protagonist's and antagonist's motivations. Also, the stakes will determine how long your scene runs.

Low stakes lend themselves to short scenes—possibly no more than two or three paragraphs.

Moderate stakes might cause a scene to last as long as one to five pages.

High stakes—leading to a desperate protagonist and a vicious, cunning antagonist—can cause scenes to run possibly as long as ten to fifteen pages.

To repeat my point, a scene's length depends entirely on how much conflict it contains. And conflict fills as much as ninety-five percent of a scene's content.

If a scene's going to succeed, it's because it serves up a clear goal, strong stakes, and intense conflict.

More scenes fail from lack of sufficient conflict than for any other reason.

However, the conflict shouldn't be aimless bickering. Instead, let the scene antagonist work in direct opposition to the scene protagonist. Sometimes a scene features the story's protagonist versus the central villain. Sometimes a scene's conflict happens between the protagonist and a friend or sidekick. Friends can disagree on how to achieve a common goal. And not everyone on the same side likes each other or can get along.

In Kim Harrison's urban fantasy novel, *Dead witch walking* (2009), the protagonist quits her job and starts a new business with a former co-worker named Ivy. They also share a house to help with expenses. However, Ivy is a vampire, and the protagonist is afraid Ivy will turn and attack her. And the more nervous and uneasy the protagonist becomes, the more she gives off subliminal signals that trigger Ivy's predatory nature.

It's like exchanging your pet goldfish for a piranha. Someday, if you ever make a mistake or lose concentration while cleaning the fish tank, you could lose your fingers.

Conflict, when misunderstood or undirected, can become circular and pointless. You should understand the motivations of your two oppositional characters when writing a scene. Why does achieving the scene goal matter so much to the protagonist? How does thwarting this goal fit into the antagonist's game plan?

When you understand why the stakes matter so much to each of them, you can write strong conflict. You'll push your characters to maneuver more against each other—to cajole, trick, and outsmart each other.

Since not every scene should feature identical conflict or intensity, to avoid predictable monotony, writers can utilize a variety of conflict types such as combat, verbal disagreement, interrogation, evasion, and bickering. Let's consider each of them more closely.

Combat

Combat can be hand-to-hand, with weapons, through magic, or mental. Much of fantasy fiction features plenty of fighting, and you need to research and think through your action scenes carefully. Does this mean you should enroll in a martial arts course? No, although doing so will help you write fight scenes with more authority.

Interview an instructor and seek permission to observe a training session. Study instructional films and talk to people who are knowledgeable. Individuals who've done military service are usually eager to share their knowledge with you. Off-duty police officers can be another source of information. Re-enactment groups and historical societies offer tips on their web sites, and you can also find demonstration videos on YouTube.com.

If your protagonist is a shape-shifter, say, a were-wolf or were-leopard, and gets into a fight, be aware that such fighting is at extreme close quarters with an intimacy that's far different than someone using a gun, quarterstaff, or sword. It's violent and messy. Fangs and claws are the weapons. Such combat is primal and intense, worse even than humans fighting with knives. Take note of the psychological impact for anyone involved in this kind of battle. And no one, not even the victor, emerges unscathed.

If your characters will be using bladed weapons, don't read up on competitive fencing. The modern sport is now all about the touch or hit of the target. The fencers are wired to register electronically who touches first with the tip of their epee. You won't learn about the art of fencing, with its moves, attacks, and parries, through studying what's done competitively today.

Please don't rely on what you see in the movies. British-produced films might or might not demonstrate some accurate swashbuckling, but Hollywood is notorious for seeking whatever looks good on screen even if it means discarding authenticity.

For example, I've taken a few fencing lessons and studied scenes from famous action films such as *The mark of Zorro* (1940), *Scaramouche* (1952), *The three musketeers* (1974), and *The prisoner of Zenda* (1952). One fight scene in *Zenda* puzzled me because the actors seemed to be armed with rapiers, yet they were occasionally using wrist action for saber fighting. When I asked a competitive fencer about it, she told me this movie version cobbled weapons together from two different types of swords and mixed up the movements accordingly—just because it looked flashier.

Granted, you may not need to dig so deep into authenticity, but you do need to know that medieval fighting swords weighed less than four pounds and were edged on one side of the blade so a man could use his hand along the top blunt side to add force to the blow in close-quarter fighting. There are plenty of reference books on swords and other bladed weapons available, and *Medieval combat: a fifteenth-century manual of swordfighting and close-quarter combat* (2006) by Hans Tolhoffer is especially enlightening.

Or, if your characters are battling with swords on horseback, you should have a rudimentary knowledge of how horses are handled, what they'll do when frightened, and how they were trained to assist knights in combat. For heaven's sake, be aware that cavalrymen slash with their weapons instead of stabbing. (Do you know why? So your opponent doesn't gallop off with your sword in his chest, leaving you defenseless.)

If your characters are fighting magically, think through a logical system of the magic. What's its source? How does a character draw on it? How much magic is available? When will it run out? What's the physical or mental cost to the user?

Try to be more inventive than just letting the wizard shoot fire from his fingertips.

Mental fighting is hard to depict well. But, as with magic, if you use the powers of the mind as a weapon, think through the parameters of such ability as logically as possible. Whatever system you devise, abide by its rules and don't cheat to get your characters out of a tight spot.

Verbal disagreement

Such conflict can be quite mild or it can escalate to loud, abusive shouting, depending on the stakes and the emotional state of the characters involved.

It will require good dialogue, swift exchanges where the characters are using words as weapons—to hurt, to provoke, to manipulate, to deceive, to persuade, to cripple.

No one will be uttering long speeches. The lines will become terse and clipped. You will have to set up the scene in a way that establishes the emotional state of the characters and what's at stake, then trust the dialogue to carry the story.

Don't hinder the dialogue with description, over-analysis, internalization, or adverbs.

"I hate you!" she shouted hysterically, her voice throbbing with anger. "I always have. I always will!"

He heard the emotion in her voice, knew that she was on the verge of losing control. It always ended in screaming and crying, then she would lie in a dark room for hours, afflicted with a miserable headache because she wouldn't be tranquilized. "Marina, don't. You know you don't mean what you're saying," he said reasonably, trying to keep his voice level. "You're overwrought, tired."

"I don't care!" she cried passionately. "I *do* hate you. For what you've done to Mother, for what you're trying to do to me."

Ah, yes, there it was, the fear—that illogical terror—that she would end up as insane as her mother.

"Your mother had to be taken to Whitebrook for her own safety," he replied calmly, watching the flinch in Marina's eyes. "She was insane. Believing herself to be a vampire was simply absurd."

The above example represents a writer who is unsure of herself and can't quite trust her story or her characters to put the scene across. The result is overwritten and clumsy. Let's strip it down for a comparison:

"I hate you!" Marina shouted. "I always have. I always will!"

He heard the tinge of hysteria in her voice. "You know you don't mean that. I'm on your side, remember?"

"No! You're not. And don't look at me that way. I'm *not* insane."

"Of course not. You're just tired, overwrought."

Alarm flared in her eyes. "You won't force me into that dark room. I won't be tranquilized, held there for hours while—while —"

"It's for your own good, my dear."

"Don't call me that. What you did to Mother was unforgivable."

"She had to be committed to Whitebrook for her own safety. She was becoming unbalanced. Thinking herself a vampire —"

"And now you want to do the same thing to me! Oh, yes, I can tell by how you look at me. That tone of voice you use. But you can't trick me the way you did her. I won't let you!"

"Marina, please. You mustn't let paranoia cloud your good sense."

See the difference? The dialogue has changed slightly, alluding to what was formerly presented through the man's internalization. The context of whatever has happened prior to this scene should tell readers which character is to be believed and sympathized with.

Interrogation

One character is asking questions, grilling the other character that either refuses to answer or is lying. Interrogation lends itself to different intensity levels, but it always carries at least a hint of intimidation and threat.

It can be a mother interrogating a child about whether she actually practiced her piano lesson after school, or it can be a psi-cop probing telepathically at the mind-shields of a cringing prisoner.

Evasion

Frequently a response to interrogation, evasion can also manifest in a scene where the two opposing characters are talking at cross-purposes. They may be friends or family. They may genuinely care for each other, but one individual wants to discuss something that the other is unwilling to deal with.

The following example demonstrates mild evasion, yet the emotional level within the conflict is high:

Aunt Tamsia stood with her back to the window, silhouetted so Shilen couldn't read her expression.

"I need to know where you went last night," Aunt Tamsia said. "Was it in the woods?"

Shilen didn't answer. She hated to lie, but this was none of Aunt Tamsia's business.

"Shilen, talk to me, please. You know the woods are dangerous at night. And there was a full moon. If you're sneaking out, meeting with the fairies, then I have to know!"

"Why can't you trust me?" Shilen asked. "I do well in school, don't I? I won a prize in mathematics. Can't you be proud of me, just once?"

"Fairies are dangerous. You can't trust anything they say. If they entice you into the woods three times, you'll—you'll never come back."

Shilen stared at her hands. They were knotted together in her lap, giving her away. Deliberately she relaxed them. "I'm very grateful for you taking me in, giving me a home. But I'm done with school now. I'm grown up. You have to let me make my own way."

Writing effective evasion is tricky. If you're not careful, you can split the focus of the scene and lose control of its conflict. When this happens, you may end up in a different place than you intended and be forced to rewrite.

Scenes where the characters are at cross-purposes are often dealing with the advanced technique known as subtext, where the surface discussion isn't what the true conflict is about.

In my novel *The crown* (2008) the protagonist Shadrael is a former general and war hero who sold his soul years before to achieve military success. Now a ruined, embittered man exiled from the army and working as a two-bit mercenary, he's acting as a double-agent. His brother has hired him to start a war by abducting the emperor's sister. The evil leader of the rebel priesthood has persuaded Shadrael to turn over the kidnapped princess to him instead. In the course of the story, Shadrael has fallen in love with the girl and renounced his allegiance to the dark gods. But on the eve of battle, realizing that the renegade priests intend to destroy both the emperor's army and his brother Vordachai's forces, Shadrael has pledged a new, although reluctant, allegiance to the darkness to ensure the girl's freedom and his brother's safety.

In a long, complex scene between Shadrael and his older brother Vordachai, a range of conflict maneuvers are featured as Shadrael attempts to stop his brother from heading into a massacre and Vordachai refuses to listen. Although the brothers are arguing in what seems to be direct conflict much of the time, there are sections of subtext where the brothers betray hints of how much they actually care about each other. Each man is hindered by sibling rivalry, pride, machismo, and what lies in his past. And although Shadrael is motivated by love for his brother, his personality won't allow him openly to say so.

Shadrael's scene goal is to save his brother's life. He uses two tactics: persuasion and the magical talisman. In any scene, the protagonist will attempt the most cautious or certain strategy first. When that doesn't work, the protagonist will take larger risks. That's why Shadrael reasons with his brother before he attempts to give him the protective talisman—representative of dark magic—as a last-ditch measure. If he can't talk Vordachai out of fighting in the battle, then the amulet will keep Vordachai from harm. Here is the last segment of the scene:

The sounding of trumpets cut him off. Vordachai stood in his stirrups. "They're coming onto the field."

Shadrael gripped his arm. "Back off now while —"

"Not when they're entering the field!" Vordachai shook him off. "Now stop talking like a toothless old woman and tell me squarely—do you stand with me or do you intend to retire like a coward?"

Shadrael glared at him, but it was obvious that Vordachai wasn't going to listen to sense. It was like trying to stand against a mighty sandstorm and blow it onto a new course with his puny breath. He sighed. "I stand with you."

Vordachai beamed. "That's the spirit!"

"But in Gault's name, take this!" Again, Shadrael proffered the talisman.

Vordachai eyed it with distaste. "Why do you give me such a filthy thing?"

"To protect you from what's coming."

Vordachai's brows knotted. He stared at Shadrael. "Wear blasphemous shadow protection when my men, my barons, have none? What do you take me for?"

Heat crept up Shadrael's throat into his face, and his cheeks burned. "Damn you! I've broken my conscience to obtain this, and by the gods you're going to wear it."

Vordachai grabbed it from his hand and threw it under the trampling hooves of horses. "And here I thought we could fight shoulder to shoulder, like brothers should. If turning human has made you a coward, then I'm ashamed to know you. Ashamed, Shadrael."

Before Shadrael could answer, Vordachai wheeled his big warhorse. "Sound the horns!" he yelled at the top of his lungs, waving his sword.

As the trumpets sounded, and the men cheered, Vordachai

glared at Shadrael. "Better collect your rabble and creep away, little brother."

"I said I'd stand with you."

Vordachai didn't look pleased. "Don't expect my gratitude. I'd rather see you dead than without your nerve."

"What do you know about this? Nothing! Why, for once, won't you listen?"

"I had meant to ask you what sort of commanders we're facing, but you've wasted the time with your mewling. We'll charge straight through, and mind you keep those ruffians you brought to one side and out of the way of my men. And keep well away from me today. I want no part of you."

"Wait —"

But his brother was spurring his horse, making it rear. "With me, men!" he roared over the noise. "To victory!"

Everyone cheered except Shadrael. He sat there, fuming in his saddle, not knowing whether to curse his idiot of a brother or beg his forgiveness.

"M'lord." It was Fomo at his stirrup, his ruined rasp of a voice barely heard in the din of shouts and war cries. The former centruin held up the battered talisman that Vordachai had thrown away. "The warlord dropped this."

"Keep it," Shadrael snarled, and joined the stream of warriors galloping to battle.

Bickering

The petty, low-level picking at each other that children, co-workers, and some spouses may stoop to at times, bickering is generally mild conflict, often used for comic relief, but it can be vicious. The latter usually covers subtext, with the characters nagging and carping about a tiny issue when a much larger, more important one is really at stake. If over-used or allowed to become circular, it can become irritating to readers.

Bickering seldom advances the plot. That's why I recommend

that you reserve it for side characters. Use it to illustrate their natures. It also works very well in providing comic relief.

For example, in Brandon Sanderson's novel *The alloy of law* the sidekick Wayne frequently bickers and complains. He seems to be upset because the protagonist Waxillium has caused him to lose his lucky hat. The bickering seldom moves the plot forward, but it does establish the relationship between the two men, who are firm friends. It also vividly demonstrates a slice of Wayne's quirky personality.

Drill exercise:

Select a scene from your favorite fantasy novel that features only two characters in direct confrontation. Identify each character's opposing goal. Determine whether the scene relies on a single type of conflict or several. Identify them from the list provided in this chapter, or perhaps your example features a different variety of conflict than I have described. Examine the tactics used by each character in trying to win. How effective are they?

7

Conflict maneuver

In Chapter 6 I mentioned that one of a scene's functions is to advance the story. I stressed that a scene should depict a moment-by-moment struggle to achieve a goal.

But how is scene conflict actually written? How is summary avoided? How do we keep a scene moving forward from one character tactic to the next, without going circular and stalling out?

- Through the willingness to allow your protagonist to hit serious, always-escalating trouble.
- Through the technique of action and reaction.

Let's examine these separately.

Keeping your characters in trouble

Although it's natural for writers to protect the characters they've created and love, you must resist this impulse. Through the majority of your story, you do not want your protagonist to be successful or happy. You want your protagonist to be worried, stressed, and suffering.

Why?

Not to be cruel, or sadistic, or evil, but to force your protagonist and her friends to CHANGE.

Human nature resists change all the time. How many times

have you promised to stop doing something that annoys your loved one, yet before you realize it, you've done it again?

Our intentions are good. We mean well. We truly realize it would be better for our health if we exercised daily and ate plenty of leafy green vegetables instead of pizza and cheeseburgers, but when we sit down to order a meal at our favorite hangout, we're still eating the high-calorie junk food that we love.

Doctors can show a patient X-rays, hand out a diet sheet, and issue stern warnings, yet within a month the patient is probably off his special diet and back doing everything wrong because change is hard. Change forces us into strange territory. Change is threatening and often uncomfortable. And, most importantly of all, we just don't want to do it.

Yet in fiction dynamics, the whole point of a plot is to force the protagonist to change by the end of the story. The only way for the protagonist to survive the challenges is through change, bit by bit, step by step, until the climax is reached. What we're doing, in a way, is training our protagonist to meet the huge ordeal of the story's climax by putting our protagonist in more and more trouble with every scene.

For example, if you want to write about a teenage girl discovering she possesses the ability to start fires with the force of her mind and you want her to confront an evil, powerful wizard and stop him from enslaving all the humans, you aren't going to introduce her in scene one and feature this cataclysmic battle of Good versus Evil in scene two. The girl's not ready. She may not know she has magical power yet. And since she doesn't know how to use it, she hasn't a hope of success. (Unless you cheat by contriving some miraculous victory.)

So you introduce her in trouble in scene one. Trouble that leaves her bruised and bewildered and shocked into taking action. Whatever she tries to do in scene two will lead to a worsening of her situation. Whatever she does in scene three to solve the problem leads to more trouble. And so on.

Make sure your protagonist isn't cautiously stepping around trouble and prudently hanging back where others do not fear to tread. Your protagonist needs to run full-tilt into terrible trouble, fight her way through, and hit worse trouble.

Not because she's stupid. Not because she can't avoid problems. But because she's the hero and must lead the other characters. She must take risks the other characters won't. She must stand up and face problems to help her friends or anyone she cares about.

Also, from time to time she hits trouble because the bad guy out-maneuvers her.

You've created a bright, appealing, sympathetic protagonist that you care about. You want your protagonist to be a winner, to succeed, to save the day. But not until the end of the story.

Therefore, don't protect your protagonist. Don't shield her. Don't baby her. Whatever matters most in the world to her should be endangered so much that she can't sit passively, crying and doing nothing. She must take action. She must become—by stages, and through failures, and as a result of confrontations—a hero.

Action/Reaction units

Mastering this technique will help you write strong scenes. A/R units sound simple and easy in explanation, but writing them correctly takes thought, care, and practice. Once you're proficient with them, you'll find conflict easy to achieve, and your scenes will improve steadily.

A/R units are simply an action and its immediate reaction. A/R operates on cause-and-effect logic, which in turn ties together many elements of plotting.

Within a scene, A/Rs move the story action along, step by step in a plausible progression.

There are two types of A/R unit—the simple and the

complicated. Both can be found in any given scene. Let's look at them separately.

Simple A/R unit

In the simplest context, for every action there is a reaction.

[**A**] You drop a glass on a ceramic tile floor.
[**R**] The glass shatters.

[**A**] You run your fingertip along the back of a fuzzy caterpillar.
[**R**] The caterpillar curls up.

[**A**] You call to your dog.
[**R**] Your dog runs to you.

[**A**] You call to your dog.
[**R**] Your dog runs in the opposite direction.

[**A**] You stub your toe.
[**R**] The pain makes you yelp.

Such simple, ordinary transactions happen all the time, illustrating the basic principle of cause and effect. They happen in a certain order. They make sense. They are easy to understand. They are plausible.

Accordingly, Action/Reaction is a mechanism in fiction that makes scene action move forward in a logical, believable, and orderly way. The straightforward pattern makes sense to readers. Most successful writers have either been trained to write this way, or they do it naturally.

The clumsy or untrained writer, however, can create confusing, awkward copy by fumbling A/R order. Remember, it takes practice!

In scenes, when you write a character's action—either a

physical movement or dialogue—you should link an immediate reaction to it from the other character. (Remember that the ideal number of characters in a scene should be two characters.)

Character 1 does or says something.
Character 2 does or says something in response.

Therefore, the simple A/R unit requires a writer to present an action immediately followed by its direct reaction in a way that's clear, in proper logical order, with nothing skipped, and occurring closely enough together so the relationship between the two components isn't lost.

Writers—caught up in their story's action—can run into difficulties because they're thinking too fast and they're focused too intently on reactions.

What happens when the A/R connection isn't clear?

Lord Ichnod walked up to Sir Freheild.

Sir Freheild ducked violently.

The close juxtaposition of this action and reaction implies a cause-and-effect link, yet logic says one has nothing to do with the other. How can a reader follow this? It's confusing and implausible.

If we ask William Writer what he is trying to do with these two sentences, he might explain as follows:

"Oh! Well, uh, you see, Lord Ichnod was looking really angry and carrying a sword in his hand that he was swinging back and forth."

William Writer pauses. "I guess I sort of forgot to put that in."

Keep in mind that author assumptions, when omitted from A/R units, are the primary reason for confusion in scenes. It's vital that you remember your readers can only see what you supply. They can't read your mind, and although your story action may be crystal-clear in your imagination, readers can be easily left behind.

There's another problem with the above example besides a lack of clarity. Let's examine it again, after William Writer's hasty revisions:

[A] Lord Ichnod, looking furious and swinging his sword, walked up to Sir Freheild.

[R] Sir Freheild ducked violently.

Huh?

It still doesn't make sense, does it? That's because they aren't directly linked. If William Writer wants Sir Freheild to duck, then Lord Ichnod must actually do something that would cause such a reaction.

[A] Lord Ichnod, looking furious, walked up to Sir Freheild and swung his sword at Freheild's head.

[R] Sir Freheild ducked violently.

Ah, much better. These two paragraphs may not be stellar writing, but at least they now make sense.

Let's try another example:

Pachinal dived for cover when the goblins came swarming up from the manholes.

What's wrong with this? Isn't it exciting, featuring danger and story action? But it's out of order. Pachinal is reacting *before* the goblins take action.

When the entire unit takes place in one sentence like this and your reader reads complete lines or paragraphs at a time, the meaning won't be lost. But what if your reader is someone who reads one word at a time? It has the potential to be confusing.

The fix is easy:

When the goblins came swarming up from the manholes, Pachinal dived for cover.

Or what about this one?

A stream of rockets exploded in the night air, raining red, yellow, and orange sparks down on the screaming crowd.

Up in the bleachers, Tynex was laughing with glee, and remembering how exciting it had felt to curl his claws around the detonator and shove it down hard.

It's jumbled, isn't it? It's trying to follow the action out of order as a film would present it. There's an immediate reaction combined with action that should have preceded the first paragraph.

Now let's look at it arranged in more logical order:

[A] Up in the bleachers, Tynex curled his claws around the detonator and shoved it down hard.

[R] A stream of rockets exploded in the night air, **[A]**raining red, yellow, and orange sparks down on the **[R]**screaming crowd.

[A] As the sounds of panic grew louder,**[R]**Tynex laughed with glee.

See how the units link together? One unit joins to the next—action and reaction, action and reaction.

Look at what happens when you skip something:

The messenger knelt before the king. Screaming and tearing at his beard, the king ran out of the audience chamber.

William Writer is back to his old tricks of leaving out important details, but we can fix it as follows:

[A] The messenger knelt before the king. "I'm sorry, your majesty, but the queen is dead of the plague."

[R] Screaming and tearing at his beard, the king ran out of the audience chamber.

Another problem can occur when writers fail to keep a close relationship between the action and its reaction.

Rupert crossed the parking lot where his brother Damien was drawing a pentagram on the pavement with blue chalk. "Hey, we need to talk about Betty and her influence on you. This sorcery stuff has to stop."

Damien tossed down his chalk. "You want it to stop? Try this!" He pulled what looked like a brass knob from his pocket and lobbed it at Rupert's head.

The trouble between the brothers had begun long before Damien started dating Betty the witch. Damien had always been a troublemaker, usually shifting the blame for his misdeeds onto Rupert. For the last three years, the brothers had barely spoken to each other. But now, recently aware of his brother's dabbling in witchcraft and magical matters best left alone, Rupert knew he couldn't leave Damien alone.

He ducked. "What's up with you these days?"

Do you see the big info-dump positioned between one action and its reaction? It creates an awkward gap between action and reaction. By the time Rupert ducks, readers may well have forgotten what he's dodging. And, no, the info-dump will not convey an illusion of the brass doorknob flying in slow motion toward Rupert's head.

"But it's all there!" William Writer protests, pointing at the page. "It's not that big of an interruption."

Ah, but what if Rupert's reaction didn't happen until the

following page because of the way it's printed or transcribed to an e-reader? If someone reading it has to stop and backtrack to figure out what's happening, William Writer has failed to write a proper, easily understood A/R unit.

You can include background and context before or after a scene. You can slide in a sentence of background or explanation inside a scene if it falls between two A/R units, but please don't stick it in the middle of a unit.

To repeat: don't create a gap or interruption between an action and its reaction.

A very clear way to organize your A/R units and write without reader confusion is to set the action in its own paragraph. The next paragraph should carry the immediate reaction. This will help you avoid muddle, omissions, and writing out of order.

Also, don't get in a hurry and cram several actions together before you write a reaction. I call this practice "stacking the unit." It creates all sorts of problems because what should the character react to first?

Example:

Sir Mezikek exploded into the room. He threw his walking stick at Bartholomew, yelling, "I'm going to kill you!" before he raced past the row of empty chairs and hit Bartholomew in the jaw. "Who gave you permission to summon my familiar?" he demanded.

What's Bartholomew going to do or say first in response to any or all of this?

More importantly, a bewildered reader may never progress past the first sentence. Can a person "explode" into a room? Does that mean Sir Mezikek is no longer intact?

"No," Angie Author mumbles, wishing she'd never enrolled in my class, "I was trying to be vivid."

We can correct Angie Author's unfortunate imagery. But

more importantly, we need to unstack the paragraph and set up the A/R units one at a time, like this:

[A] The door opened, banging into the wall.

[R] Startled, Bartholomew jumped from his chair.

[A] Sir Mezikek strode inside and flung his walking stick at Bartholomew.

[R] Ducking barely in time, Bartholomew backed up to keep his desk between the angry man and himself. **[A]** "Sir? What's wrong?"

[R] But Sir Mezikek was racing past the row of empty chairs, straight for Bartholomew. **[A]** "I'm going to kill you!" he shouted.

[R] "Kill me?"

[A] Sir Mezikek socked Bartholomew in the jaw, **[R]**sending him staggering off balance.

[A] "Who gave you permission to summon my familiar?"

Do you see how the action is now moving one step at a time to Sir Mezikek's question? Even better, we've produced nearly a full page of manuscript copy instead of a single messy paragraph. The writing is choppy, but easy to follow. Of course, Bartholomew doesn't know why Sir Mezikek is acting like a crazy fool, other than he appears to be angry about what's happened to his familiar, but it's okay if protagonist and reader are equally puzzled. As Bartholomew finds out the answers, so will the reader.

Remember that it's better to write a chain of A/R units than an awkward, stacked paragraph. Think through what you want to happen and what you want your characters to say. Choreograph their movements. Who will do what first? What will the response be? Write it thoughtfully and logically.

Just because readers race through scenes that are dramatic and filled with conflict, you needn't attempt to create them at breakneck speed.

Complicated A/R units

Not all give-and-take story action is straightforward. Human beings are illogical, unpredictable, contradictory, inconsistent, and complex creatures. They don't always tell the truth. They are seldom direct. They enter confrontations with hidden agendas or they play psychological games with each other. Sometimes they're impulsive and thoughtless, blurting out comments they regret afterward. There are also people in real life who don't know what their true feelings are. They're baffled, unable to figure themselves out, and they certainly can't express what they feel.

Think of a little boy developing his first crush on—eeeuw—a girl. Little Timothy is feeling emotions he doesn't understand. He's caught in an unfamiliar place between the past, when he simply hated all girls, and the future, where he eventually will reach the realization that he likes Emily. Meanwhile, he can't stop thinking about her or watching her. Confused, he may run past her, shouting. Or he may come up and punch her in the shoulder. Equally confused by Timothy's behavior, Emily thinks he's weird and ignores him when he offers her a frog.

Where your characters are concerned, scene conflict isn't about playing by rules. It's about winning. This means that at least one of the characters involved in a complex scene won't be fair or honest.

Therefore, complex scene conflict will involve two levels: what the protagonist and antagonist are saying and doing, and what the protagonist or viewpoint character is truly thinking and feeling.

This means that as you write a scene, you must manage

the element of contradiction—i.e. some degree of tension between what the viewpoint character is saying versus what she's feeling inside.

For example, if my viewpoint character Dain is a naturally honest boy who has been raised to tell the truth and be open with others, then Dain must be pitted against someone who is less honest or toying with him. Let's say that Dain arrives at a market fair to sell the swords his guardian has made. A well-dressed man walks up and examines the weapons. He selects the best, most beautifully made one. But instead of buying it, he criticizes it, declaring it shoddy and ill-forged. Dain will counter this by pointing out the blade's craftsmanship and strength. The man becomes angry and loud. He accuses Dain of trying to cheat his customers by selling cheap goods. He claims such a weapon would shatter in a fight, leaving him defenseless.

If Dain is naive as well as honest, he may remain completely baffled by this customer's behavior. If Dain is a bit more clever, he may think the man is criticizing the sword in order to drive down the price. If Dain has some experience, he may suspect the man of trying to distract him while a colleague steals items from the booth.

Whatever may be running through Dain's mind about the situation, he should remain aware of gawking onlookers and his responsibility to stay courteous despite the customer's angry, insulting remarks.

In such a scenario, the A/R units can't all be simple ones. We need more.

When a character does or says something (Action) and the other character reacts in a complex or illogical way (Reaction), the writer must explain it to readers.

The only means you have to accomplish this is viewpoint. Through viewpoint, we can insert internalization between an action and a complicated reaction.

For illustration, here's a simple A/R unit:

"Hello," Michael said.

"'lo," replied the pixie.

There's nothing confusing in this exchange, is there? But contrast it with the following:

"Hello," Michael said.

Screeching, the pixie flew at his face, trying to jab his eye with a sewing needle.

We can take several guesses as to why the pixie would react to Michael's friendly overture in such a violent way, but unless prior events show us context, we have no way of knowing what's going on.

When an A/R unit is complicated, provide internalization so the reaction makes sense to readers.

"Hello," Michael said.

Rage filled the pixie. This Michael, this *human*, had betrayed his dear wife. Thanks to Michael, Iria was now dead. Screeching, the pixie flew at Michael's face, trying to jab his eye with a sewing needle.

The internalization makes quite a difference. But what if we're in Michael's viewpoint instead of the pixie's? What if Michael genuinely doesn't understand what's causing the pixie's violent reaction?

Then Michael will have to guess why the pixie is upset, or he'll have to demand an explanation, or he may become angry enough to strike back.

"Hello," Michael said.

Screeching, the pixie flew at Michael's face, trying to jab his eye with what looked like a sewing needle.

What the hell? **Baffled by the tiny creature's rage, Michael swatted it away. "What's wrong with you?" he shouted.**

Michael's puzzlement about the pixie's behavior will mirror reader confusion. As Michael seeks an explanation, readers are never left behind. Together, readers and the viewpoint character are trying to discover what's wrong.

Now, there's a certain logical order to follow when writing internalizations for A/R units. This order exists to keep things clear for readers. It also enables writers to avoid stopping the story to drop in awkward lumps of explanation.

We're not trying to explain anything within a scene's activity. We want to keep scene conflict snapping, moving quickly through lively back-and-forth exchanges. Instead, we acknowledge through our scene protagonist the comments or behaviors that don't make sense and move on. Once a scene has ended, the story can pause for the scene protagonist's reflection and explanation.

Internalization components fall in a specific order as follows:

- Feeling/emotion is first.
- Then thought.
- Then action.
- Then dialogue.

I use the term "feeling" to indicate either physical pain, or numbness, or being stunned. For example, if my protagonist Sam has just been walloped with a pikestaff, he's not going to sit on his duff, thinking about what just happened. The first thing he's going to feel is pain from the blow that's knocked him off his feet.

Years ago, I was backstage at a dance recital when I went hurrying up a flight of steps in the dark. Hindered by the gloom, I hit my head on the corner of a wall-mounted speaker. I didn't quite lose consciousness, but for what seemed to be a very long moment my entire awareness was centered on the burst of agony in my left temple. I don't even know if I stopped in my tracks or kept moving. But time slowed until my body was able to recover and go on.

If you've ever broken a bone, you know how agonizing that moment is. Your body is stunned. Everything shrinks to intense pain.

When a writer is depicting physical conflict but omits such reactions, the scene becomes cartoon-like and implausible, as superficial as a video game. Recently I was proofing an old science fiction adventure of mine, written early in my career before I'd ever broken any bones or suffered serious injuries. I came to a chapter where my viewpoint character was trying to escape a fortress. He was hindered by a broken arm, which he kept tucking in his belt or otherwise ignoring. The story seems silly to me now because it lacks plausible feeling. Granted, the character was a tough special forces operative, trained to keep going even if injured, but I should have at least acknowledged that he was sweating with agony every time he shifted that arm.

Emotion receives double billing with feeling as the first component of internalization because we're humans and we operate on our emotions. They're instinctive and natural to us. We govern them largely through suppression. We aren't usually sociopaths and we certainly aren't Vulcans. So if you're writing about human characters, their emotions are going to happen before anything else.

Fiction written without emotion lacks a common touchstone between writer and character, and character and reader. It's hard for readers to feel sympathetic toward any viewpoint character lacking in emotion. Readers become detached from the story situation, the story problem, and the events themselves.

If you recall, the whole point of a scene is to keep the story moving forward. That means everything in a scene is happening quickly. We don't want to stop a scene to let a character emote at length. That's why, even within complicated A/R units, emotion is simply a burst or a snap of raw reaction that's then suppressed so the scene action can continue.

(Once the scene is completed, you can allow your protagonist's emotions full rein.)

Thoughts follow feelings and emotions on the list because although we're mammals first, we humans are also rational beings. We possess the capacity for reason, although whether we use it is another issue. Emotion is instinctive and sometimes primitive. Thought is more under our control.

One writing principle that was hammered again and again by my writing instructor, Jack Bickham, was that thoughts do not substitute for emotions.

Each has its place. Each serves a purpose in advancing plot or revealing character. But one does not substitute for the other.

Again, and again, I find student writers reaching for a character's thoughts to convey reaction instead of utilizing that character's emotions. Although it's often a mistake to do so, I understand why students do it. It's easier, for one thing. It's less messy. It's also less effective.

Let's say that you see a house on fire. Neighbors have gathered in the street to watch the firemen at work. Whatever could be saved has been dragged out. All the family is safe. There are two little girls with soot on their faces, now sitting on the curb in their bathrobes and slippers.

One little girl (Judy) is in tears, sobbing her heart out. The other child (Trina) sits in stony silence, watching her home collapse in a shower of sparks and flames.

They're wrapped in blankets. Each child is handed a teddy bear. The sobbing Judy clutches her bear, hugging it tightly. Trina accepts the other bear politely before laying it aside without interest.

Which sister pulls at your heart most? Which sister is more appealing? Which little girl would you reach for first to offer comfort?

Would you gravitate toward the one that's crying? Judy's emotions are simple and heartfelt. We understand what she's going through. From kind compassion alone, we want to help her.

As I writer, however, I'm very intrigued by the stone-faced sister, Trina. She's more complex, isn't she? I want to know if she's in shock or if she's sociopathic or if she set the fire.

I'm intrigued by her, but I don't like her better.

Not unless Angie Author puts me in Trina's viewpoint and shares her heart with me will I care about her. Maybe Trina's unresponsiveness is a means of survival. Maybe sobbing Judy is the monster that set the fire. Maybe Judy is the pretty one who always manipulates people and when she doesn't get her way, takes out her rage on Trina. Maybe hiding her emotions is the only way Trina can cope with the horror hidden inside her home. Maybe she's glad, glad, *glad* the house is finally dying. Maybe she's secretly feeling alight with hope and letting herself dare believe that escape is possible. Still, she's not safe yet. She knows better than to show what she's feeling inside because grownups—the ones now petting and comforting Judy the monster—won't understand why Trina is so happy.

Getting back to reaction component order, we write action after thought because, technically, people should think before they act.

And dialogue comes last because it should be the component most under our control. Of course, some people never filter what they say. Do you find it a trial to be around them?

There's another reason why the components fall in this order. Feelings, emotion, and thought are internal responses. We can't know them unless we're in viewpoint.

Internalization alone cannot stimulate conflict. Therefore, it cannot be the action half of an A/R unit.

If you write conflict where a character hops over a wall and then thinks about it, you've left no link for the next A/R unit to connect to.

For example:

> **Paulina smiled at Sam, then shifted into her wolf shape. As usual, the transformation hurt but she wanted to frighten him.**
> **Sam stumbled back against the alley wall. "Whoa!"**

You can follow the action here, but it doesn't read very smoothly. By the time we reach Sam's reaction, the link has weakened. He's somewhat like people being interviewed via satellite. The reporter asks a question, and the interviewee sits there with a silly grin on her face for a few seconds until she hears the question and sobers her expression. The brief time-lag makes her look stupid.

Let's look at a corrected version:

> **[Internalization] Paulina hated shifting because it always hurt, but it was important that she gain Sam's attention. The best way to do that was to frighten him. [A] Baring her teeth, she shifted into her wolf shape.**
>
> **[R] Sam stumbled back against the alley wall. "Whoa!"**

Notice how much smoother the A/R unit flows? Internalization occurs first, expressing Paulina's motivation and reluctance. Then we see her action, which Sam can respond to.

Now, consider another A/R error:

> **"I'd love to go," Jazbo said eagerly, then cringed inside at his own stupidity. Why had he lied like that?**
> **"Would you?" Alix said. "I expected you to hate the idea. Well, come on if you must."**

This example shows Jazbo reacting to his own dialogue. How can the person to whom he's speaking respond directly? The muddled order creates sloppy, weak story progression.

Here's a corrected version:

"I'd love to go," Jazbo said eagerly.

"Would you?" Alix said. "I expected you to hate the idea. Well, come on if you must."

Following her through the woods, Jazbo wanted to kick himself for lying. How could he be so stupid?

Jazbo's internalization now has been deferred until the conversation is over. If your viewpoint character must react to his own actions or dialogue, wait until the scene is over to do so.

Remember that your protagonist is not on such a vain ego trip that he can only internalize and react to his own behavior. Instead, direct his attention to the person he's in conflict with. Let your protagonist react to what the antagonist is saying or doing because, in scenes, conflict is external.

Drill exercise:

Select a scene of conflict from Jim Butcher's novel *Fool moon* (2001) or examine a confrontation between Harry Potter and Dobby in one of J. K. Rowling's books.

First, determine the scene protagonist's goal for that encounter. Underline it in green.

Once the author has established character positioning and motivation, what is the first action taken by the protagonist to achieve that goal? Bracket it in red or make a check mark next to the paragraph where it appears.

What does the antagonist do in response or retaliation? Mark that in blue.

Mark the conflict with red and blue. Can you determine the A/R units? If you lose the linkage, go through the passage again. It's possible the author has written something out of order, or you overlooked it. ➡

Antagonists often try to throw scene protagonists off-kilter by distracting them or using evasion to confuse them. Pay close attention to where—and how—the scene protagonist gets back on course toward pursuing the scene goal.

After you've marked and studied a published example from either Rowling or Butcher, select a scene that you've written. Mark the conflict in blue and red. Are your A/R units clear, closely connected, and in proper order?

8

Resolving scenes

As soon as your scene conflict becomes repetitious, circular, or loses steam, it's time to end the confrontation. And scenes should end in complete or partial failure for the protagonist.

Every time.

Until the story climax.

Sounds like a total bummer, doesn't it? Of course it is. It should be. Mind you, this practice isn't to discourage readers. It's not to make the hero look lame or stupid. Instead, it's to prepare the protagonist to meet the biggest challenge of all in a book's or short story's climax.

Years ago, when I bought my first dog, I chose a Scottish terrier puppy. At six weeks old, the little guy could fit in my hand. I'd researched and thought long and hard before I chose a Scottie. Two notable characteristics of the breed were stubbornness and problem solving. Very quickly, I saw them demonstrated.

There was a small porch on the back of my house, with three wooden steps leading to the ground. Every day, attempting to housebreak my puppy, I would carry him down the steps to the grass. And every day, he would struggle to climb those steps by himself on our return.

At first, because his legs were very short, he could barely reach the first step with his front paws. He struggled and pulled until finally he could gain the first step up. But when he tried to gain the middle step, he always fell through the gap. Thud! He'd plop onto the ground on his side, catch his breath, and try again. Thud! Down he'd go. And he'd try again.

Now, as his anxious and kindly owner, I wanted to help him by scooping him up and carrying him inside. But that wasn't what he wanted. He was determined to conquer those steps, and I realized that I had to let him try. As he grew daily and kept at it, he became stronger, taller, and better coordinated. Finally he could bound up those steps in a small black blur and race into the house.

So must you, as a writer, allow your protagonist to try and fail, try and succeed partially, try and fail, try and succeed at terrible cost, try and fail at even bigger cost, try, and try, and try some more.

The failures and semi-failures that end scenes aren't there to make readers unhappy, but to force the protagonist to take bigger risks next time.

It's human nature to avoid risk. Aside from a few intrepid souls who thrive on thrills, most of us prefer comfort and a safe, steady environment where we feel confident, content, and secure.

That's why change is so upsetting and threatening.

Think of Bilbo Baggins in J. R. R. Tolkien's 1937 classic, *The hobbit*. Bilbo has a snug home and a comfortable life. He doesn't want to go on any wild and dangerous adventures, yet he's caught up in one and soon swept far from his pleasant, safe hearth.

If every scene goes well for your protagonist, pretty soon your story will be over, or—if it's some kind of quest—the adventure will become boring and lifeless. Why? Because nothing is going wrong.

Ever sit down to watch your favorite ballgame on television? In the opening play, your team scores points. That's exciting. You're happy and cheering. But the other team doesn't rally and doesn't score. By halftime, your team is so far ahead there's no possible chance of losing.

You may still be happy, but are you truly enjoying the game? Are you watching it with close attention, or have you wandered off to the refrigerator to make yourself a snack? Have you taken a phone call and put the TV on mute? If the outcome is a foregone conclusion, why stay tuned? Why cheer every play? You continue to watch, but from a sense of celebration rather than suspense.

Compare that to a game where the teams are evenly matched or perhaps your team is the underdog. Every point is scored after a battle of plays. Every mistake is agony to watch. Your team is down slightly on the scoreboard, the star player has been taken out with an injury, and time is running out. In such circumstances, are you going to wander off to make a sandwich or will you stayed glued to your set?

If, in the closing seconds of the game, victory is achieved by some impossible dazzler of a play, how much sweeter is your sense of elation. After all the worry and suspense, your team won!

The same effect works in fiction. The more difficulties your protagonist faces, the more reading enjoyment you're providing to your audience.

You want your readers gripped by the unfolding events, by the tension, by the danger, by the likelihood that things are going to become even worse. You don't want readers to put your story down until it's finished. You want them staying up late into the night, determined to cheer on your protagonist and her friends. You want your readers surprised, astonished, shocked, perhaps even crying. You want your readers unable to predict what might transpire next.

Ambitious? Yes!

Achievable? Yes!

One of the ways you accomplish such tension and suspense is by having scenes end in failure despite the protagonist's very best efforts.

Conversely, if your protagonist succeeds at the end of each scene, your novel will end somewhere between page ten and page thirty. A short story will be over in the first scene.

Failure, hardship, defeat ... or outgunned, outsmarted, outmaneuvered ... such outcomes enable you to keep spinning the story out, longer and longer, until you have a full-length manuscript.

Your protagonist doesn't fail because he's stupid. He fails because the antagonist tricked him, or outthought him, or outmanned him.

Result?

Once your protagonist recovers, dusts himself off, and picks up the pieces, he's angry. He's angry and determined to keep that from happening again. He's a bit more willing to take risks than he was before. He's like my little Scottie, falling between the steps, but coming back to try as many times as it takes to succeed.

Now, in fiction it's best if the scene's setback is derived partially from the protagonist's own efforts. In other words, don't have your protagonist capably fighting off the swamp-dwellers, only to have a gigantic dragon fly past and randomly drop a boulder on him.

That's just dumb bad luck. The hero doesn't deserve it, and it seems contrived and unfair.

Instead, let's say the protagonist is a bit too cocky. She's been hired to deliver the baron's new sword from the swordmaker. Despite warnings against venturing into the swamp alone, she's running late and decides to take a shortcut through there. She's done it once or twice before without a problem. As a result of her decision, however, this time she meets up with swamp-dwellers. Her dagger is no match for their talons, so she pulls out the sword—gleaming and new—and uses it to fight. For a few minutes, the odds seem fair. She regains her confidence. But then the creatures split up and surround her. One of them strikes her from behind, causing her to stumble. They overtake her and knock her down. They leave her battered and half-dead. Even worse, they steal the sword.

So, yes, the swamp-dwellers beat her up and stole the weapon, but it wouldn't have happened if she hadn't chosen to take the shortcut. The outcome is partially her fault. The disaster is organic to the story, not contrived and tacked on.

In the same way that we use cause-and-effect logic in crafting conflict within a scene, so do we also utilize it with disasters and setbacks. And the harder they push a protagonist back from achieving his story goal, the more determined he must become to keep trying until he prevails.

Options for scene resolutions

In elemental story design, the four possible ways in which to end a scene are

1. Yes,
2. No,
3. Yes, but,
4. No, and furthermore.

Notice that each option is some type of yes-or-no variant. That's because each scene goal can be inverted into a scene question. At the conclusion of the scene, the answer is yes, Hero achieved his goal or no, Hero did not.

For example, let's say I'm writing a scene where young mage-to-be Firwyn wants the wizard Nilrem to accept him as an apprentice. Firwyn arrives at Nilrem's abode at the edge of the village, and knocks on the door. Firwyn's scene goal is *I want an apprenticeship with Nilrem.* That means the scene question is *Will Firwyn land the position with the wizard*?

Yes

If the scene question is answered with our first option, the scenario might happen as follows:

Firwyn knocks on the door. Instead of letting him inside, Nilrem shouts from a window for him to go away. Firwyn pleads and cajoles. Finally Nilrem lets him in.

"I suppose I do need a helper," he concedes. "You're hired."

We'd like to be happy for Firwyn here, but the event feels a bit flat. We're let down, aren't we? Because although we might be curious as to how he'll be trained, there's no suspense. If Firwyn is talented and does well, the story has nowhere to go.

So a Yes scene resolution—if the scene is in the protagonist's viewpoint—should be reserved for the story's ending because otherwise it's a) too easy; b) story tension can't be sustained; and c) it doesn't lead to real plot advancement.

Why, then, have I even mentioned it as a possibility? Because if you are writing in the antagonist's viewpoint, you will be ending some scenes from his perspective with a Yes in order to raise threat over the protagonist. Each time the antagonist succeeds with his nefarious scheme, you are making the outcome less certain for your protagonist.

Also, in a novel the subplots need to be resolved before the central storyline reaches its climax. You will be using Yes to tie off those smaller story questions.

No

As for our second scene-ending option, let's see how it works:

Firwyn knocks on the door. Instead of letting him inside, Nilrem shouts from a window for him to go away. Firwyn pleads and cajoles, but Nilrem is adamant.

"Begone! I don't want an apprentice. I've never had one and I don't intend to change my ways now. No!"

Firwyn has certainly met a setback. He's tried and he's failed. Although the No setback works, it's not ideal because it hasn't changed Firwyn's situation. He began the scene as a boy seeking an apprenticeship and he ends the scene as a boy seeking an apprenticeship. He got precisely nowhere.

If Firwyn returns the next day and asks again, and again Nilrem shouts "No!" nothing has changed.

If Firwyn returns the third day and asks, and Nilrem refuses, nothing has changed.

If Firwyn returns the fourth day and asks, and Nilrem refuses, nothing has changed except the reader will start to feel impatience. The story has stalled. It's going nowhere, despite the conflict and setbacks. Firwyn had better change his strategy to make something happen.

From time to time, mainly for variety, it's okay to use a No setback. Just remember that it leaves your protagonist stonewalled, in a corner. Whatever he tries next will have to be from scratch.

Yes, but

I've found this one to be the most useful of the four options. It's effective and flexible, and it's my favorite.

> **Firwyn knocks on the door. Instead of letting him inside, Nilrem shouts at him to go away. Firwyn pleads and cajoles, and finally Nilrem opens the door a crack and peers out.**
>
> **"Yes, all right, you can work here cleaning up the place but as my servant, not as my apprentice."**

That's not what Firwyn wants, but at least he can stay. Although he hasn't achieved his goal, he can cling to the hope of possibly changing the old man's mind. He's been set back from his larger goal of being trained in magic, but at least he hasn't been sent home. The story has advanced, if only by a small fraction. It allows the protagonist to make a slight amount of progress despite disappointment.

Another example of Yes, but can be taken from Victor

Hugo's *The hunchback of Notre Dame*. In the 1939 film version, when the army of beggars storms the cathedral, Quasimodo drops a large wooden beam on the crowd from the bell tower. His goal is to drive them away. Does he achieve that? Yes, for a moment as they scatter back in fright. But then the king of the beggars announces that they now have a battering ram to use in breaking down the cathedral doors.

Quasimodo tried his best at that point, but as a result things are worse for him and Esmeralda.

The Yes, but resolution comes in two versions—the strong and the weak.

The strong version is where things are definitely made worse for the protagonist.

The weak version is where the goal is achieved, but it's led only to new doubts or raised new questions that will trouble the protagonist in some way. It's not dramatically suspenseful like the strong version, but it can still do its job in ending a scene.

No, and furthermore

This setback option delivers a mighty big defeat. It can be considered a scene-ending disaster. It's often used to conclude large, high-stakes scenes, although it can work elsewhere. While it's very effective, I recommend that you don't overuse it. Save it for major turning points or portions of the story where you need shock or a plot twist.

Firwyn knocks on the door. Instead of letting him in, Nilrem shouts from a window for him to go away. Firwyn pleads and cajoles, until finally Nilrem opens the door a crack.

"For the last time, I don't want an apprentice. And since you're such a pest, I'll teach you never to bother me again."

As he speaks, Nilrem conjures a spell and turns Firwyn into a duck.

This example is so silly it may elicit a laugh, but it does leave Firwyn in a pickle. He's not an apprentice. And now, he can't even speak, let alone go home. His situation has changed, but not at all for the better. He's much worse off than when the scene began.

Remember that you want your protagonist to keep trying, but you also want him or her to be in progressively worse shape. By intensifying trouble and making the obstacles harder, you are raising the stakes.

When your protagonist falls into terrible difficulties because she's done her absolute best and took the risks no one else in the story would, how can readers not sympathize with her? She's given her all. She's dared to try, which makes her more heroic than most people will ever be in real life.

By trying, by breaking his pride to beg for a favor to help a friend, or by exposing a weakness, the protagonist will have made himself vulnerable. If the antagonist takes advantage of that vulnerability to strike hard, then the story makes excellent dramatic progress.

By regrouping and finding the last bit of determination to get up one more time and try again—despite injury to pride, emotional hurt, a bruised spirit, or a battered body—the protagonist is showing herself to be heroic. A hero is the kind of character readers want to cheer for.

Drill exercise:

In the following scene, a gladiator and his trainer are discussing events the day after Caelan has won a major victory in the arena. Notice how the story action remains focused between the two characters. No one else is allowed to come in and interrupt. See how quickly the conflict starts. Observe their opposing perspectives and motivations. Take note of each man's tactics and where he shifts his strategy. Can you find clearly linked A/R units? Pay attention to where a longer internalization falls within the scene protagonist's reaction. Why is it provided?

Can you spot any subtext? If so, notice when—and how—it is brought to the surface.

How does the non-viewpoint character show emotion? And at the scene's conclusion, can you identify what type of setback is used?

Example from *Shadow war* (1996) by Deborah Chester:

"You are tired," Orlo said, watching him. "Please rest. No matter how fancy the healer, it is still old-fashioned rest that makes the best cure."

"There is not time for rest," Caelan said, frowning. "And I am well."

Orlo touched his shoulder gently. "A lie," he said, but the reproof was mild. "Stop the lies, Caelan. You lie to the world. You lie to the prince. You lie to me. Worst of all, you lie to yourself."

"I don't understand."

Orlo's gaze never wavered. "I think you do. You threw yourself on the Madrun's sword as though it was nothing. Stupid or courageous, who can say? But why can't you throw yourself on the truth?"

Caelan's temper slipped. "Speak your mind, Orlo. Not these riddles."

"He won't free you."

It was like having the sword pierce his side all over again. Caelan lost his breath and struggled to regain it.

"You are wrong," he said, his voice weak against the intensity of his emotions. His fist clenched on the coverlet. "Wrong."

"I have made my share of mistakes," Orlo said, "enough to know that it is stupid to walk about in blindness. His highness will never free you as long as you are valuable to him. No matter how many times you guard his back when he goes where he should not. You have served him with all your heart and soul. Yesterday you nearly got yourself killed for him, and none of it will avail you."

"I will be free again," Caelan said grimly, staring into space. "I have his word."

Orlo snorted, his square face branded with cynicism. "Oh? You have the word of our kind, honest master. Soon enough there will be betrayal to balance the honey. I have warned you enough, but you never heed warnings, do you?"

Caelan glared at the trainer, hating everything he said. "Careful, Orlo. You're stepping close to treason."

"No. He is."

Caelan surged to his feet.

Orlo took two quick steps back, balancing on the balls of his feet, his eyes watchful and wary. "Defend him," he said in what was almost a taunt. "You always do."

"It is my duty to defend him."

"Why? Do you have hopes of becoming his protector when he takes the throne?"

The accusation hit Caelan like a glove of challenge. Caelan's eyes widened. How much did Orlo know? How much had he overheard? Or was this only speculation?

He was not quick enough to keep his reaction from his face. It was Orlo's turn to stare with widened eyes.

"Great Gault," he breathed, taking yet another step back from Caelan. "So he has promised you that."

Caelan felt stripped and vulnerable. To deny it would be useless, yet he could not confirm it either without condemning himself. He said nothing.

Orlo frowned and slowly shook his head. "You great fool," he said at last, pity in his voice. "Can't you see he is—"

"He does not use me," Caelan broke in. "You understand nothing of this matter. Nothing!"

"No wonder you pulled the Madrun's sword into your side. With that incentive, what man would not take tremendous risks?" Orlo glanced sharply at Caelan. "But can't you see that he is jealous of you?"

Caelan's mouth fell open in astonishment. "Jealous?"

"Whose name were they screaming yesterday?"

"But he is the prince."

"And you have the popularity," Orlo said with scorn. Glancing at the door, he kept his voice low. "When you ride through the streets at the prince's side, cheers from the populace are guaranteed. He can pretend the cheers are for him. It sends a message to the emperor, does it not? But inside, the prince knows the truth. His popularity is purchased, and at the crux it will not hold."

"Take care, Orlo."

"No, *you* take care. Prince Tirhin is a desperate man, and I tell you to watch yourself. When you cease to be of use, he will discard you as he does all his worn-out possessions."

Caelan's chin lifted with dignity. "I have his word."

Without warning Orlo closed the distance between them and gripped Caelan's shoulder hard. "And what is the worth of a promise made to a slave?" he snarled. "Nothing! Nothing at all." He gave Caelan a shake and released him. "He doesn't see you as a man. You belong to him as his dog belongs to him. As that chair over there belongs to him. He owes you nothing, do you hear? No matter what you do for him, there is no obligation from him in return."

How scenes can fail

The following types of mistakes happen frequently in amateur fiction, but they can also creep up on experienced writers.

A muddled or missing scene goal

I've reiterated the importance of clear scene goals many times already because they're so important. Know where your characters are going and what they want to do. Do not be vague. Do not keep the scene goal a secret from your readers.

A forgotten scene goal

Sometimes scenes start out strongly but crumble in the middle and never quite go anywhere. That's because the antagonist has pulled the scene off track. Chances are that through maneuver, trickery, or evasion, the antagonist has shifted the conflict to a different issue than the one that began the scene. As a result, both the writer and the protagonist have forgotten it.

A split focus

This error can occur because the scene goal is lost or because viewpoint is allowed to shift partway through. If you begin your scene with Morwinia wanting her older sister to give her a pet unicorn and halfway through you shift to the sister Brigitta's perspective, where she wants to stop being a useless princess in the tower and instead drive out the invaders who've taken control of their realm, we've lost the entire thread of where we began.

Split focus often happens when the protagonist is a weak or poorly defined character, allowing the antagonist—or any stronger character—to take over.

A passive protagonist

Aside from insufficient conflict, a passive protagonist is probably the worst error that can happen to a scene. A passive protagonist stands around, lacking any kind of oomph or drive. A passive protagonist is not goal-directed. A passive protagonist simply reacts to what other characters are saying or doing. A passive protagonist often internalizes in reaction to what his opposing character says or does, thereby throwing the A/R units off balance.

Check your scenes to be sure your protagonist is actually talking, and not just thinking.

A bystander protagonist

Beware the protagonist who skulks around behind the activity, eavesdropping on conflict happening between other characters. This may seem exciting as you write it, but it's false drama. The protagonist and readers are not taking part in the event; the result is unsatisfactory hearsay.

Another way to sideline a protagonist is by tying her up and making a hostage of her at the critical point. Now she's helpless and must wait until she's rescued. Unless she can escape, she's not proving to be very heroic, is she?

A problem that's too big

The situation should be dire, but if it's well and truly hopeless, and literally there's nothing the protagonist can do—why bother?

The hand of fate

This is a variation of the problem that's too big. If Destiny is against your protagonist, then he stands no chance. Why should anyone read about a character that's truly doomed? What's the point?

Weak conflict

Don't let your protagonist give up at the antagonist's first tactic. Remember that if the scene goal is worth anything at all, then the protagonist won't fold so easily.

Drill exercise:

Plan a scene. Choose a scene protagonist. Give this character a name. Invent a scene goal for this character. What is his or her motivation for attempting the goal?

Choose a scene antagonist. Remember that this character should be directly and strongly opposed to the protagonist's achieving that specific scene goal. Figure out why.

List three or four tactics the protagonist will attempt.

List the tactics the antagonist will counter with.

Determine a setback that will resolve the scene. Be sure that your scene's resolution fits one of the available three options: no; yes, but; or no and furthermore. Remember that the setback should belong to the scene protagonist.

Write the scene.

When you've finished, switch the characters into opposite roles. Make the antagonist of Version 1 into your scene protagonist. Make the protagonist of Version 1 into your scene antagonist.

Go through the steps again, this time from the perspective of the new protagonist. Has the goal been tweaked? Do you need to change the tactics? How will the scene-resolving setback be affected?

Write the scene, then compare the two versions:

Which of the two characters is the stronger protagonist? Why? ➡

Which shows the most sympathetic motivation? Why?

Which version do you like best? Why?

What do these comparisons tell you about how a character drives the scene's action and its outcome?

9

Sequels

Sequels are the second type of dramatic unit that—along with scenes—comprise plot. While scenes tend to attract the most attention, never underestimate the power or usefulness of sequels. They're the key in whether your story will ever make sense.

Please don't be confused by the term sequel. I'm not talking about the follow-up film to a major motion picture or volume two of a book trilogy. Those are the next installments of a long story, and "the next installment" is only one definition of sequel.

According to Webster's dictionary, sequel first of all means "consequence or result; a subsequent development."

Therefore, I'll be discussing sequel as the result or the consequence of a scene.

When creating plot, we can't write all the story action in scene structure. A novel would run to a truly immense length, and short stories would stretch to novella length or longer. Even worse, there would never be a break from all the dramatic intensity. Too much intensity sustained for too long causes readers to break away. They are overloaded, and either they will stop caring because all the action simply blurs together or they'll start laughing in the wrong places because the story has become too melodramatic and campy, too absurd to believe in.

So, following a scene, with its escalating conflict and tough ending, it's necessary to give your readers a breather. You do this by allowing your protagonist some processing time, plus a chance to react to whatever hurtful things have been said or done to him.

After all, let's say you desperately want that rare blue dragon's egg in the pet shop's window, and you've been saving enough money to buy it by eating minimal groceries, surrendering chocolate and sweets, not buying cups of coffee on your way to work, etc. Finally, after weeks of scrimping and saving, you have enough. You head for the store with all your savings in your pocket, only to find the window empty. The egg is gone, sold that very morning.

Wouldn't you need a few moments to deal with your disappointment? Of course!

You're crushed. You're sad. You're angry. You'd been forming wonderful plans. You were going to keep the newly hatched dragon by the kitchen stove, so it would stay warm and dry. You were going to buy a license for it, so it would be a legal domestic pet. You'd already bought a harness and leash. You'd been making lists of names. Aware that your butcher's bill would be increasing, you'd even worked out a tight budget to accommodate the amount of meat young dragons supposedly consume during their first six weeks out of the egg. You'd talked to other dragon owners and located the best trainer to consult on how to housebreak a young dragon while teaching it not to spit or steal all the forks from the kitchen to start its treasure hoard.

And now, there's no little dragon to call your own.

You need time to absorb the shock. That's why novels pause after scenes. The story's movement freezes while the protagonist suffers through reaction to the disaster that's just concluded the preceding scene. The story's movement remains static while the protagonist calms down and begins to think about what to do next.

Therefore, if scenes are dramatic units that are all about conflict and change, sequels are dramatic units that feature internalization, emotion, and planning.

Scenes supply your story with action and excitement. Sequels supply your story with motivation and logic.

This teeter-totter effect provides the so-called peaks and valleys of fiction. The rise and fall of action. The buildup and the drop of drama. It's a balancing act, and reading fiction should help you hone your story instincts about how to manage scenes and sequels. Remember that sequels are valuable. They're never inferior to scenes and shouldn't be underestimated. Although readers may be less aware of them than scenes, experienced writers recognize their value. Good sequels allow you to explain and describe. They allow your viewpoint character a chance to react to what's just happened in the preceding scene. All those deferred feelings, analysis, and motivators that are held back in scenes are given a chance to develop in sequels.

Sequels also show readers why your protagonist is doing what he's doing. They show readers what your protagonist is going to do next and why he's willing to take such a horrendous risk. Sequels remind readers of what's at stake and how the situation is growing worse.

They also allow writers to summarize portions of the story that can't really support scene action. So when your characters need to travel from Xyni province to the Kingdom of Umlaw—and nothing exciting or threatening will happen on the way—describe the journey in one brief paragraph and move your characters to where the action will be. Such a summary should occur after a scene between the protagonist and her mother who's against the journey, yet before the scene where the protagonist arrives at the Umlaw city gates and is robbed the moment she steps through them.

Furthermore, sequels allow writers to adjust the story's pacing because the general effect of a sequel is one of slowing down. (In contrast, the general effect of a scene is speed. Refer to Chapter 15 for additional explanation.) We don't want a story to maintain the same pace from start to finish. That would become predictable, monotonous, and boring. But alternating scenes and sequels vary how quickly or slowly the story moves.

Sequels provide opportunities to fit in background and explanation—elements so necessary in fantasy fiction yet so deadly to scenes.

Sequels are where in-depth characterization belongs, where analysis of motivation occurs, and where explanation of character behavior appears.

I like to think of sequels as bridges. They're connectors linking scenes together. Without a sequel spanning the distance between two scenes, you can't plausibly cross from one scene to the next. If you just ignore sequels and write scene after scene after scene, you're basically allowing your character to leap over chasms in a contrived, unbelievable way.

Sequel construction

A sequel contains certain components designed to work together in a plausible system, and those components fall in a certain order, as follows:

- Emotional aftermath.
- Analytical thought.
- Review of previous story events.
- Weighing of options.
- Making a decision.
- Taking action.

As the viewpoint character works through these steps, we're moving that character away from the scene and its disastrous outcome toward the new scene that will come next.

Now, let's examine each sequel component separately.

Emotional aftermath

This is all about raw feeling, the sheer, overwhelming, unfiltered sweep of emotion that will hit your character following partial or complete failure in the preceding scene.

You know how you feel when you attempt something and fail, don't you?

Because we're human beings and not Vulcans, we feel things intensely. We may be able to suppress our feelings enough to hide them from others, but we pay a price for such suppression—either through social isolation as we shut out friends and family—or through a breakdown of our health.

(In crime fiction such as mysteries and thrillers that deal with sociopaths, ever notice how you seldom find yourself in such a character's viewpoint for long? Modern popularity and/or public fascination notwithstanding, a sociopath is *not* normal. Dabbling in such a viewpoint provides readers with a taste of that existence without immersing them in what could prove to be a very uncomfortable reading experience.)

Sometimes, the scene-ending disaster is so shocking or terrible that the protagonist may be emotionally blitzed and too numb to comprehend it. Savvy writers don't skip that reaction. They play the numbed shock. Then the dam will break, and real emotion will come.

Certain emotions won't work in sequels. For example, happiness, satisfaction, glee, hope, contentment, or delight will seldom appear because why would the protagonist feel any of them if she's just experienced a setback? (On the other hand, a villain might feel glee and satisfaction if the protagonist has just performed a face plant in the mud while jousting in a pseudo-medieval tournament.) The higher the stakes or the more effort the protagonist has put into the endeavor, the more intense the emotions will be.

Accordingly, familiarize yourself with how it feels to be angry, sad, disappointed, grief-stricken, appalled, horrified, bewildered, shocked, and flummoxed.

Or, if the scene setback was a physical one where the protagonist is knocked cold, the first component of its sequel will involve regaining consciousness and all the physical misery that goes with it.

Example from *The queen's gambit* by Deborah Chester:

Icy cold water ran beneath Talmor, filling his mouth and nostrils. He jerked up his head, snorting and coughing, dragged himself forward a few inches, then sank down. More than that required too much effort. He wanted only to sleep. Water surged beneath him again, hoisting him a little higher on the beach. Revived a second time, he had better luck in keeping his face out of the water.

He did not know where he was, but as he rolled onto his back and gazed at the sky, he expected to see daylight. Instead, the stars were twinkling in an indigo sky. The surf roared in his ears. The usual scents of seaweed and fish filled the air, but when the wind shifted he smelled smoke and the stink of burning hair.

The sea ran under him again, unpleasantly cold, and this time he thought, *tide*. Rolling onto his side, he sat up with a groan. Every inch of his body hurt, his head and side most of all.

Sitting up seemed to make the pounding in his skull more violent. He moaned, lifting his hands to his face, and realized vaguely that he must have been moaning for quite some time. His throat was terribly dry and there was sand in his mouth. He spat out the unpleasant, briny stuff and stared at the bay in muzzy confusion. There was something he needed to remember, but memory and coherent thought swirled dizzily through his mind. Just as things started to make sense, they were gone, too elusive to grasp. He did not try very hard.

In the above example, the viewpoint character is experiencing the emotion of confusion combined with the physical effects of concussion. His actions are minimal. The story is on pause while he tries to come to. Prior scene action involved

Sir Talmor in an intense battle that concluded with him caught in a gunpowder explosion.

Following intense, exciting, disastrous scenes such as Talmor's battle, readers need a chance to relax as they assimilate the fast and furious depiction of combat that just ended. The lost battle carries serious ramifications that will affect the rest of the story. There's much to be described and explained, and the sequel is the place to do it. To hurry would be to short-change such crucial details.

You can also write about a viewpoint character that feels intensely, yet is unable to display his emotions. Only readers are able to share what he's truly experiencing, and they will bond with him even as other characters feel frustration in dealing with someone they perceive as emotionally cold. (Although not a fantasy writer, Dick Francis was a master at depicting protagonists who are emotionally reticent yet extremely sympathetic.)

Please keep in mind that your protagonist shouldn't wallow in prolonged, super-charged levels of emotion for every single sequel. Readers will soon draw back from such histrionics.

We're not seeking to provide hysteria. What we want is for the protagonist to sort out her feelings in order to take new action.

Also, you should understand that at certain points in a fantasy novel, combat and danger will be increasing, moving the protagonist rapidly from crisis to crisis. In such instances, there may not be time to react emotionally.

Usually what happens is that the protagonist will start to experience an emotional reaction, but will have to cut it off, suppress it, or defer it until later simply because new danger is crowding in.

Sequels should never be skipped, but sometimes authors will defer them, playing them later in a story. (Refer to Chapter 19 for a more in-depth explanation.)

How long should the emotional component run?

Emotion should last as long as your viewpoint character

is experiencing sheer reaction, whether there's time between story events to fully develop the appropriate emotions, how you intend to manage the pacing of your story, the stakes of the scene that just ended, and the personality of your protagonist.

After all, sequels serve to deepen reader understanding of characterization. Not through description or a heavy-handed info-dump, but through showing readers how a character reacts to shocks and difficulties.

Is your character emotionally strong, able to feel intensely but in control of herself? Is this character emotionally reticent, able to open up only with one or two trusted individuals or perhaps as emotionally damaged as television's Doc Martin, who's unable to share with anyone?

Is your character tenderhearted and compassionate, feeling everything with such sensitivity that she cries at sentimental television commercials and blubbers tears over movies and books?

Is your character emotionally weak, someone who falls apart whenever tragedy strikes? People like this may indulge in hysterics or lose their tempers and lash out. Such self-centered folk disregard the needs of others. They make no effort to control themselves, and can even be even proud of it. You can certainly dabble briefly in such a viewpoint, but I don't recommend such a personality type for your central protagonist.

Creating and delivering emotions

Although it's easy for me to insist that stories contain emotional content, you may be wondering how it's done.

When your manuscript is criticized for "holding back," what should you do?

When your characters are described as "flat" or "lifeless," what does that mean?

And when readers just can't relate to your protagonist, what haven't you done?

Emotions are messy things. They take a toll on the person

experiencing them, and when they're exhibited in public, it's uncomfortable to witness them, isn't it?

Do you feel tempted to tuck them away in your stories by alluding to them vaguely, pointing in their direction, and hoping readers can imagine the rest?

That just won't do.

Just as plumbers are paid to roll up their sleeves and reach into the cold, messy water flooding your house from a broken pipe on Christmas Eve, so do readers pay writers to wade into the emotional upheavals of their characters.

You've created your protagonist. You should know what makes this individual tick, how this individual reacts, what this individual will do when the story situation goes terribly wrong. When your protagonist hits trouble, you—as his creator—can't distance yourself.

Like it or not, it's your job to put yourself in your suffering, beleaguered character's heart, soul, and mind. As writers, trying to imagine what our character is feeling at any given moment, we must draw on the same techniques as method actors.

We must experience—either through our memories or our imagination—what our characters are coping with.

That's hard work. As I've already said, it's messy. It's exhausting and at times unpleasant. And it's our responsibility.

Emotional transfers

Before I was ever published, I came across the advice, "Write what you know."

Haven't you encountered a similar suggestion?

But I wanted to write about castles and dragons and shapeshifters and supernatural creatures. How could I experience any of that? I couldn't.

So is this dictum stupid?

Not at all. It's very true. We just have to figure out what we actually know.

"Not very much," you might say.

Are you so sure?

"Well, I haven't had much life experience yet. I—uh—mostly read and play video games. I don't get out very much."

To believe you know very little is to shortchange yourself. As a human being, you've already experienced most, if not all, of the major and minor emotions. You may not know how to capture a bogart, much less the necessary spell to use, but you know what you'd feel if you actually encountered one.

That's right ... fear. Maybe terror. Possibly even panic.

Now, think about some moment in your real life when you were afraid. Where were you? How old were you? What were you doing? What was happening around you?

Perhaps you were five years old. Your parents were away for the evening, leaving you with a thirteen-year-old babysitter. The night was stormy. The electricity went out. You were supposed to be in bed, but you were afraid of the thunder. Instead of comforting you, the babysitter was shining a flashlight on her face and telling you ghost stories in a weird, ghoulish voice.

Maybe you were so scared you cried or wet the bed or pitched a temper tantrum.

Maybe for years afterward, you couldn't sleep without a night light, or you would lie in bed, frozen stiff as you listened to the creaks and groans of the house around you. Did you wait to hear that slow, dragging step approaching your bedroom door and the rattle of the knob that would signify the monster was finally here ... to claim you?

Or perhaps you were eleven and about to play in your first public piano recital.

You could see the silhouetted heads of the audience beyond the stage lights. You could sense that mass of people, those unseen strangers who soon would be staring at you. Your feet felt rooted to the stage floor as you waited in the wings for your turn. You wanted to throw up. You wanted to die. You wanted to run away and never come back. You couldn't remember a single note of the Chopin etude you'd been practicing daily for the past several weeks. You wished with all your heart that you'd never taken piano lessons, and you hated your teacher and your parents for insisting that you go through with this.

Or perhaps you remember going riding with your cousins at their country farm.

They promised to put you on a gentle horse. Just as everything was going well and you were having tremendous fun, someone shouted, "Let's race!" Instead of pleasantly ambling, your mare suddenly transformed into an iron-mouthed monster that broke into a gallop, going much too fast. You tried to stop her, but she got the bit in her teeth and ran faster. Everything was out of control. You could feel yourself slipping in the saddle and feared you'd fall off and break your neck. And now you were heading for the creek and the woods beyond them. You knew the animal was running to the trees to drag you off. You'd fall. You'd be killed.

Or let's say that you were a teenager, supposed to be watching your younger brother for the afternoon.

But he was little and a pest. You left him digging in the sandbox so you could read your book in peace. Then you heard him calling out, "Pretty baa!" When you looked up, you saw that he'd left the yard and was standing next to the road, pointing at the neighbor's sheep pastured on the other side of it. You could hear a car approaching beyond the curve. At any moment, it would roar past. And there was Johnny, who at any moment was going to toddle across the road to the sheep. You knew you were too far away to reach him. You were afraid that if you shouted, he would stubbornly dart into the road, away from you—as he'd done in the past. You couldn't think what to do, but you were suddenly running faster than you'd ever run before, knowing that you weren't going to reach him in time.

Or perhaps you were seven, walking home every day from school past a ratty yard and decrepit old house.

A large, aggressive dog was chained in the mud. It always growled and snarled at you as you hurried by. You were afraid of it and you hated it. One day, when you'd had trouble at school and were feeling upset, the dog barked at you as usual. Angry, you threw a stick at it and shouted at it to "Shut up!" The dog went crazy and lunged, snapping its chain. Before you could run, it was on you, tackling you so hard it knocked the wind from you. You couldn't even scream. It was heavy and snarling, its breath hot and rancid in your face as you struggled to hold it off. And then came the searing pain as it bit you.

In each of the above examples, I've provided some variant of fright, fear, or terror. In our lives, we may not have ever experienced these situations, but we've known similar moments of overwhelming helplessness, fright, or the instinctive primitive fears of childhood. We've lived through imaginary fears and actual fears born of terrible events that we somehow survived. We've faced down nervousness and conquered it, emerging triumphant and stronger as a result. Or perhaps we've been damaged physically or psychologically, and now are weaker, less able to cope with a world that's too big or scary for us to handle.

We have irrational fears—fear of heights, fear of spiders, fear of clowns, fear of crowds. We have rational fears—fear of a neighborhood stalker who's breaking into homes and assaulting women, fear of financial loss as the worsening economy erodes our life's savings. We have fears that have been ingrained in us or taught to us by others—fear of snakes, fear of pathogens. And we have fears born of past experience—fear of planes after surviving a crash, fear of loud noises after bombs are dropped on our community, fear of a drunken and violent father.

The key to effectively employing emotional transference is to pinpoint the exact emotion you wish your character to feel, then examine your memories for a time or experience when you felt the same emotion. Think about how you felt inside as you lived through the event. Then transfer the sensations and feelings—not the past event—to your character in your present plot situation.

Once we know which emotions we intend to use and we've drawn on emotional transference, we have to think about which method we'll use to present character emotion to readers.

After all, it would be so much easier to write, *The vampire felt sad after he'd drained his victim's blood.*

But that doesn't work, does it? It's too flat, too dull. It's telling what the vampire feels, but readers seldom believe what they're told. They're usually convinced only by what they're shown through description, action, and dialogue.

Description

How do you feel internally when you're unhappy, or upset, or disappointed, or angry? Can you write a description of such feelings? Close your eyes and think about the internal physical details. When you're nervous, does your stomach flutter or feel nauseous? Do your palms sweat? Do you fidget?

You may find that describing emotions comes naturally to you, or you may feel inept with the process.

If describing emotion gives you trouble, examine the scene that occurred just before the sequel you're now writing. Did that scene end with a strong disaster for the protagonist?

If not, it will be much harder for you to scrape up an emotional reaction in your character.

You never want your character to enter a sequel feeling *meh*. Indifference is a loser in fiction. We don't want it, and it won't contribute to the success of any story we want to write.

Tepid, apathetic reactions poison a good story. They will damage it and probably kill it.

Also, keep in mind that heroic, epic, high fantasy will require a more florid style of emotion than urban fantasy—which will be underwritten in the *noir* mystery tradition. So your chosen subgenre will affect how flowery, snarky, or low-key you go.

Example from *The queen's gambit* by Deborah Chester:

Pheresa lay in her bed, watching the shadows of a snowy dawn lighten to gray around her. That's what she felt, cold and gray and empty. So very empty. She had carried life, but it was gone now, extinguished and taken from her. Her son had never cried. His blue fists had been so tiny, so miraculously perfect. She glimpsed him once, wrapped in a cloth and rubbed by Oola before the fire, but then Oola's efforts had stilled and all was silent as the servant carried him away.

A door clicked open, and someone came inside, skirts rustling. A tray was set down beside her, and a lamp lit.

The light hurt Pheresa's eyes, and she turned her face away.

"Your majesty?" Oola said in concern. "I've brought you some good, hearty broth and bread. Have a little, won't you?"

Pheresa ignored her, and after a while Oola sniveled in her apron and left. Then the physician came. He asked questions in his calm, deep voice. Pheresa ignored him, too. What she wanted was gone, taken from her forever. She had never held her son, and she ached for him desperately, so desperately she wanted to scream aloud for Thod to give him back.

But her child could not come back, and she wanted nothing else. She could not cry out for him, and so she said nothing at all. She lay in this empty place, listening to her own breathing, and she did not want even that.

In the next example, the villain, a sorcerer, has been tricked by his young hostage into destroying his beloved pet.

Example from *The king betrayed* by Deborah Chester:

She went on laughing that false laughter of mockery and contempt. Appalled at what he'd done, at what she'd tricked him into doing, Tulvak Sahm felt his wrath gathering into a fiery ball inside him. He curled his hands into claws, shaking with the effort to control himself. After a moment he turned and left her, for only his fear of Ashnod's wrath kept him from destroying her on the spot.

Character action

Conveying emotion through character action means you must study people's body language—their stance, their gestures, their tics, and their habitual mannerisms. You need to convey emotion through these external signals when dealing with non-viewpoint characters.

Observe actors at work. Dig into acting craft to learn what a change of expression can convey. I suggest that you particularly study older films, the black-and-white classics from the late 1930s and 1940s. Often you'll see a different style of acting craft than is utilized today, and it can be very helpful. (Although I love movies that are even earlier than the mid-1930s, many of the pre-Code films and early talkies feature a "stagey," heavily theatrical acting style derived in turn from the silent films, and the silent films such as *Metropolis* (1927) sometimes display influences from Victorian stagecraft. These styles are interesting from a film buff's perspective, but less useful for writing prose.)

You may be put off by the lack of color, absence of computer-generated effects, and a different style of pacing in old movies. You may find the characters' manners, formality of speech, and clothing odd, but give them a chance. Especially observe what the actors are doing in close-ups. How they walk, or how they stiffen and turn around. Look at how their eyes grow steely. Observe what they're doing with their hands. It can also be useful to study how one actor steals attention from another. Remember that you aren't trying to learn the craft of movie-making, but instead non-verbal signals, gestures, and body language to incorporate in your own characters' mannerisms.

With your non-viewpoint characters, you must remember that they're acting and speaking from their emotions, just as your viewpoint character is. The challenge for you lies in conveying what they're feeling without shifting into their perspective.

Any combination of actions—such as dabbing at wet eyes, sniffling, or turning his back to everyone—can demonstrate emotion clearly.

The risk of showing emotion through action is that readers may misunderstand. However, the more adept you become at showing the correct behavioral signals, the smaller the risk of being misconstrued becomes.

The advantage of showing emotion through action is that readers are allowed to figure things out for themselves. As in real life, where we constantly observe and draw conclusions, emotion shown through action is very convincing and plausible. Another advantage stems from increased reader involvement. As readers empathize with characters, they will draw on their own imagination and past experiences to share in what they believe the character is feeling.

Through showing emotion through action, you are, in effect, enticing readers to make emotional transfers of their own.

Discussion

This method of presenting emotion comes through character dialogue. Sometimes in sequels, the protagonist may confide her feelings, doubts, and distress to a confidant or mentor.

Such a conversation centers on how to cope with the preceding scene which has gone wrong. It usually doesn't feature conflict because it's about helping the protagonist move past her emotions so she can plan what she'll do next.

Therefore, in this method, you aren't internalizing. Your readers may mistake a sequel discussion for a scene since two characters are talking and moving about, but the purpose isn't goal oriented. The discussion should be designed to convey emotions in the protagonist.

For example, let's say your protagonist is about to infiltrate the inmost lair of the vampire headquarters. He's studied a map of the place stolen from a captured messenger so he knows the layout. He's put on the messenger's clothing, and he's drenched in a lab-formulated chemical designed to mask his "alive-ness" from the vampire predators that will soon surround him. His boss is giving him instructions and asking him to repeat them aloud, over and over. At one point in the preparations, the boss grips the hero's wrist and takes his pulse.

"Hmm, too fast, but you'll do," the boss says.

That's presenting emotion (raw nerves) through a spoken comment.

Here's a prose example of emotion presented through subtext and discussion:

Example from *The king betrayed* by Deborah Chester:

Thum put his hands on the desk and leaned forward to scowl at Dain. "You should rest."

"I've had all winter to rest. Now there's too much to do." Impatient for his friend to go, Dain looked up, meeting Thum's worried eyes. "When I grow tired, I'll stop. My word on it."

Thum shrugged. "Nothing I say seems to persuade you."

"That's right," Dain said briskly.

Very often, writers will employ a combination of all three emotion methods in sequel. Emotion and physical feeling can be conveyed through a blend of description, character action, and discussion.

Drill exercise:

Select three emotions that are likely to make a person take action. For example, anger, love, and envy.

Make a chart for each emotion, then deal with one at a time. Think back to one of your memories when you experienced this emotion in a powerful way.

Write down on your chart how you felt physically or from the inside. Don't edit details or censor yourself. Just jot them as quickly as you can.

When you've finished, think about some occasion when you've witnessed a person in the throes of this same emotion. How did the individual look—externally? How did you know what the person was feeling? What signals, behavior, expressions, etc. did you observe?

When you've finished your chart for each emotion, both internally and externally, make a list of variants. For example, earlier in the chapter I addressed the emotion of fear. Variants would be nervousness, stage fright, terror, etc. Try to think of lesser or milder versions of an emotion as well as the strongest possible ones.

Which internal details would be the same as before? Would there be any different ones? List them.

Repeat this procedure for the external details.

Compare your charts. If there are other emotions that interest you, go ahead and make charts for them as well.

Remember that self-pity is an emotion that destroys reader sympathy for your character. Avoid it.

Also, I've already warned you against using apathy. Don't confuse it with the character cynicism so popular in urban fantasy. Cynicism means a distrust of sincere motives or the best aspects of human nature. It's often a superficial mask worn by characters to hide their true natures. (Refer to Chapter 14 for more information.) Apathy is true absence of emotion or involvement and is extremely hard to depict well or sympathetically. It will not help you move a story forward. Fantasy stories are about heroes and people who dare strive for achievement. True losers and slackers will not make the effort, or will fold at the first scene setback.

10

Dilemma and decision

As long as a character is caught in the emotional or physical backlash of a scene's disaster, the character will remain frozen there. But in order not to stop the story indefinitely, it's important to let the protagonist move past sheer emotion and start thinking about the dilemma she's landed in.

After all, she tried very hard to attain the previous scene goal. As a result of her having taken risks and made an attempt, she's been outmaneuvered and defeated. At this point in the sequel, as she calms down and her emotions lessen enough for reason to return, she should be thinking along the lines of *What am I going to do now?*

This forms the second component of sequel structure.

Any character strong enough to carry a viewpoint should be capable of analyzing a problem and coping with it.

Depending on the stakes, the scope of a disastrous setback, and the character's personality, the transition from emotion to thought may happen very quickly or it may involve relapses into pure emotion again.

But rational thought must return for the character to move forward in the story.

In analyzing her dilemma, the protagonist is taking her first—possibly shaky—steps forward. And once she can think, we have another structural pattern order to follow:

Analyzing the problem

How a person analyzes a problem demonstrates how he thinks, observes, and reasons. That gives readers additional insight into this individual's true nature.

Think about the musical film, *Doctor Doolittle* (1967) starring Rex Harrison. Perhaps you saw it as a child. It's a whimsical, fantastical, light-hearted film about a Victorian doctor who likes animals better than he likes people. With the help of his century-old parrot Polynesia, he learns to speak the language of nearly all the species in the animal kingdom and becomes an animal doctor. The humans in his village think he's mad and want to lock him up.

With the help of his companions, the doctor escapes and they set sail around the world in search of the elusive pink sea snail, which the doctor is eager to meet and observe.

Shipwrecked by hurricane, they fall into more dangers and adventures before everything works out in an unusual way.

The point is that the doctor's perspective is always different than that of the other humans. He thinks outside the box. He sees opportunity where others see disaster. He's almost never discouraged. His approach to problems is unique, and he possesses a spirit of adventure that never leaves him.

In other words, his analysis of the problems and setbacks he encounters tells us a great deal about his true nature as a man.

Review

In this stage, the viewpoint character mulls over the key points of the scene that just occurred. She remembers the disaster that concluded it and internalizes what it means in terms of her hopes.

The character also reiterates her story goal and why it's so important to her.

While review isn't necessary in all sequels, if the preceding scene was strong or created a significant turning point, review is definitely needed.

Sometimes, the character will find it necessary to review even earlier aspects of the story. Perhaps your protagonist was tricked into meeting someone on a poorly lit street at midnight, only to be ambushed and nearly killed by werewolves. He's managed to escape, but now he's wounded and in trouble, hiding for the moment while he tries to figure out who he can trust.

In such a scenario, he might need to review important aspects of several prior scenes or comments, seeking a new interpretation in the actions of the person he thought was his friend, the person who betrayed him tonight.

The story situation, and its degree of urgency, will determine how long the review process will be. Review allows writers to remind readers of key plot points disguised as the protagonist's musings.

Planning

In this stage, the protagonist tries to formulate a new plan of action so he can continue striving to attain his story goal. Accordingly, he must weigh options. Some will be discarded. What remains will be ranked in some kind of order according to risk and degree of feasibility.

Now, of course, what's really happening in this portion of the manuscript is that you're planning the next steps of the plot for *yourself.* You're also playing fair with the reader in sharing what your protagonist is going to attempt next and why. And you're doing all of this in a way that disguises the process and creates the illusion that your protagonist is driving the story.

In fact, it's you—the writer—that drives the story. But of course that must always be hidden from readers.

Be very careful with your plot outline. For those of you who take the time and trouble to work out your story before you write it, there's a tendency to grow tired and just shove your character into the next event and the next and the next. Yes, you're following your outline and checking off the plot points as you go, but there is the danger of failing to sustain the illusion that your protagonist is reasoning his way toward his next step.

When the illusion falters, your story looks contrived.

Even when you know clearly what your character will do next, take the time to show your protagonist figuring out a solution and planning the next step.

Yes, you know where you want the story to go, but you must take your character emotionally and rationally through the decisions that will cause him to attempt whatever you want him to do next. Doing so supplies your protagonist with motivation. The most risky, outlandish, or possibly foolish course of action will make sense to readers because they understand how the character reached his decision and why he wants to take such risks.

Skip this process at your peril.

Reaching a decision

The third component of sequel construction is all about positioning the viewpoint character to take new action. The setback has been processed. The worsening problem has been reviewed and analyzed. Options have been narrowed to two or three possible courses of future action.

But which one?

The decision should not be a vague one. It should not be philosophical or left dangling as a generality. *I ought to try again to stop Esmelia from poisoning the servants. I really should. But I'm so tired, and counteracting her magic spell exhausted me. I'll sit here wearily and pet my beloved talking horse. Maybe tomorrow we can do something.*

Excuse me while I go find something better to read.

Such limp, self-indulgent blather makes me hate this character who's sitting on her duff instead of figuring out how to save her friends and servants from the evil Esmelia. I don't want the languid protagonist to sit under a tree and regain her strength. I want her to DO something, and do it right now.

A sequel decision should be about forming the next scene goal.

Whatever went awry for your viewpoint character in the preceding scene, there is now some new chance, some slender means by which to succeed—however risky or dangerous. And by working through the emotions, review, and analysis, and by weighing options, the character is now psychologically prepared to choose a new course of action and try again.

Making decisions—especially when the stakes are high—isn't always an easy matter.

In real life, I have a friend who's very decisive. She makes up her mind quickly and grows impatient with anyone who's slow to reach a decision. Affluent and married to a successful businessman, she knows that should she make a mistake, she can afford to shrug it off and purchase a replacement.

But if someone relies on intuition and feelings instead of pertinent facts, and if this individual lives on a small budget, then important purchases must involve a slow, careful decision because a mistake will be too costly to rectify.

In fiction, your character will have reached the best decision he can according to his personality, circumstances, and what's at stake. The reader will have gone along as the character worked his way toward reaching that decision. Even so, for a touch of plausibility, it's okay to let the character still feel doubts and uncertainty about the new course of action. This reminds readers that the stakes have gone up. The trouble ahead is likely to be harder than before, although last time was pretty rough.

It's important that the new decision—or goal—be very clear

to both the character and readers. Don't leave things vague and unresolved.

Clarity helps you stay focused on exactly what's about to happen next. Perhaps you're thinking, however, that you want to surprise the reader. You don't want to share the new goal. You're planning to spring a plot twist instead.

A surprise will work much better if the reader is led to expect something very specific. Then, when the twist occurs, readers will be much more shocked by it.

It's important for readers to understand a new goal has been chosen and the character is moving into position to act on it.

When readers know the new goal, they can start anticipating the next scene and the confrontation to come.

When readers know the new goal, they understand the new stakes.

Taking action

This last element of sequel is where the viewpoint character actually resumes an active role in what happens next.

The character is no longer sitting around, weeping over her potion book and thinking about how unhappy she is since she flunked out of Hogwarts. Instead, she's ready to take action.

Decision alone isn't enough for a hero in carrying the story forward. The character must *do* something to bring about the next scene.

It can be as small as making an appointment with the matriarch of the local vampire hive, or knocking on the door of the village wizard, or driving through the woods instead of taking a shortcut home. This action puts the protagonist somewhere that will provoke confrontation with the opponent in a new bout of conflict.

When your protagonist acts on a new decision by reaching for a new goal and is opposed by a scene antagonist, you are in the next scene.

Sequel chart

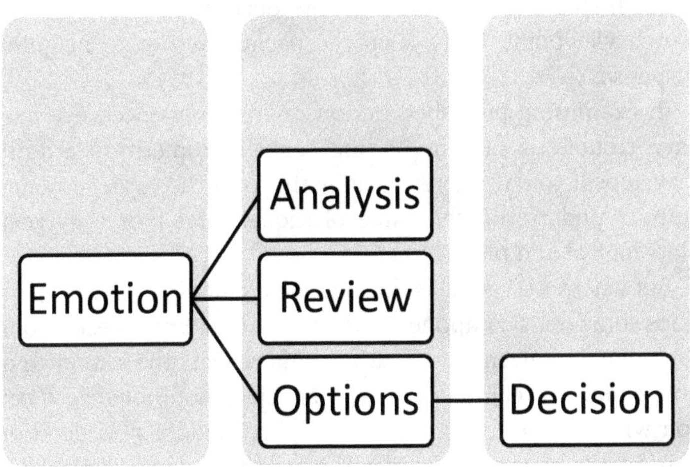

Scene and sequel linkage

Remember that sequels are bridges that connect your scenes smoothly. They show readers how your viewpoint character repositions from one scene to the next—emotionally, mentally, and physically.

In a larger sense, you can think of scenes and sequels as hugely expanded A/R units. The scene is the action—something happening externally—and the sequel is the reaction—something happening internally to your protagonist.

So, just as A/R units link together, with one causing the next, so do scenes and sequels connect, with one leading to the next.

It's helpful to keep in mind that sequels can skip components if motivation and decision are obvious from the story's context. Some sequel components crowd into others. And at times, if there's enough urgency or danger, sequels are interrupted or deferred.

Therefore, not all sequels are written fully, with a complete and thorough exploration of each component as I've explained them in this chapter. Some writers delay sequels in order to switch viewpoint, or to keep the pacing fast, or to heighten suspense.

In examining published fiction, the inexperienced eye may have trouble at first in finding sequels. Sometimes a story may appear to have none. Usually this isn't the case. Seasoned authors understand the value of sequels and how they keep plots logical and plausible.

But whether a sequel is thorough and complete or whether it skips some of its components, the components are presented in the order I've given you. That formula reflects the sequence of how people in real life cope with shocks and problems. When you write in the order of emotion plus thought plus decision plus action, your story carries the power of plausibility.

Remember, a well-written sequel will help you—and your readers—stay bonded with the viewpoint character; explain future developments in the novel; establish and reiterate logic within the story; explain and reinforce character motivation; and allow room for background explanation.

Sample sequels

In Example 1, notice how brief it is and how the components have been compressed into the briefest wordage possible.

Example 1

[**Scene-ending setback**] Liam slumped over the steering wheel with a groan, his blood soaking through his shirt. As the car veered toward the guardrail, Emma [**emotion**] froze with terror. [**Analysis component deferred**] There was no time to think. [**Decision**] All she could do was steer the car to safety. [**Action**] She gripped the wheel with one hand, pulling Liam back.

Example 2 provides a longer sequel. However, review, weighing of options, and decision are missing. That's because review and options aren't needed here. Decision is implied by the character's action.

Prior to this excerpt, Queen Alexeika has been informed erroneously that her husband the king is dead. Now his body has been brought home.

Example 2 from *The king betrayed* by Deborah Chester:

For this was not Faldain's body.

[**Emotion**] She stared, hardly daring to let herself believe the evidence of her own eyes. And inside her, as the hard twisted knot of her emotions and fears uncoiled with joy and relief, she knew astonishment that Faldain's men and attendants could be so mistaken.

[**Analysis**] *But am I seeing the invention of my own hopes?* she asked herself. *Am I deceiving myself?* She was determined to be sure.

"Fold back more of the shroud," she commanded.

The man complied, baring the corpse to its waist. As Sir Pyron had warned her, it was in poor condition, yet this was not her husband's frame, not his musculature. Those were not his ears. His blood was pale, courtesy of his eldin heritage, not clotted black like this. His old scars were not to be found. His sword Mirengard still lay atop the body, held beneath swollen, fingerless hands. Of course it had not worked its magic, for this corpse was not its master's.

For a moment, her heart sang; [**Action**] then she reached out and pulled Mirengard off the body.

Although this sample has been taken out of context, you can see something of how Alexeika's mind works from how she examines the body. She's not cold-hearted. She feels emotion, but she's also capable of controlling what she's feeling in order to think. She's quick and decisive. She's not going to wring her hands and dither. When she removes the king's sword from the corpse, she's declaring that it's not Faldain and should not lie in state to be mourned by a grieving kingdom.

It is also possible to break a sequel in half, delaying its second part until later in the story. This serves to set a hook and heighten suspense while delaying what the character involved will finally decide to do. Although story time will have passed, it's important to remember that the viewpoint character will have remained in the same psychological state as when he last appeared. This is the key to a successful interruption or delay of a sequel.

In Example 3, there's a small amount of background summarized to remind readers of who Perrell is since they saw him last and what's troubling him. By not repeating his emotions, the sequel shows that he's recovered from his initial shock in the days since the cardinal first mentioned murdering the queen. But although Perrell evidently spent the time procrastinating making a decision, the summons now leaves him no more time to make up his mind.

Example 3 from *The queen's knight* (2004):

Sir Perrell—clad in a fresh white surcoat over a polished hauberk, the emblematic black circles interlocked across his chest and embroidered with the symbol of his order, sword clean and shining in its scabbard, helmet carried correctly beneath his left arm—strode down the long, silent passageway once more to Cardinal Theloi's apartments.

[**Background explanation**] In the past few days since discovering evidence of plague, Perrell and his men had been busy indeed. The affliction was spreading rapidly through the poorer sections of Savroix-en-Charva. The port had been closed, and travelers by road were being turned back at the city gates. No one could use the road between town and palace without a signed warrant, and even then Perrell had been stopped at a checkpoint, leaving his horse and companions behind while he journeyed the rest of the way to the palace by boat.

It was believed the air on the river had cleansing powers. Even so, at the landing, he'd had to stand in the cloying smoke of incense for quite a while until he was permitted through guarded gates into the wing of the palace where Cardinal Theloi resided.

Now, Perrell strode along impatiently behind the cleric escorting him to Theloi's chambers. His mind was on a hundred details still undone, for his order was exiting the town at dawn, assigned to escort the cardinals, cathedral bishop, and other high-ranking church officials who were scattering across the realm to safer towns and monasteries for the duration of the summer. [**Review**] But he could not help but recall the last summons he'd received from Theloi and the questions his eminence had put to him.

Is this the night that I'll be ordered to murder the queen? he asked himself, and felt a chill sink through his body.[**Emotional bounce**]

Theloi had warned him to be ready with his answer. Despite prayer and much searching of his conscience, Perrell had no idea whether he would obey the order or refuse it. [**Weighing options**] He was an officer, trained to follow orders. If the Circle of Cardinals believed her majesty to be a secret heretic and a danger to herself and others, then their decision must be obeyed. And yet ... she was the queen and crowned sovereign, and Perrell believed in the Thod-anointed sanctity of her majesty's right to sit on the throne.

Dreading what was to come, Perrell told himself to stop being a fool. [**Decision**] He must follow orders. An officer could do nothing less. An officer's conscience was the same as his duty; and part of his duty was to believe in the chain of command, to follow it, to obey it without hesitation. If he could no longer do that, then he would have to break his oaths and withdraw from the knighthood. The prospect made him sweat.

A door opened before him, and [**Action**] he was ushered into a small, oppressively furnished sitting room.

Transitions

When you're delaying a complete sequel for a valid dramatic reason—i.e. you want to keep the pacing very fast in a particular section of the book; or you want to withhold a character's decision or reasoning from readers for a short time; or, you're using the plotting strategy known as a scene cluster (explained in Chapter 12)—you should signal to readers that you're changing the time or locale of what's about to happen next.

Readers need the signal to avoid becoming confused. When you drive your car, you're supposed to indicate your intentions to turn or change traffic lanes to avoid confusion among other drivers. When you write, you need to remember that without these prompts, readers can't always keep up with what is probably crystal clear in your imagination.

We have simple transitions and long transitions.

Simple transitions consist of short, simple phrases or paragraphs that serve only to inform readers of a change in time or locale.

For example:

At the same time as the werewolf "Wilderness Rocks!" convention, the Coalition for Vampire Safety was holding a meeting of its own in another part of town, where the gathering was considerably more serious in tone.

Here's another:

It was the following Thursday before Alyssa received her shipment of silver bullets.

Or this:

Up in Jenny's room, all was peaceful slumber, but downstairs, ghosts began gathering in the kitchen from all directions. Some

came from the basement. Others slid out from beneath the antique stove or emerged from the end of the sink faucet.

And this:

Meanwhile, back at the castle ...

The long transition usually consists of dialogue between the viewpoint character and a confidant, where the preceding scene is discussed. It may also be where the viewpoint character seeks out someone with information and they talk without conflict. Often the long transition is a passage of narrative where background is presented or events are summarized instead of being dramatized in scenes. The long transition allows room in the story for romantic subplots to develop—whereby the two characters involved aren't in conflict with each other but instead are flirting, courting, or becoming better acquainted.

For example, if you're writing an epic quest story, your characters may have come through an exciting but perilous story event. Perhaps someone is now injured and needs recovery time and tending. Perhaps the food supplies have been exhausted, and the characters should pause on their journey to hunt. Maybe the horses have gone lame. It's time to camp for a few days, and allow everyone a chance to lick their wounds, replenish the food pot, sew up torn clothing, and plan a revised strategy for reaching the stronghold of the Dastardly Evil Villain.

So the story is allowed a lull. Narrative provides what's happening, but there's no dramatic conflict or scene action.

Despite its name, such a long transition shouldn't last more than a handful of pages. It should follow a very intense portion of the plot. In other words, don't pause story action for a long transition when nothing else has been happening.

Drill exercise:

Select a scene from your manuscript. At its conclusion, what happens in the very next paragraph?

Have you remembered to write your protagonist's emotional reaction to what just happened?

If not, why not? Is your scene missing a definitive setback? Is there a setback, but perhaps only a weak one? Can you strengthen it by making the situation much worse?

Once you've done so, write a new or revised sequel hot on the heels of that disaster. What would your character feel first? How will your character analyze the problem? Is review necessary? Have you remembered to let your character weigh options? Has your character decided what to do next?

Think about it first, then write as quickly as you can without self-editing as you go. When you've completed the sequel, print out your pages and mark them as follows:

- Green for emotion.
- Blue for thoughts or memories.
- Purple for considering options.
- Red for decision.
- Yellow for action.

If any colors are missing, evaluate your sequel. Did you omit a component for a dramatically valid reason, or did you simply forget to include it?

11

Entering the dark dismal middle

Beginning a novel is fun. It's exciting. You're eager to establish the fabulous story world you've invented. You have characters you like and want to set in action. But once those first few story events are written, you've introduced your characters in vivid entry action, and you've plunged your protagonist into several complications, what then?

The vaguest middle portion of your plot outline now looms ahead of you like an iceberg in the north Atlantic. Fog and mist swirl around you. Your path is becoming uncertain. All the momentum of the first act is dwindling. Perhaps your enthusiasm is waning. Before you know it, writing each page has become a slog. Perhaps you're beset by a creeping certainty that if you force your story forward, you'll be lost forever in some Dreadful Land of No Return.

Many writers, myself included, find the middle section of a novel to be the most challenging part to write. For one thing, it's so darned long! You know where you want your story to end, but how do you get there?

When I was a child, my grandparents lived about two thousand miles away. We visited them once or twice a year, setting off for a twenty-two-hour drive to get there as quickly as possible. My parents would alternate driving—with one behind the wheel while the other one dozed. I remember how thrilled I would be when we set off, usually at night after my parents got off work. There was the novelty of sleeping in the back seat, dozing and rousing to the flash of lights or the sounds of traffic. But once morning dawned, boredom set in. Our route always took us across the widest part of Texas, and it is mighty wide when a child has nothing to do but sit quietly in the backseat and stare at miles and miles of empty landscape. Bad vision wouldn't let me read in a moving car. No genius had as yet invented DVD players for backseat entertainment. I had no sibling to squabble with. I was so very anxious to reach our destination, but meanwhile there was Texas, Texas, and more Texas to endure first.

So here's the novel's second act before you, stretching as empty and long as the widest portion of Texas. How will you fill it? How are you going to sustain your interest in the story? How can you be sure your story events will keep readers intrigued by the story?

Well, writing a book involves a process. When you train yourself to understand the process, master the skills necessary to perform the process, and—most importantly of all—*trust* the process by sticking with it even when you aren't certain of what you're doing, then you'll survive the dark dismal middle.

There are several tactics available for a writer's tool kit to help him or her survive the middle.

We'll start with the basics. As you leave the first section of the story, continue to write scenes with clear scene goals. Monitor them to be sure the conflict in each scene is focused on opposing goals. Don't forget to end scenes with setbacks linked directly to the scene protagonist's goal. And make sure you write fully developed sequels between each scene.

Stick with the structure. Trust it. It's like following a narrow trail through a spooky old forest. If you grow careless and wander off, you'll soon be lost. If you stay on the trail and don't lose your nerve, you'll make it across.

A lost writer is one who panics and forgets about basic writing principles such as scene and sequel structure. A lost writer is one who stalls, slowing down the story action and stretching events too thinly. A lost writer pads the story with excessive description and explanation. A lost writer lets sequels run longer and longer while avoiding scenes. A lost writer stops controlling the structure, allowing conflict to become circular or worse—allowing the characters to just chat aimlessly with each other as they travel mile after mile on a quest that no longer seems to matter.

The tactics of a lost writer are futile and useless. They undermine the story. They serve no purpose. They waste time. They result in pages that have to be cut out if the novel is to stand a chance of being read.

If you're writing aimless drivel because you've lost control of your story, or you're stuck, or you simply don't know what to do next—STOP!

Examine the following seven strategies that can help fill the middle with compelling plot and exciting story action, and then reassess your plot.

Juggling plates

"Plates" is a term some writers use for tiny questions thrown into the story, solely to keep readers curious or concerned. The technique gets its name from the type of old-fashioned juggling act where a juggler spins a china plate on top of a pole, then starts a second plate spinning atop another pole, then another until he has several going at the same time. As he sets the last one spinning, the first will be slowing and wobbling. So the juggler runs back to the start of the row and sets it spinning again, then corrects the ones in the middle as they slow.

The fun for audiences lies in the anticipation of whether the juggler can manage to keep all the plates spinning at different speeds, catching some and starting others, without dropping and breaking anything.

The plates plotting technique is simply a story-long juggling act that writers either learn or do instinctively. Its effectiveness lies in where and how the tiny questions are raised or answered.

Miniature hooks or small hints of potential trouble serve to generate additional problems for the protagonist and reader to worry about besides the main plot or subplots. Don't confuse plates with the central story question. They aren't individual scene questions. They're extra bits of complication, like candy sprinkles scattered atop the icing on a child's birthday cake.

Why do we need plates?

Because you can't set up a novel with only one, super-huge, overwhelming plot question ... and nothing else.

You do need a super-huge plot question. It's the central story question that's going to be answered at the end of the book. But you need more than that because no matter how clever or intriguing it is, if that's all there is, readers will grow tired of it.

Savvy writers, therefore, throw in plates to keep readers interested.

As the juggler holds his audience with anticipation, so do writers hold their readers with dramatic scene action, setbacks, plot twists, hooks, and lots of plates.

The more plates raised in your story, the more readers will be enthralled, wondering how everything will turn out.

It's all about suspense. *What will happen next? When will the curse be invoked? How many bad omens does it take to create a really bad feeling? Is someone really following Danielle as she walks home, and is it mortal or demon? What's really scratching and thumping in the attic at night under the full moon? Why does Maxil Mordechai Macneilius Mordant Mufesant insist on being called by all five of his names? What's buried in the garden under the gnarly rowan tree, and why does the dog keep sniffing and digging there? Will the potion work? Is my mother someone—something—other than she claims to be? Why do the ghosts only speak to Sarah? When will the goblin steal another child, and who will it be this time? What drove Gustav mad? Can the mummy be reanimated? If so, can we control it?*

As you can see, I could go on with this forever. But of

course, the key to successfully managing plates is bringing them down properly.

If you raise a question in your story, you must answer it. Failing to do so simply isn't fair to readers. So don't throw plates up and forget to catch them. It's a juggling act, which means you are—for dramatic purposes—setting some to spin, letting one wobble until it's almost gone and then spinning it anew, and bringing down a plate while putting up three more.

This constant flow of new hooks and questions, of answering a question only to immediately spin more, creates the illusion of many things happening. Avoid predictability by not following a set pattern.

Perhaps you raise a question in one sentence and answer it in the next phrase. Then you raise a question and delay answering it for three pages, or fifteen pages, or six chapters.

Just remember that if you plan to delay answering it for more than three to ten pages, mention it periodically (re-spin the plate) so readers don't forget to worry about it.

Now, I hope you realize that it's inadvisable to wait until the middle of the second act before utilizing plates in your manuscript. That wouldn't make sense.

No, you need to include plates from the very first page, but don't worry. There's a good chance that you've been inserting some instinctively without being consciously aware of it. In revision, you'll want to go back through the first act and make sure you have enough plates.

The reason I waited until this chapter to mention them is because in the middle of the story, you need to remember plates you may have tossed in and subsequently forgotten about.

The middle section is a good place to revive some of those earlier plates. Certainly you need to introduce new ones.

There's no limit on how many plates you might use. I've counted as many as thirty plates in a single chapter and as few as ten. But again, remember that you must answer each one, bringing it down adeptly.

If you check over the middle portion of your story and find few or no plates—especially no new ones—that's usually symptomatic of a dull and lifeless yarn. And once you pass the mid-point, you should be bringing down more plates than putting up new ones.

Moving conflict forward

Has anyone advised you to keep making things harder for your protagonist? Well, you should! It's a fairly common writing suggestion, but how exactly is it accomplished?

Be sure every scene you write ends with a setback for the scene protagonist. But there's more to it than that.

Progressive conflict means escalating conflict—or story trouble that grows steadily worse. To express this writing principle another way: each major event or turning point in a story should top the one that came before it.

Does that mean you'll be inventing wilder, more hare-brained plot events? Not necessarily. Even in the fanciful, bizarre, and exotic realms of fantasy, we want our stories to make sense and to be plausible within their parameters.

Merely concocting random, crazy stuff won't accomplish story advancement.

Or perhaps you've thought of an opening event for your story that's a stunner. It's amazing. It's big. It's going to deliver the wow factor that modern readers want.

Great! I'm delighted for you. Use it on page one, by all means. But if you do, how will you top it?

If you can't think of anything that will surpass it in scope or intensity, then you need to change your plotting strategy. Save the super-amazing event for the middle of your story.

Yes, I know. I advised you in an early chapter to open with a strong hook. I haven't changed my recommendation. You'll have to think of a new opening hook if your stunner is going to fall in the middle. That's okay because I'm sure you can do it.

Your new opening event, while exciting, won't be as big and ambitious as the stunner you're going to build toward.

On page one, your protagonist faces a change in her circumstances—one with consequences that can't be ignored. She starts trying to solve her problem, but the first thing she'll try will be the least risky course of action.

For example, the sink faucet in my laundry room recently began to drip. Do I immediately call a designer and remodel the entire room? No, that's too extreme and costly a reaction. Do I rush to the store and buy a new faucet? No, that's also costly and probably unnecessary. Do I call a plumber to come and repair it? Yes, perhaps. Do I know a guy that's handy enough to fix it without charging me a hefty fee? Yes, I might call him and save myself half of what the plumber would charge. Or do I decide not to deal with such an unexpected expense this month by turning off the water line under the sink? Aha! Yes, that's where I'll start.

It may not be the most sensible course of action. I realize that it means inconvenience, especially because I can't wash my hands there after gardening and I won't be able to fill the dogs' water bowl without traipsing to another sink in the house. But it won't cost money this month.

When I have saved a little money and am very tired of slopping water through the dining room as I carry dog bowls back and forth, will I call the designer and order a remodel? No. I'll call my handy friend for an economical repair. If my handy friend has left town on vacation or can't fix the problem, then I'll call the licensed plumber. If the necessary part is no longer manufactured, only then will I consider springing for the cost of a new faucet. And only if the leaking faucet has dripped water inside the wall and created black mold will I consider gutting the room.

Do you see how I've progressed from least risk (or expense) to most?

That's the way fiction is plotted.

Each setback that ends each scene creates a point of no

return. The protagonist *must* keep going forward because retreat is no longer an option. When minimal effort and caution won't work, what will the protagonist do next? The harder the protagonist tries, the stronger and more ruthless the antagonist becomes in opposing these attempts.

As risk increases, the setbacks become harsher. The stakes grow higher. Antagonism and conflict grow in each confrontation. As a result, by the center of the story, the protagonist's situation should be rough. She may have started the story in trouble, but it's only gotten worse.

Take care that in the middle of your story, you don't inadvertently let off the pressure of escalating trouble. This can happen as writers grow tired. Often a story loses impetus and stalls out in the middle, not because there's anything wrong with the outline but because the writer has stopped increasing the conflict.

Be vigilant in watching for this tendency. Don't ease up on your characters.

Take care that you don't become so protective of your protagonist that you're guarding her from trouble. You may not realize that you're shielding her from the villain or preventing her from blurting out something unwise that will create a new enemy for her.

Before you write a scene, think about what your protagonist wants to accomplish, her motivation for trying, and what she most dreads might go wrong. Within those parameters, what's the worst thing that could happen to her? Then go there.

This is not to be cruel to your characters or unpleasant. It's to test them, to force them to draw upon their true natures and discover what they're really made of.

Therefore, imagine what your protagonist most fears—externally and internally. In the central part of the story, bring him to that fear and make him face it. He won't overcome it then, but you're laying the groundwork for what he'll face in the climax.

Remember that in a novel of about twenty or so plot events,

you'll be writing perhaps as many as forty to sixty scenes. (A short story will have perhaps four or five scenes.) Every scene should be building on what's gone before it—in the opening section of the book, through the middle, and then in the rush toward the climax.

Does this mean you need to lengthen your fantasy by inventing additional events? Perhaps not. There are, after all, three types or levels of conflict: the internal, the relationship, and the external conflict.

If you've only plotted external conflict, escalating the trouble progressively will have you reaching for more and more things to go wrong. But if you can also write about an inner flaw within your protagonist, something he must overcome as he deals with his external problems, then you will find a new layer of depth and richness to add to your story. Or if he's so battered by his external story problem that he can't deal with his inner flaw enough to keep the woman he loves, now you're writing on three conflict levels. And by doing so, you're creating a much more complex story.

Increasing suspense

Regardless of its genre, every story contains some element of natural suspense. From the moment your protagonist forms a central story goal, the question goes up: will he achieve it, or fail? From the first sentence that launches a new scene, there's suspense as to the scene's outcome. From the setback itself, there arises the question of what will the character do next?

However, in urban fantasy there tends to be a strong element of mystery/thriller crossover requiring much more suspense than merely the outcome of a protagonist's actions. So let's consider some methods used by thrillers to make urban fantasy more compelling.

Sympathetic protagonist

Until readers care about the protagonist (or additional viewpoint characters), why should they worry about the danger this individual is in? Creating a bond between the protagonist and readers is essential.

In the middle of the story, be sure to reveal vulnerability or a new facet of the protagonist's true nature. This "opening up" of the character makes a terrific setup for danger to come. It raises the emotional stakes.

Set the mood

Don't make the mistake of thinking atmosphere is too cheesy to be effective. If Edgar Allen Poe remains in print and is still creeping out readers, then establishing a spooky atmosphere continues to be a useful technique. J. K. Rowling takes the trouble to describe Harry Potter's surroundings, whether it's sneaking through the forbidden passages of Hogwarts or venturing deep into the gloomy forest at night.

Plant threat early

Raising some form of danger over the protagonist or people the protagonist cares about is equivalent to suspending a Sword of Damocles over them. Keep in mind that the middle is where the Sword will drop like a guillotine toward your protagonist's neck.

Use plot twists

A story's outcome is always less certain if the writer can utilize twists and unpredictability. The middle should showcase your very best plot twist. Don't hint at it. Let it happen at an unexpected moment so you can shock readers.

Danger must be real

Readers grow exasperated with any writer who cries wolf. Building up heavy amounts of anticipation, and then revealing that the threat was a false one, does *not* constitute a plot twist. Instead, it's an aggravation. Let villains be cruel. Show them doing evil deeds. Don't let them wimp out in a crisis. Also, remember that in the middle, you need some kind of intense confrontation between the protagonist and villain. Just be sure you can top it in the climax.

Space out the moments of shock

A writer eager to keep his readers on the edges of their seats may become too extreme in piling one terrible event on top of another and another. Cram too much too tightly together, and the story will become absurd. Instead it's important to build to a shock, then provide a sequel to help the protagonist—and readers—cope with it. Sequels help cushion the shocks within scenes. Then build to the next twist or danger point. Study Alfred Hitchcock's film *Psycho* (1960) for tips on how to space out jolts. He bides his time and waits until the character—and audience—feels safe before he strikes with the next surprise.

Use a series of obstacles

This technique works nicely in helping to fill the middle. Let's say that the hero must sneak into the evil sorcerer's castle alone in order to steal back the Sacred Vessel and return it to its rightful place in the Peaceful Village. A deep moat with flesh-eating fish circles the castle. The hero must get past that obstacle. Beyond the moat rise tall walls clad with poison ivy. The hero must find a way past that obstacle. Then there are zombie guards patrolling the grounds at night. Past them, a three-headed dog and a ten-foot python protect the chamber door where the Sacred Vessel is kept. Above the pedestal supporting the Sacred Vessel, an enormous, razor-sharp blade hangs suspended. If the Sacred Vessel is moved, the blade will swing down with deadly force.

See how this is going? Each time the hero succeeds in getting past one of the obstacles, anticipation rises. Readers know he's going to encounter something worse each time. Sooner or later, he's bound to make a mistake or be surprised by a danger he didn't plan for. Not because the hero is stupid, but because the villain is smarter and nastier than expected.

Will the hero escape with the Sacred Vessel or be caught just as he grabs hold of it?

That's right. He'll be caught.

Don't open that door

This is a variant of the series of obstacles, and it also works well to fill up the middle. In this technique, the protagonist is faced with one obstacle, and it's one better left alone. It could be a locked door leading to the treasury vault. Or a locked portal between one dimension and the next. Or a locked box containing a potion recipe for immortal life. Or a locked book of spells so evil that to read them is to go blind.

The protagonist will have a very, very good reason for opening the locked door. But we all know what happened when Pandora opened the box. Beware!

Dangerous isolation

Splitting up a band of friends is an ideal way to endanger them. Remember the old adage about safety in numbers, and at a key point in the story—say, the middle—divide them up. Maybe one sidekick is injured and has to be left behind. Maybe another goes for help, but never returns. Maybe another companion is killed, or knocked unconscious. One by one, these helpers are removed, until the protagonist is left cornered and alone.

One of the best suspense stories using isolation is *And then there were none* (1939) by Agatha Christie. It's not a fantasy novel, of course. But it's well worth your study for how to use this technique.

Darkness falls

Evading darkness is an elemental principle of basic survival. Darkness is dangerous. Humans can't see well in it, and it hides the shadowy creatures that might be closing in. So whenever possible—especially for the big confrontation in the story's middle—make the setting gloomy, dark, or nightfall.

Utilize a chase

Think of this ... a lonely, isolated moor barren of habitation ... twilight is falling ... in the distance we hear the sound of dogs baying ... or are they dogs? They sound ... peculiar, unworldly. From the rocks stumbles a lone figure. It's a man, weaving and staggering with exhaustion as he tries to keep running. He keeps glancing over his shoulder each time the dogs howl. Then he trips and falls. He lies there as though stunned, and from the ridge behind him there comes the first hound, followed by a pack. They're hellish creatures, their eyes glowing red, their black oily bodies half transparent in the failing light. They're huge, larger than wolves, and they bound toward their prey with eager shrieks.

Ready to stop reading? No, indeed!

How many suspense techniques did I use in the above paragraph? Take a moment and identify them.

Now, in writing chase scenes, we have a couple of rules to observe. Rule 1 is that if the hero is being pursued, it must be by several villains.

Rule 2 is that if the hero is doing the chasing—whether she's a cop or an agent with the Federal Bureau of Spook Investigations—then the hero and villain must be evenly matched.

Regarding Rule 1—if there's only one villain in pursuit, and the hero flees, he'll appear cowardly. So if there's only one villain, it should possess supernatural powers that give it a huge advantage over the mortal hero. An acceptable variation is when the hero runs away in order to lead the villain into a trap.

As for Rule 2—a lone individual chasing after a gang of demons is both foolhardy and stupid. She's outnumbered, and as soon as they figure that out they're going to turn and tear her to pieces. Remember that we want to worry about the hero, not dislike her for being a doofus.

But if the hero is chasing a lone villain, there's always the chance that the villain will turn and confront him in a fight.

Chase scenes most often appear at the climax, but they can work also in the middle of stories. They won't be as long or as involved as they would be at the ending, but they are still a viable option halfway along.

Ticking clocks

This term refers to any type of deadline or any dangerous situation where time is running out. Ticking clocks work well to create suspense because they generate a sense of urgency and pressure as the hero struggles to solve the problem before she's out of time.

It's important that the deadline be legitimate danger, and the penalty for not reaching it should be drastic. If, for example, the protagonist's best friend—a vampire—has been poisoned, how long can he hold on before he crumbles to dust? The threat is real. The penalty for missing the deadline will be the destruction of a dear friend.

The higher the stakes and the tighter the time frame, the more suspense your story will generate.

Drill exercise:

Read through the first chapter of George R. R. Martin's *Game of thrones* (1996). Then use a red pencil to check every plate you can find—anything, however small, that makes you want to know more. When you've done that, use a blue pencil to check where a plate is brought down or the small question is answered. Use a green pencil to check where a plate is repeated.

Next, mark the first chapter of your story in the same way. Compare how many red marks appear in your chapter. How many are in Martin's? How many blue marks do you have in comparison to his? How many green?

You may have twice as many plates as Martin, but perhaps you've also answered all of them. Or he may have introduced more plates than you, but he's answered very few.

What conclusions can you draw about how to set hooks and plates that will keep readers turning pages?

12

Surviving the dark dismal middle

If you loosely hold a piece of string between your hands, what does the string do?

It sags in the middle.

If you pull the string taut, it stretches out straight, but it won't stay that way without your sustained effort.

Therefore, to continue with this analogy, if you don't plan out the second act of your novel and if you let your characters wander aimlessly, the story will sag, lose focus, and go nowhere.

If, however, you work at keeping your scene and sequel structure going, the storyline will advance but perhaps that's all. Monotony and predictability may set in. You're likely to become tired and bored with your characters. If so, the plot will plod along and anyone reading it will be tempted to abandon it.

Instead, what we want in the mid-section of a novel is novelty, excitement, and a change of pace. (Observe how the following graph illustrates placement of a book's strongest points. Note the opening spike, the middle demonstrating more intensity, and the climax topping all previous excitement levels.)

One of the ways we can jazz up the middle is through the introduction of new subplots. Of course you don't have to wait until the second act to do so, but writers frequently use a new subplot as a bridge from a novel's opening into its middle.

A subplot is secondary to the main plot or central storyline.

Plot event intensity graph

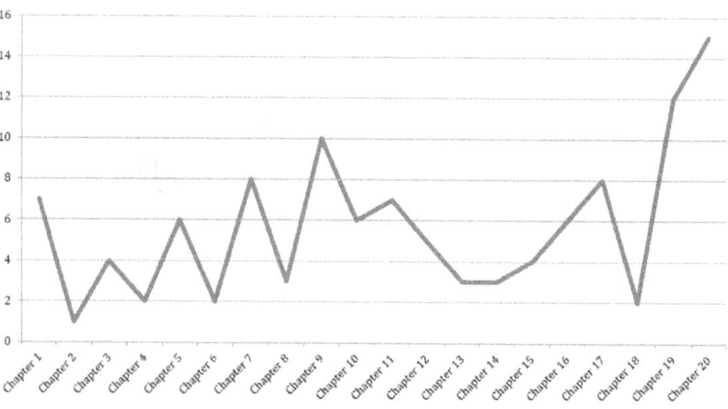

It's not as long. It receives less emphasis, less attention, and fewer pages. It may involve secondary characters or be centered on an additional complication in the protagonist's life. It may belong to the primary antagonist.

If the subplot involves the protagonist, it often deals with that individual's internal conflict or inner flaw. Or, it may deal with a relationship conflict. Such issues are related but not a key element of the main plot.

Also, if you intend to use multiple viewpoints in your story, keep in mind that you will be devising a subplot for each viewpoint character besides the protagonist. (This is why I recommend a limited number of viewpoints.)

Think of a subplot as a plotline in miniature. The viewpoint character serves as the protagonist of his or her subplot. For example, in Brandon Sanderson's novel, *The alloy of law,* Waxillium is the book's protagonist. But when Sanderson takes us into the villain's perspective, showing us what the villain is up to, who the villain's sponsor is, and what the villain's plan involves, the villain has become that particular subplot's miniature protagonist. For each subplot, there will then be a small central goal and story question. The miniature story question must be answered yes or no at the subplot's resolution in a miniature climax.

Always remember, though, that the subplot remains secondary. If you become enthralled by a side character's personal story, you may allow that individual to steal too much from the book's protagonist. When that happens, you split your story's focus and run the risk of seriously damaging or even killing your plot. If a secondary character is taking over, rethink your plot outline. Have you chosen the wrong protagonist? It's possible.

Avoid the temptation to divide a book evenly between two equal plotlines or two important viewpoint characters. Most novels lack equality. The protagonist is the star. The protagonist is the book's primary focus. The protagonist should have the most viewpoint pages, if not all of them. The protagonist's goal drives the central plot and forms the main story question. The protagonist stands in the final confrontation against the central antagonist in the book's climax.

Anything else muddles the structure and splits the focus.

Are you sputtering right now, wanting to interrupt me and protest about the exceptions you've found? Go ahead!

George R. R. Martin's massive, broad, multi-volume story features so many viewpoint characters I don't want to count them all. Readers love what he's doing, but he's one of the few writers with the ability to pull off such an uncommon novel structure. The farther he goes, the harder it becomes for him. Will he be able to tie up and conclude the story eventually? I don't know. I hope so, for the sake of his readership. But strictly from a structural standpoint, the task will be extremely difficult.

For most writers, every element in a fantasy novel is there because of how it connects to other story elements. The relationship may be structural or thematic, but it unifies the work. Readers generally seek that unity on an instinctive level. If they can't find it, they may enjoy the feeling of chaos or they may toss the book aside in confused dissatisfaction.

Although your traditional fantasy heroes may be George R. R. Martin and Robert Jordan, you may lack the skills necessary to manage six or a dozen—or more—viewpoints, shifting perspectives, and plotlines. That's okay. Start with what you can do. Even in your first effort, you can write a compelling story featuring only the protagonist's viewpoint, a single villain with a few minions, and perhaps one or two subplots. As you practice and gain experience, you can add more layers. Remember also that a single-viewpoint novel can serve up several subplots, if needed.

Advantages of subplots

Besides just filling up the middle, subplots serve other purposes. Here are a few:

A subplot can make a plain story special. One of the factors that helped Jim Butcher's early Harry Dresden novels rise to prominence was when he developed the subplot about Harry's relationship with his father.

Give the protagonist enough internal conflict or angst, or develop a protagonist with conflicting loyalties, and you will enrich your story immensely.

A subplot can complicate the central storyline. This is accomplished by bringing in additional antagonism and trouble. For example, Harry Potter's fondness for Hagrid leads him to help keep Hagrid's dragon egg a secret. Yet Hagrid is breaking the law and risking trouble not only for himself but also the children and the school.

Or, consider Harry's difficulties with Professor Snape. Harry is beset by Snape's dislike of him from the very start. Although Voldemort is the chief villain, and Voldemort's minions wreak all sorts of evil, the subplot of Harry's dealing with Snape's antagonism creates additional complications for the young protagonist.

A subplot can keep the story moving when the beginning or a major event is delayed. Although in this chapter my primary focus is on the middle, sometimes a writer needs a longer setup before she can start the central storyline. Usually it's a risky idea to delay the central story, but on occasion that's the way the plot works out.

For example, in Scott Westerfeld's steampunk/alternative history novel *Leviathan* (2009), the two central characters don't meet and join forces until the middle of the book. Westerfeld needs to establish his story world and a complicated political climate. He wisely avoids a massive info-dump and instead *shows* the world by plunging his young characters into trouble and plenty of action. He runs two subplots parallel to each other, until they finally—in the second act—converge, and at last the central plot can get going.

As another example, in Naomi Novik's enchanting *His Majesty's dragon* (2006), there's a long delay before the storyline takes the protagonist and his dragon Temeraire into actual combat when England fends off an invasion by Napoleon's forces. Novik feeds in numerous early subplots, including Temeraire's training, the mysterious question of his breed and background, and a poignant account of a smaller dragon being neglected and abused by his handler.

A subplot can help us find our best story. Sometimes, subplots take over our imagination. So much so that we may eventually decide that the subplot should be the central plot. Of course, making such a change means an enormous revision after completion of the first draft, but if this happens to you, don't bemoan the extra work. Be glad that you figured out which plot was better.

Subplot hierarchy

Usually the plotlines in most novels fall into an established ranking of importance, as follows:

1. The main storyline or central plot should have the greatest importance.
2. The top subplot should deal with the protagonist's inner problem, and it should be solved by the end of the book—thus demonstrating an arc of change for the character.
3. The second subplot belongs to the second most important viewpoint (probably the antagonist's).
4. Additional subplots will be assigned to the third most important character, then the fourth, etc. Or they'll deal with the protagonist's other problems—whether relationships, finances, old troubles with past mentors, bad deals with devils, etc.

The hierarchy not only helps you keep control of your story material, especially as you revise, but should an editor ask you to cut a sizable portion of your manuscript, you'll be able to chop the least important subplots first.

Finally, your climax will be more manageable if all the subplots don't run exactly parallel to each other. They shouldn't begin at the same time. They shouldn't all continue to the very end of the book. Most of them will enter the story near the end of the first act or in the middle.

One of them might end in the center of the second act, with its miniature climax forming a rather exciting event or plot twist. Another might extend past the climax of the main question in the third act, serving as the denouement of the entire story.

Just try to resolve them at different points in the plotline to stay less predictable.

Central story event

The middle of the book will be hugely improved by inclusion of a pivotal event, something with high stakes and strong consequences.

As you plan your fantasy story, be sure to set a huge, shocking, unexpected, dangerous, frightening plot twist in the center.

As you write your story, start laying the groundwork for this central event from the beginning. You have two approaches for this shocker. One is to hit the characters completely out of the blue with an unexpected plot twist. The other option is to build anticipation for a stunner of a confrontation.

What we're trying to deliver here is maximum entertainment value at least up to this first half of the story. (Remember that the climax at the end will be even bigger.)

Think of it like this: you want to open your story with a strong hook—an event that's attention grabbing and will pull readers into your story. You want to hit readers in the middle with something exciting and high stakes. And you want to finish in a really throat-gripping way. That's at least three huge, major events in your book, plus everything else you may have planned.

The central event serves the dramatic purposes of punching up the sagging middle and signaling that the story will now be racing toward the climax. It's a flag indicating that the dark dismal middle of the story is coming to an end, and we're about to dive through a portal that will lead to the third act of the book.

In the central story event, your protagonist steps past a point of no return. There's no backing out. All the safety nets are cut. The stakes rise. A challenge is issued, and accepted. Events are set in motion that can't be stopped. From the central event onward, every scene will be pushing the protagonist and antagonist toward a final showdown.

How, then, do we present this big story event to readers? We can do it through what's known as a Big Scene or we can use a scene cluster. Although they have different structures, they both fully develop this awful, dreadful, stupendous event that's taking place in your protagonist's life.

There's a writing principle that mirrors Einstein's law of relativity. It says that the lesser word count you give an event, the more trivial it appears to readers. The higher word count you assign it, the more importance it gains in reader perception.

In other words, in the world of fiction, length equals importance.

Because the central story event is so tremendously important, it must be long. If you don't feel capable of writing a scene that's 4,000 words long—or 5,000 words long, or 7,500 words long — then write a series of normal-sized scenes and group them together for dramatic emphasis. One large sequel can follow the scene cluster.

Let's deal with these two constructions separately.

The Big Scene

In fiction, scenes should be of different lengths, different levels of conflict, have different stakes, lead to different consequences, and end with different types of setbacks. This variety keeps the story less predictable and far more interesting.

Therefore, some scenes deliver more dramatic oomph than others. As I've stated, you will need a minimum of three Big Scenes in a novel, and at least one in a short story.

To qualify as "big," a scene should meet the following criteria:

The setback is a no and furthermore, and the furthermore contains a startling surprise beyond anything expected.

The conflict should be intense and powerful.

There should be desperation, either in the characters' actions or emotions.

The scene should build in momentum, with escalating conflict.

The scene should substantially affect at least one or more of the major characters.

The scene should be long, without padding.

Generally, Big Scenes aren't just dropped into the story as a total surprise. They work most effectively when a foundation is laid for them.

Step one

When creating a Big Scene, build anticipation. You do this through spinning plates, hinting at trouble to come, planting for looming disaster, and by taking your time. For example:

Uncle Matok came late to the breakfast table that morning, casting off his coat and hat and sitting down with us. He seemed larger than usual, swollen with news.

"Word going 'round in the village," he said, reaching for the puffcakes. "Been sightings of deer migrating out of the valley. Yup, and the smaller game's going, too."

Pa stopped chewing. "Bad winter coming?"

"War, more likely."

Pa looked at me, then at my little brother Nat. I saw his fork digging into his puffcakes, but he wasn't eating. "No," he said, his voice too casual. "No need to take fright because of an omen or two."

A clever writer would move the story to other issues, then in a few pages mention the coming war again. There would be more talk in the village. Then word would come of a farm burned out. Then rumors. Then a sighting of the king's garrison pulling out. Then talk among the adults about whether to evacuate before invasion or stick it out. Then extra work for all the field hands, laying up supplies and selling less of the harvest than usual. Then definite news that the invaders have crossed the northern border and are heading this way.

Enough of this, and readers will realize that sooner or later the family will be facing attack unless they abandon their farmstead and flee like their neighbors. When Pa decides to stay put, readers will be certain of what's coming.

Boring? Not if the writer has built anticipation well.

Predictable? No, because readers enjoy anticipation. They don't want it skimped or rushed.

Learn to draw it out. Learn to set it up and then build it until readers are anxious for the battle to happen.

Anticipation is a valuable tool and is as enjoyable—if not more so—than the actual story event itself. Make it work for you.

Step two

Put your characters through an emotional wringer. Let them scoff in disbelief, then worry. Let them receive good news and think the invasion isn't coming, then let them experience shock and grief when their neighbors are burned out. Put them on an emotional rollercoaster.

Step three

Deliver a scene worthy of the buildup. Supply readers with all that you've promised, plus more.

Scene clusters

Big Scenes can be intimidating, especially when you're still learning how to handle ordinary scenes well. Also, the major story event may be long enough and complex enough to require a cluster of scenes grouped together.

Today's readers tend to favor shorter scenes with faster cuts from action to action, which makes the scene cluster structure more in line with modern attention spans.

If there's enough danger, conflict, trouble, and urgency so that characters aren't allowed time to react as they move from one scene to the next, the cluster will generally read as one huge event. Readers may be caught up in the intensity, excitement, and quick pacing so that they're scarcely aware of how many scenes or scene fragments are actually grouped together.

Scene clusters are also ways in which to pit multiple characters in conflict with each other without becoming hopelessly entangled.

The scene protagonist is still directly opposed by one individual at a time, but in short, intense bursts that end in setbacks. The sequel is then deferred or compressed, and another scene of conflict with a different character present in the situation begins.

What's important is that once the large event is over and the dust settles, you should allow space for a long, thorough sequel to all that has happened to your focal character.

In my novel, *The queen's knight,* I use scene clusters to deal with what immediately happens after Queen Pheresa is abducted by evil forces during her coronation ceremony. Talmor—her ex-protector and lover—has nearly died trying to rescue her. He and several others have been severely injured from breathing a toxic mist used in the abduction. Ill and frantic, Talmor tries to persuade the palace guardsmen to go in search of the queen, but they are in chaos following the attack. These guardsmen may be brave in combat, but they're deathly afraid of the dark magic that can possess the dying and reanimate new corpses. No one can agree on what to do. The queen's disappearance threatens the political stability of a realm already torn apart by recent civil war.

Talmor's goal is to spearhead a rescue effort, but the men are arguing, interrupting each other, and all but accusing Talmor of being in league with the evil forces since he seems to be the only survivor of the poisonous mist. With so much intense conflict happening, Talmor can barely start a plea before he's stopped or interrupted. His sequels are fragmented and compressed. The general effect across the chapter is one of tension, fear, and despair.

Drill exercise:

Select your most important, most intense event from whatever story you are currently writing. Have you written it as a Big Scene or with a more ordinary approach? Can you intensify the conflict, raise the stakes, or throw in an unexpected plot twist? Has it ended in some sort of disastrous setback for your protagonist?

Is there a sense of urgency compelling your protagonist to take more drastic action right away, or have you dropped the story tension to allow your protagonist a long rest? If the latter, consider whether your story would improve through eliminating the chance to rest and recuperate. Think about plunging your protagonist into a continuation of the crisis and whether that might make your plot more readable and exciting.

13

More dark dismal middle

Another strategy for a novel's second act concerns multiple story lines. Novels often contain as many as three—the ongoing story, the back story, and the hidden story. These are not subplots.

While you should plan them from the outset, it's in the middle where they either appear or intersect.

The ongoing story

This is the main plot, the central line of events from beginning to end, all built on the protagonist's major story goal. This is what you'll have outlined. It's what your scenes are connected to.

It's also the story action that readers are allowed to experience as it's unfolding. It's the protagonist's viewpoint and perspective. Ongoing story events take place in the "now" of the story, not in the past.

The back story

Remember how in Chapter 1 I urged you to set aside the history of your story world until later? All the events that have taken place before the action commences on page one, all the old feuds and quarrels, all the past relationships and secrets and mythology and legends are part of your story's background. They are part of your protagonist's past and part of your antagonist's past. Even the more important secondary characters will have pasts that may be pertinent to the ongoing story.

While not all novels need or contain a back story, most fantasies do. Inventing a rich backdrop of myth, culture, and history adds rich color to your story world and brings desirable texture to your audience's reading experience.

However, the problem lies in where to put it and how to contain it so that it doesn't engulf the ongoing story.

The past may be intriguing and fascinating, but the ongoing story should always take precedence over it.

If you can't control that balance, then you need to consider writing the back story in its own dramatization and get it out of your system. Such books are sometimes referred to as prequels.

Also, if you don't need a lot of back story—and again, not all books do—don't use it. There's no need to encumber yourself unnecessarily, for example, in simple tales of sword and sorcery or deconstructed fairy tales. A few paragraphs of cultural backdrop should suffice.

However, if your fantasy story relies more heavily on character development, keep in mind that back story is the well that supplies character motivation. It can provoke character reactions that are far more extreme than the ongoing story's present circumstances—thus revealing some issue that's been building inside the character for a long time.

The dismal middle of a book is a good place to inject back story. Not, mind you, a heavy chunk of invented cultural history that will stop the story dead and possibly sink it, but a plot twist or complication coming from a character's past. It's a good source for bringing in an element of surprise, increasing the drama, and piquing reader curiosity about the character.

In Brandon Sanderson's *The alloy of law,* the villain (I won't reveal this character's name as a spoiler) and the protagonist Wax once knew each other on an amiable basis. Something changed the villain. Time and events have affected this character, twisting the villain's nature into something darker than before.

J. K. Rowling's character, Professor Snape, despises Harry Potter because of events that happened between him and Harry's father. The past motivates and torments Snape.

Such secrets, such long-ago encounters, betrayals, and disappointments, can fester in certain characters for years before bursting forth with a bitterness that may be shocking to an unsuspecting protagonist.

Often the central event in the book's middle derives from either the back story or from motivations caused by what occurred in the past.

If you intend to rely heavily on the back story, then you should plot it in outline form exactly as you would the ongoing story. Once you've done that, do NOT inflict all of it on your readers via long-winded lectures from enigmatic wizards sporting long white beards.

The back story outline is to help you choose where in the ongoing story you will drop hints, or reveal ancient secrets long buried, or bring up old conflicts that need resolution.

Flashbacks might as well be mentioned here. They are complete scenes drawn from back story. While I recommend avoiding their use as much as possible, the dismal middle is an appropriate place for one if you feel it's absolutely necessary.

No matter how much—or how little—back story you invent, please avoid the temptation of sharing all of it with readers. Hold back as much of it as you can and reveal only occasional glimpses. Such a tactic will entice reader curiosity without becoming boring.

Please understand that what's necessary for you to figure out your characters' motivations and why they behave in certain ways is NOT necessary for readers to know in order to follow your story.

Your needs are not the same as your readers'.

Also, don't fall in love with the back story to the point that you forget about the ongoing story. Writers can become side-tracked and lose their way if they don't stay focused.

You need back story for character motivations. You need it for a sense of a larger story world than an urban pixie's favorite alley on the dark side of town. You need it for character consistency of design. That's all.

Back story tips

If any of the following advice seems repetitive, it's a deliberate emphasis on points that are important for you to remember.

Establish the ongoing story *first*. It's always more important than past history. (If the past is proving to be more exciting than your present story, perhaps you should rethink your project.)

Avoid massive info-dumps early in the plot. Throw up plates. Hint at things. Hold off explaining until readers are bonded with your characters and very interested in knowing more about them.

An important back story still comes second to the ongoing story. Mention the past *only* when it has a direct bearing on what's happening at present.

Use sequels to drop in small bits of back story. Remember that sequels sometimes use a review component. Let this work for you when you need to draw on back story as a character motivator.

Pull back story material from your protagonist's and antagonist's dossiers. If you've reached the dismal middle and need something to enrich the plot, search those character outlines for some hint of the past that you can now develop.

Avoid flashbacks whenever possible. If you absolutely must use them, do so in the middle of the story—not at its opening. You can also use small flashbacks in sequel review.

The hidden story

This is the story action concealed from the protagonist and readers. It's what's happening behind the scenes and narrative that you're presenting to the reader in the ongoing story.

While back story is a simple, fairly straightforward plot to handle, the hidden story is more difficult. It's running parallel to the ongoing story, although most of the time it's not on view.

Readers are unaware of it, but writers have to know what's happening off-stage to their nonviewpoint characters.

So when Voldemort isn't present, sipping unicorn blood or trying to annihilate Harry Potter, where is he? What is he doing?

Readers don't know. Harry doesn't know. However, you can be sure that as she was writing her stories, J. K. Rowling knew.

When we don't see the central antagonist, where is she? What is she doing? What is she plotting? What happens in her sequels, when we don't shift viewpoint to show them? Where and when will she appear next?

Just because some of your characters aren't present all the time doesn't mean they're frozen in limbo or caught between dimensions. They're somewhere in your story world. They're doing something, all the time.

Because of this, hidden story usually is much more important to how a novel moves forward than back story is.

Back story is about secrets and motivations.

Hidden story is about where the next confrontation will be coming from. It's about the trouble that's due to hit your protagonist next. It's where the plot twists come from.

We invent back story as we need it. We use it primarily for enrichment and extra texture.

We need hidden story in order for the conflict to flow consistently and plausibly. Although readers can see an antagonist in action in a scene, they don't experience the antagonist's emotions or plans of retaliation (unless the viewpoint is shifted). But the antagonist's actions still have to connect and make sense, in each appearance. That means the writer must think through the antagonist's sequel and know it, even if none of it is shared directly with readers.

In stories—long or short—of single, limited viewpoint, the hidden story is very much concealed. Readers have to piece together hints and allusions from nonviewpoint character action, behavior, reaction, and dialogue. They may not know for sure if the character is telling the truth.

But in novels featuring multiple, limited viewpoint, readers are given glimpses of the hidden story because the viewpoint may shift to the antagonist or perhaps even a secondary character who's about to betray the protagonist. That shift of viewpoint allows readers to vicariously experience the sidekick's anguish as he makes a Judas decision to turn against his best friend. Readers know his motivation for this, and although they won't approve, they'll understand what he's going through.

Now, in terms of hidden story's connection to the dismal middle, very often in the second act, viewpoint may be shifted for the first time to the central antagonist. This allows the writer to reveal a great deal of hidden story to readers. It will usually spike interest.

Adept management of ongoing story, back story, and hidden story can enhance a plausible connection between character motivation and goals. Later in revision, these story lines also assist writers in achieving a better dramatic effect as plot events and story elements are rearranged.

Drill exercise:

If you have a complete draft of your manuscript in progress, create a chart of the chapters in chronological order from start to finish. List the events of ongoing story that occur in each chapter in a single color—blue perhaps.

(If your manuscript is still in progress, create a plotting chart from your working outline. You may need to generate a fresh copy of your intended ongoing story. List the events in blue as suggested above.)

Next, select a different color, such as purple, and mark the intersection points or chapters where back story appears.

Finally, choose a third color—green—and mark where small amounts of hidden story will be revealed.

Look at your chart and ask yourself if you have too much purple. Or perhaps all the purple occurs early on, in the first act, and none appears elsewhere on the chart. That should tell you that you've loaded the story too heavily with explanation too soon.

Maybe you don't have any green at all.

If you've been writing from a single viewpoint, perhaps you might consider shifting to the villain's perspective a few times. Be sure, however, that doing so doesn't give away your plot twists. Or, if you want to stick with one viewpoint, then allow a few allusions to hidden story to spill out in dialogue.

Consulting your chart should help you in revision when the time comes to rearrange some of your scenes and sequels for optimum dramatic effect.

14

Unmasking true nature

In Chapter 2, I dealt with how you create character complexity. You set up a design for your character's surface—including age, intelligence level, gender, occupation, personality, values, mannerisms, possessions, etc. All of this takes time and thought to assemble into a package that will interest readers.

Beneath the surface lies a character's true nature. And although glimpses of it may occur early on in a book, often true nature is revealed in some large way in the dark dismal middle.

As I've explained earlier, true nature is shown through what a person does or says *under stress*. The greater the stress, pressure, duress, or strain—the deeper such a revelation is likely to be. Put a character in enough trouble, and the character will act closest to his basic nature.

We learn the truth about people through what they do and through their choices and decisions in life. I often encounter individuals at writers' conferences who sigh dramatically and "confess" that they'd love to write but they never find the time. I've learned to smile and murmur politely while inside I'm thinking of the student who's working on her Ph.D., juggling a job, raising a child as a single parent, and taking care of her elderly father, all while writing a novel and meeting her deadlines. In real life there are the people who get things done and the people who make excuses. When you truly want to do something, you make the time for it.

And what you choose to do—in school, at home, in your daily lives—defines you as an individual. If you choose not to clean your home, then you either have to hire a cleaner or you live in filth. If you choose to party instead of writing your daily quota, you miss your deadline. If you choose to steal your roommate's identity and open a fake credit card account for a spending spree, you go to jail once you're caught.

When we write about a character, we're not merely putting that protagonist through a rough spot. We're revealing his or her true nature to readers a little at a time, from the beginning of the story to its conclusion.

In each scene, the protagonist's actions either reveal a glimpse of her true nature or continue to hide it.

In each sequel, the protagonist's emotions and analysis show what she's really like, bit by bit.

A story needs strong conflict and compelling scenes, not just to advance the story but to also pressure the protagonist into either growth or devolvement. Scene conflict and setbacks push the protagonist into making choices under stress. By contrast, decisions made in comfort mean nothing dramatically.

Who cares if your lead character is a teenage vampire girl who attends a party and is asked if she prefers type A blood or type O? She has a considerate host, right? Hand that young lady a glass!

But what if this girl is newly turned, is still trying to adjust to being undead and a predator not yet in control of herself? What if she's forced to attend a ritual, and when she's asked if she prefers type A or type O, her best friend and sister (both living) are shoved forward. To be welcomed into the hive, Vampire Girl must now mesmerize one of them and feed—without assistance. She can't choose some random victim off the streets. It must be either her friend or her sister—both of whom she cares about. Both girls are frightened and sobbing. When they see Vampire Girl, they don't understand that she's turned. They plead with her to save them.

See the potential here to reveal true nature in each of these three characters? We would give Vampire Girl most of our attention of course. Writing in her viewpoint, we would explore how she copes with her dilemma, how she struggles to control the primal urge to tear out someone's throat, and how she reaches a painful decision. But we can also show Best Friend in action. Her life is at risk here. Does she cry, plead, pray, or stand silent in shock? What about Sister? Does she try to save herself by manipulating Vampire Girl's choice toward Best Friend? Does she try to push Vampire Girl's emotional buttons or play off their sibling relationship? What does doing so show readers about her?

Compelling scenes pressure characters in hopes that their masks will slip and readers will glimpse what they're really made of. As each scene escalates, with stronger problems, higher stakes, and harder setbacks, it becomes more and more difficult for the protagonist to cling to the same persona he or she had at the story's beginning.

Think of Tolkien's *The hobbit*. The protagonist starts off as a content little homebody, as non-controversial and non-confrontational as an individual can be. By the end of the story, he's shown himself to be fierce, resourceful, clever, and brave. His mask of a complacent, well-off, slightly pompous person slips then erodes as the adventure winds along. Would he have ever changed if the story hadn't forced him to? Would he have changed enough to not only discover his true nature but embrace it? Probably not. Safe by his hearth, why would he have needed to? And what would there have been for Tolkien to write about?

Very often, readers stay hooked by such insights into true nature. They want to see how much the protagonist will change as the story progresses. Will he become a better, stronger, more heroic person? Or will he let his first lie take him down a path to bigger lies, self-deception, and cowardice?

Glimpses of true nature are fine for a while. But in the central portion of a book, it's time to reward readers by pulling down character masks.

Very often, the actual villain is unmasked in the middle.

In some stories, perhaps a character that seemed to be a friend is exposed as a scoundrel. Or the protagonist discovers that he's been manipulated or cheated.

For example, let's say that in Lisbon a pack of young were-wolves are fed poisoned raw meat. Most of them die. The few survivors remain deathly ill. Investigation commences, and at mid-point in the story the protagonist learns that the poisoner must be a member of the pack. The assassination didn't come from a rival pack. It came from within.

But who is it? Which pack member is responsible? Why would a friend or relative commit such a terrible act?

Often, the huge plot twist that spikes the sagging mid-section of a novel brings revelation of a character's true nature with it.

Fundamentals of revelation

Contradiction between what lies on the surface (the mask) and a character's inner, true nature is tremendously important to good storytelling. I often joke that writing would be so much simpler if we could just type a list of characters on page one, stating their attributes, personality, and background after each name, and then expect readers to remember all the information we've provided. That way, we wouldn't have to weave such details constantly into our story fabric.

Alas, it's not that easy.

Giving characters dimension comes easier to some writers than others. But from our toddler years, when a playmate smiles at us before grabbing our favorite toy and hitting us with it, we learn that people are not what they appear to be. Traits are a facade. True nature lies concealed beneath that facade. Who do we trust? Who do we stay away from? Part of growing up is learning to read the signals, to trust our gut, and to be careful.

In writing fiction, whether short story or novel length, we might create a plausible shallow, non-dimensional character, but do readers want to read about such a flat, boring, predictable person?

No.

Part of the writer's job is not to waste a reader's time. Therefore, we shouldn't create characters where the mask and true nature match, where a questing knight rides into a village, apparently a good, true, valiant man, and—when the village is attacked—he turns out to be a good, true, valiant man.

In real life—bully for him! What a wonderful fellow to have on hand to fight off the Viking invaders.

In fiction—dull, dull, dull. Readers will be able to guess exactly what he will do or say next, and when he does or says exactly that, they'll be disappointed in the character, in the story, and in you as the writer.

In *Storm front* by Jim Butcher, Harry's investigation into gruesome murders takes him to the lair of a vampire called Bianca. We're shown Harry getting ready for the meeting by preparing some hocus-pocus. His care and attention to detail as he makes these preparations are signals that the meeting with Bianca is important and dangerous. After all, no one should visit a vampire queen casually.

Harry arrives at his meeting. When Bianca appears, she's described as a stunning woman, expensively dressed. They chat in a formal way, each sizing the other up as they spar verbally. Then something is said that triggers Bianca's true nature. It's shocking and unexpected—despite the obvious plants for it.

When Bianca is unmasked, readers are shown what she really is. The contrast is unmistakable, vivid, and very effective.

In the charming Halloween comedy film *Arsenic and Old Lace* (1944) Mortimer Brewster discovers that his two adorable elderly maiden aunts have been murdering homeless men and having them buried in the cellar. Their matter-of-fact admission of how they poison their victims and their cheerful belief that they're committing acts of charity with each murder reveals they're quite insane. Yet their sweet dispositions and kindly actions as they hand out Halloween treats to children and prepare the afternoon tea continue to mask this key aspect of their true natures. You don't want to believe the truth about them because they're so charming and delightful, and yet there sits the poisoned elderberry wine on the table. (They use the homemade wine instead of tea because tea just won't mask the flavor of strychnine, arsenic, and cyanide.) What might they decide to do next?

In J. K. Rowling's first Harry Potter novel, from the opening lines, we learn that Voldemort is a dreadful, villainous creature—so horrible, in fact, that people are afraid to speak his name. When Voldemort actually appears in the story, he more than lives up to his reputation. He's truly dreadful and villainous, so where's the contrast?

Answer: there's no contrast in Voldemort.

What? Aren't I contradicting myself?

Nope.

Voldemort himself isn't a complex, dimensional character. He works because he stays behind the scenes, stays hidden except for two or three glimpses through the course of the novels. So the masking and unmasking of Voldemort is a physical instead of psychological one. The question for readers becomes one of anticipation ... when will we catch one of those glimpses?

Of course, if that's all Rowling gave us, the stories would be much less intriguing, but each time she supplies readers with a secondary villain—the visible one who appears masked as an ally and trustworthy friend, yet at some point always is revealed as Voldemort's minion.

Let's turn our attention to Professor Snape, a character who is very multi-dimensional. He's torn inside between conflicting loyalties. He's assigned to help Harry yet hates him. He supports a cause despite the personal pain it brings him. As we read Rowling's series, we're never sure which way Snape will go. We are shown a mask of angry loathing so effective we believe the man is a villain and yet from time to time Rowling lets the mask slip, showing glimpses of Snape's true nature.

Voldemort is a flat character—never intended to be complex. Snape is a dimensional character, who fascinates us more and more as the series progresses. We never know when we'll catch a glimpse of his better nature. We aren't sure we can trust those glimpses. Rowling tantalizes us by concealing and revealing his true nature.

Although revelation is an extremely important writing technique to employ for all of your major characters, take care that you don't reveal too much too soon. If, for example, you completely unmask your protagonist midway through the story and her true nature remains exposed for the rest of the story, what is left to entice readers to the end?

Think about Superman—a heroic figure of comics, television, and film. He constantly hides his true superhero identity from the public in the persona of Clark Kent. Yet whenever danger threatens, he steps out in his blue-and-red supersuit and saves the world. As soon as that's accomplished, he dons the mask again.

The same principle works for many beloved heroes of fiction and comics—including Zorro, the Scarlet Pimpernel, the Incredibles, James Bond, and superheroes in general.

From the middle of a story to its climax, all sorts of pressures and dangers must increase, until it becomes harder and harder for the major characters to retreat behind their masks.

The entire span of a story, whether short or novel length, is about forcing the protagonist to change in some way. It may be slight or profound, but this progression is called the character arc of change. Without this arc, the story is simply a depiction of characters standing here and running there with little accomplished that makes it worth a reader's time.

Unless the protagonist learns new skills or perceptions—or alters his behavior—he won't pass the final test at the story's conclusion. Sometimes, the ability to change, or to admit vulnerability, or to apologize, or to trust may be what saves the protagonist at the end. The inability to change or learn may be the deciding factor in the antagonist's defeat.

Writers like George R. R. Martin fascinate readers by creating characters that are very complex, with divided loyalties and divided natures. As long as readers are kept guessing as to what a character will decide or do, they remain fascinated with Martin's vast canvas.

Progression of character arc

Step 1: novel beginning: Establish protagonist's personality and situation.

Step 2: fleshing out first act: Story complications open the protagonist's heart. Story conflict reveals glimpses of his true nature.

Step 3: the middle: The protagonist is torn inside by inner conflict. His behavior should contrast with his true nature.

Step 4: turning point and leaving second act: With the protagonist's true nature exposed, increase pressure on him. The story should force him to face harder choices.

Step 5: novel ending: The third act deals with the story climax and resolution. The protagonist's choices have changed him. Demonstrate this through his sacrificial decision and final heroic action.

Plot and character function

The plot's function is to provide a progression of more and more difficult problems that force characters to face increasingly difficult dilemmas. To meet the escalating challenge of horrible choices, characters must take bigger and bigger risks. In doing so, they move beyond their comfort zones. They cannot remain static and survive. As they overcome challenges, take risks, and change, they slowly reveal their inner character—whether they realize it or not.

Your characters' function is to bring enough humanity, emotion, and inner quandary to the story to capture reader sympathy and keep readers bonded with the characters as they make choices and take action.

Drill exercise:

Select the protagonist of your favorite novel and list the following attributes:

- Age
- Name
- Physical appearance
- Personality traits
- Background
- Occupation
- External story problem
- Internal story problem
- Deepest personal secret
- Biggest flaw

Now skim through the book and note where the protagonist's true nature is revealed. Mark chapter and page number for each instance.

Once revealed, does the character resume his mask or leave his true nature exposed? To what effect? ➡

Ask yourself if you like this character *because* of his true nature or *despite* it.

If you could change the character in any way, would you? What would you do?

15

Pacing

When you're writing fiction, you should understand that the speed of your story depends on which techniques you use at any given point in your plot.

Pacing is directly affected by viewpoint changes, length of scenes and sequels, and modes of discourse.

While the majority of fantasy readers are believed to be process-oriented rather than results-oriented—meaning they're more interested in the progression of the story than reaching its conclusion—that doesn't mean you should write with complete disregard of pacing and its management. Nor should you deliver a massive tome of traditional epic fantasy that moves with the speed of a crippled tortoise.

Viewpoint

If you choose to write in a single viewpoint from start to finish, it has no effect on the story's speed.

However, if you're writing a novel from two or more perspectives, you should be aware that viewpoint shifts will slow down the pace briefly. They don't stop it, but they affect it.

Modern readers are used to rapid cuts from one character to another, due largely to novelists adopting numerous screenwriting techniques. If your book is an action-packed, sword-and-sorcery tale, for example, and it's crammed with danger and excitement, and you've been shifting viewpoints among three established characters from the opening chapters onward, the drop in speed at each shift will be negligible. Readers will be oriented to what you're doing, and can stay with you without confusion. They'll be largely unaware that there's much variance in tempo whenever you employ a space break and change viewpoint. That's because you're keeping the conflict strong and the suspense level high.

On the other hand, if you thunder along in the same viewpoint for ten chapters and then abruptly shift viewpoint in the middle of scene action, you'll create a confusing stumbling block and an inadvertent pause as the reader scrambles to re-orient to a new character. It's certainly fine to shift viewpoint late in the middle of the first act or even do so in the second act, if you wish, but signal clearly to readers what you're doing. Write a transition, and remember that the new viewpoint needs to be established clearly before you plunge that character into scene action.

Savvy writers will position such a late viewpoint shift at a point where the novel needs a lull.

Let's say you've written the first eight chapters of your urban fantasy from the viewpoint of Meriden—a tall, red-haired Amazon working as an enforcer for the city's goblin king. She's been assigned to track down and capture a rogue mage called Eric, who's offended the goblin king in some way. Perhaps Meriden's investigations have led her into vampire territory. Although she's not supposed to venture there unless invited, she's so certain that the vampires are hiding Eric that she breaks protocol, lands herself in trouble, and has to fight her way out. Limping and exhausted, carrying her dead partner, she crawls into an alley and hides before passing out at the end of chapter eight, vowing that she isn't going to bring Eric in as ordered. No, when she finds him, she's going to kill him.

Now, shift viewpoint to Eric. Readers will have heard plenty about him in the first eight chapters, but you'll need to introduce him in dramatic action and give him some kind of memorable entry into the story. You'll need to establish his perspective, show him through both action and introspection.

Give readers a chance to compare the man they're finally meeting and how he fits or contrasts with what Meriden thinks of him.

Doing all of this will slow the story, but the story needs that breather. Readers won't dare skip the slower Eric section because they can't be sure when you'll shift back to Meriden, who's really in trouble.

If you're clever and listen to your innate story sense, you'll make readers sympathetic to Eric and then leave him in dire straits when you shift back to Meriden.

Scenes and sequels

In their respective chapters, I've already mentioned that scenes and sequels affect story pacing organically. Scenes carry the intensity and drama of conflict, and therefore are perceived by readers as moving very fast. Sequels carry the rational side of processing and planning, and therefore are perceived as moving slowly.

When you're revising a story and perhaps you feel that it's bogged down or moving slower than it should, look at the lengths of these dramatic units. Are your scenes too short or fragmental? Is the conflict within them too trivial? Are your sequels too long, running several pages in length? Do your sequels end with definitive decisions, or are your characters wallowing in emotion without ever addressing their problems?

Or, perhaps you're revising and you've been told that your story is too fast and shallow, and that it's too difficult to follow. Chances are, your scenes are dominating, and you're omitting sequels or skipping the analysis/planning phase of your sequels.

Perhaps you've been told that your story is dull and predictable despite your having written every scene with a clear scene goal that leads to a definite setback. You've taken great care to write every sequel fully and completely, without omitting any of the components. How, then, can there be a problem?

Once again, look at the lengths of your scenes and sequels. Are they identical? Is every scene the same number of pages, ending in the same type of setback? Is every sequel exactly like the one before it?

While I recommend that you write your rough draft as completely as possible, not skipping components until you've mastered writing technique—you should, when you revise, vary the units to mitigate predictability. Too many identical scenes create a dull, stodgy, wooden effect. They shouldn't be the same length. They should feature different kinds of conflict and end in a variety of setbacks. Find key turning points in your story and cluster two or three scenes together, followed by a long sequel. Keep your readers guessing what you'll do next.

The pacing will be uneven and irregular. That's fine. Don't worry if one scene is three pages long and the next one is eighteen. What matters is the conflict within the scene and whether it advances the story.

Modes of discourse

Naturally there's more to constructing a novel than just writing scenes and sequels. Learning to handle the various types of discourse brings extra kick to your story. It makes it richer, more textured, and less predictable. It helps you manage pacing to your readers' increased enjoyment. It will make you a better writer.

Novels feature combinations of scenes, sequels, narrative, dramatic action, dialogue, description, and factual exposition. When should you use what? How do you know when to use description? Can there be too much dialogue? What should you do when you need to shorten a story but its plausibility depends on all the events you've plotted?

The answers to such questions lie within the modes of

discourse. Let's look at them in more detail, in order from fastest to slowest.

Narrative

This is sometimes known as narration, summary, or narrative summary. It's the fastest way to inject information or present an event. Writers use it to condense what's happening as briefly and economically as possible.

Narrative is primarily used to convey background and clarification or to further reader understanding of a place or situation.

Fantasy relies heavily on narrative because fantastical story worlds have to be explained. Readers need to understand what a "terclock" is, for example, and how it works if it's going to matter at some point in the story.

In Scott Westerfeld's steampunk World War I novel, *Leviathan,* British technology is based on DNA and gene-splicing. So talking lizards run to and fro on the airship, delivering messages between officers and crew. The airship is created from a whale and jellyfish, held aloft through internal gas chambers. Such a "natural" kind of living technology requires considerable explanation for readers to understand and embrace Westerfeld's unusual setting.

Advantages of narrative

It conveys information extremely fast.

Use it for quick transitions within sequels—for example, when it's necessary to position the character in a new setting.

Use it to condense long journeys –such as those in Ursula LeGuin's *A wizard of Earthsea* (1968)—when nothing dramatic is happening. Quests may be a beloved tradition in fantasy; however, remember how bored you were as a child when your parents took you on a long road trip and you had nothing to do in the car's backseat except stare at the passing scenery? Moment-by-moment depiction of travel is dull.

Use narrative when you want to shorten your story without losing any plot events. Choose the least dramatic scene and, instead of portraying it in A/R units of dramatized conflict, summarize it in a narrative paragraph.

Use narrative when your characters are performing mundane tasks that need mentioning for story veracity but you can't make a scene from them. For example, your characters pause in their quest to rest the footsore horses, make stew, wash their laundry, and hunt for fresh food supplies. It's not worth a scene, is it? But you don't have to leave it out completely.

Disadvantages of narrative

It *tells*. It does not *show*. Readers tend to disbelieve what they're told. They want to be shown.

Therefore, use narrative with caution. Be aware that although it's fast, it keeps readers at a detached distance. Reader involvement is sacrificed, and if readers aren't involved, they soon stop caring. If they stop caring, they stop reading your story.

Narrative lends itself to the dreaded info-dump that goes on for pages and pages. Avoid this at all costs.

Narrative is best used in small doses. Employ it in sequels or long transitions to move characters to new locations or to skip over chunks of time. Don't flood readers with more information than they want.

Example of narrative in a long transition, compressing time

Observe here how the narrative is also providing details of the setting and the viewpoint character's internalizations without utilizing dialogue or dramatizing the meetings between characters.

Example from *The chalice* (2001) by Deborah Chester

Megala, her serving woman, had vanished without explanation, and Pheresa feared the worst. A deaf-mute caretaker, terribly disfigured, and afraid of her, came limping in twice a day to build a meager fire in the tiled stove and to bring trays of food. Sometimes Gavril appeared to eat; often, however, he forgot and simply went on wandering aimlessly about the palace, prowling and talking to himself. If he did not come, there was no one to feed Pheresa. Unable to move more than her fingertips, unable to grasp a bowl of thin, greasy soup, much less lift it to her lips, she sometimes had to sit there with the food tantalizingly close yet impossible to reach. Hours would pass until the soup congealed and the bread grew stale. If the bold rats ate it in front of her, she would cry, averting her eyes and holding back her screams.

She knew instinctively that if she ever broke, if she ever let herself utter those internal screams, she would never stop.

The only brightness to her dreary days was when the potion was brought to her by Master Vlana, a court physician. Sometimes Count Mradvior came along. He would chat with her after the potion's effects took hold and she regained enough strength to converse. But on the days when the magician, the creature called a sorcerel, came to observe her condition, Pheresa's fear left her trembling and silent.

Dramatic action

This is the second fastest mode of discourse. It's scene action, written in moment-by-moment detail in A/R units. Confrontations in dramatic action can be violent or quiet. Either way, however, the conflict will carry intensity as the scene unfolds to its conclusion.

Nothing is summarized in dramatic action. The encounter is happening in the "now" of the ongoing story.

Advantages of dramatic action

It delivers plenty of detail in its give-and-take exchanges of conflict between characters. The pacing is almost as quick as narrative, yet dramatic action offers the benefit of strong reader involvement.

Disadvantages of dramatic action

None for readers. However, writers must think through every detail of action and its immediate reaction. The A/R units should follow a logical cause-and-effect pattern. This requires a lot of planning from a writer, and creating a dramatic passage will often be slow and time-consuming. Just remember that readers are oblivious to how long it's taken you to choreograph and write a scene. Your hard work will result in a quick, enjoyable read.

Example of dramatic action delivered in A/R units

Example from *Requiem for Anthi* (1990) by Jay D. Blakeney:

Her cadre drew their weapons, and Asan cut off his sentence, cursing himself for having trusted her. A rough hand drew his fire-rod from his belt, then gestured for him to enter the cell. He stood where he was, feet planted. At his side Saar released his musk.

Alarmed, Asan flung out a hand. "Saar, no!"

But the Bban was already leaping at the nearest warrior. They went sprawling in a tangle of legs and cloaks. Asan saw another aim his fire-rod. Desperately Asan snapped his rings forward, seeking to deflect the blast from Saar, but Dame Agate's rings slammed him to one side. He fell, scraping his cheek upon the stone floor, and the moment was lost.

Blue fire flashed briefly, and Saar screamed. The stench of seared flesh and Bban musk filled the air.

In the stillness that followed, the man Saar had attacked rolled Saar's body to one side with an oath and staggered to his feet. One of his arms hung useless at his side.

Asan climbed upright, fury sawing through him. He faced Dame Agate, whose face was haughty, closed, without regret. He wanted to crush her.

Dialogue

It takes practice to write effective dialogue, and this mode of discourse can come across as very fast when stripped to its essentials. However, because dialogue is a give-and-take exchange between characters, its general effect is slightly slower than straight dramatic action, and usually it's perceived as slightly less intense than dramatic action.

Direct dialogue is what characters say to each other in a dramatized scene of conflict. The exchanges are delivered in A/R units. There is no summary, and what's spoken is punctuated with quotation marks. The comments of each character are placed in separate paragraphs for clarity.

Indirect dialogue is the summarized allusion to what characters have said in narrative. It does not appear in quotation marks. It is not depicted in A/R units. The reportage of the characters' remarks may all be lumped together in the same paragraph. Take care that you don't allow yourself to slip into indirect dialogue when you're writing scenes. It belongs in sequels and narrative.

Advantages of direct dialogue

Readers love the illusion of eavesdropping. Dramatized dialogue puts readers vicariously right in the middle of a scene, privy to everything that's being said within the viewpoint character's hearing.

Disadvantages of direct dialogue

Although it should be written in A/R units, dialogue can sometimes become bogged down by excessive character internalization as a writer struggles to record full responses to what's being said.

This effect can be mitigated by positioning the scene protagonist and antagonist clearly at the beginning of the scene, making their opposing stances known, and then stripping the dialogue down to bare bones. This keeps the pacing fast, the conflict intense, and reader involvement high.

Most scenes in published fiction are a combination of dramatic action and direct dialogue. If you seek separate examples, you'll be more likely to find scenes of straight dialogue than ones of straight dramatic action.

Example of direct dialogue

In the following excerpt, the sorcerer Sien has summoned the injured Prince Tirhin's shadow for information on his condition. Note how the dialogue seems to flow more quickly as the conflict intensity rises. Note also how limited usage of dramatic action is here. Just the barest amount supplements what's being said.

Example from *Shadow war* by Deborah Chester:

Sien almost smiled. He was pleased, but he could not indulge in his emotions now while he fought to hold this shadow.

"Stay," he commanded. "Tell me."

"The slave has been accused and taken away. He will be silenced."

"Good. No one believed him?"

"He made his accusations only to the healer," the shadow said and tugged against him.

Sien grunted, straining to hold it. "Stay. Tell me more."

"The servants are afraid. They will send word soon to the palace, asking for help."

"Will Tirhin recover?"

"Unknown. Without him, I shall die."

"Will the healer treat him?"

"No. The healer is afraid."

"Then I must take action."

"Free me," the shadow said.

"Not while you are useful."

"I must return," the shadow said, and wrenched away.

Description

Usually description is used to depict the setting, a non-viewpoint character's appearance or expression, and the viewpoint character's internal feelings. While your story world may be vivid in your imagination, you must remember that readers can't see it unless you provide description to help them. Therefore, you can't overlook it or skip it.

It's needed to describe emotions and reactions. It's used to display character tags. It's used to jog reader memory when an absent character reappears later in the story. It's needed to make the story world plausible.

There are two techniques of description—what's known as the laundry list and dominant impression.

Laundry list description starts at one side of a room or space and covers every detail as it moves the mind's eye around the perimeter.

Example from *The crown* by Deborah Chester:

The battlefield was cramped and tight, bordered by low ridges to the east and a series of arroyos to the west—time-consuming to travel through. The north was blocked by a canyon too deep to cross. The south lay fairly flat, opening to desert devoid of water holes or much life.

Do you see how even this brief paragraph is slowing down into one static detail after another? Although the information is important for the battle that's about to begin, readers will have scant patience for a topography lesson. Three sentences of laundry-list description are pushing the limit, and this is where the passage stops.

Although laundry-list description can be useful, remember to keep it short. Readers will never be as fascinated by the number of blotches on your goblin villain's face as you are.

The technique of dominant impression is much more

dramatic and effective. It recognizes that readers are more likely to remember one strong, vivid image than innumerable small details. Accordingly, choose the most important aspect that you want to get across and focus your description on that.

Example from *The crown* by Deborah Chester:

Blinking, Pendek knuckled sleep from his eyes and glared at his aide, half seen in the early light. "Is it attack?"

"I don't know, sir," the aide said briskly. "Alarm has sounded. Dragons are flying in."

Scowling, Pendek tossed down his sword. "Is *that* all? You know better than to panic over a courier."

"We've counted a hundred of them, sir."

"Are they attacking?"

"They're flying in the Imperial formation."

Astonishment rooted Pendek in place before he rushed to his window and flung it open. It seemed at first to be a dream. The sky was glowing pale above the horizon in hues of red and gold from the rising sun. And against this backdrop, the dragons, their enormous wings silhouetted against the sky, were approaching in a single V, perfectly aligned, instead of their usual flying clusters.

This excerpt uses the faster dialogue mode of discourse to lead into the descriptive passage. Note the shift in pacing, the effect of slowing down from rapid dialogue to slow description. The story action pauses while Pendek stares at the dawn sky. The dominant impression is a single image of the dragons flying in formation. If that can ignite a reader's imagination, the description is successful.

Example from *The call of Eirian* (2012) by C. Aubrey Hall:

A raft was approaching on the channel, poled along by a Fae robed in silver. As the raft drew up to shore, the silver robes began to move. What had appeared to be cloth now separated into individual fish that wriggled free and leaped into the water. The boatman stood there as dark and insubstantial as shadow.

On the following page, this image is repeated:

There was a splash, and a glistening fish leaped from the water and clung to the boatman. Another fish did the same, and another—until he was robed in silver once more. He stopped poling, and the raft glided to a stop against a flight of stone steps leading up to a railing.

Next, we have a combination of the two techniques. Dominant impression provides a focus for most of the details that are described, but the length of the passage tends to pull it toward a listing of information. Decide for yourself whether such a combination is effective or would work better had it been shortened to a simpler dominant impression.

Example from *The sword* by Deborah Chester:

The gallery looked magnificent in the sunlight. Its tall mirrors, even more costly and rare than the glass in the windows, hung on the right-hand wall, reflecting back the sunlight streaming in. The place was all dazzle and glitter, prismed light refracting on the walls and shimmering from the faceted balls of bard crystal hanging on chains of gold from the ceiling.

It was the Gallery of Glass, famous throughout the kingdoms. His passage beneath the bard crystal balls set them swinging lightly, and he could hear them sing in faint little sighs of melody. The gallery had never failed to enchant all who entered it. Dignitaries from foreign lands often came and sat here by the hour, marveling at the dazzling array of light and color and sound. During festivals, it pleased Tobeszijian to allow dances to be held and madrigals to be performed in here. The fine carpets would be rolled up, and the floors polished. Candles would be lit everywhere until the mirrors blazed with their reflection. The ladies would swish and spin about, laughing to see themselves in the mirrors. The jewel-like colors of their

gowns glittered like kaleidoscope pieces on the faceted surfaces of the bard crystal balls overhead, while the crystal sang with the melodies, their tunes eerie and soft.

I've shown you examples of short description versus long. Now, considering the danger of pausing a story too much to paint a lengthy word picture, why would a writer ever want to take such a chance?

Strategically, when you want to increase or build suspense, deliberately painting a long passage of imagery can work very well to create anticipation. In other words, set a threat looming over your characters. Readers know or guess that terrible danger is coming. Soon.

Your protagonist has made a deal with the devil and now demons will be coming for her at nightfall. Twilight is stretching across the city park, where she sits alone on a park bench. Her time is running out. Shadows are lengthening. She's terrified, but she has nowhere to run where they cannot find her. She's trapped, with no way to avoid paying the horrifying debt she now owes.

This is the type of set up where a savvy writer will stretch out description and internalization. Not only will the character's emotions be described, but the writer will paint a detailed image of the sunset. Every moment of the slow fading of light will be delineated.

Why?

Because of the writing principle that says readers love anticipation. Why rush description when it can work for you to such advantage?

Conversely, if there's no danger and no tension, don't lavish description onto your story. If the action is already flat, with nothing happening or about to happen, don't slow down further.

Advantages of description

At its best, description is lyrical and filled with vivid imagery. It paints exquisite word pictures. It gives readers a sense of place and grounds the story action in a setting. Fantasy relies heavily on description to depict usual, highly imaginative locations. Without description, how can readers understand the story world or its invented concepts?

The more specific the details provided, the more plausible the story—however bizarre—will become. Vagueness, however, undermines believability.

Disadvantages of description

Description is slow and static. It puts the story action on pause while it paints that word picture, leaving readers with the general impression that nothing is happening. If it's too long or too focused on minutiae, it becomes boring and readers will skip it. Writers must use a great deal of it in fantasy without letting it bog down the story. This requires a balance between useful description that keeps readers oriented, and endless, mind-numbing imagery.

Factual exposition

This is the slowest mode of discourse. Straight factual information is dull reading at best.

Now, whether the facts are true in the real world or exist only in your invented story world, they still can be labeled exposition. For example, you might have one character explain the ceremony of knightly investiture to another. Even if part of the ritual involves stepping into another dimension and selling one's soul, it's still factual within the story parameters.

Don't confuse exposition with background information or explanation.

Exposition is factual information about how many drops of blood go into a potion, or how to capture sunlight in the corner of a handkerchief before you face a vampire, or techniques of flying on magic carpets, or what behaviors in mortal humans will trigger a goblin attack.

Although fantasy seldom requires as much exposition as

science fiction—which is more focused on explanation—it can't be avoided entirely. Often traditional fantasy will feature passages of exposition when the young hero or heroine is being trained in the arts of combat or sorcery.

Joseph Delaney, in his *The last apprentice* series for young readers, utilizes Tom's training as an intrinsic part of the plot, and Tom shares all sorts of knowledge with readers as he learns, for example, the exact dimensions to dig a hole for imprisoning witches.

Advantages of exposition

Facts—whether real or invented for the story world—create a sense of belief and plausibility. They reinforce the setting.

Disadvantages of exposition

Boring, boring, snore. Exposition should always come in short passages. Wise writers usually combine it with dialogue or summarize it in narrative.

Example of exposition

Example from *Reign of shadows* (2015) by Deborah Chester:

As yet, Caelan had not been inside the arena. He wondered what it would be like. Supposedly the ring was divided into six sections. In the first game, twelve gladiators were positioned, two to a section. The six victors then fought, until there were three. Then there would be a free-for-all among the three men, or lots would be tossed to see who fought first. Only one victor left the ring each day.

On the following day, the lone victor would again be a member of twelve gladiators. The same procedure would be followed. Usually the least trained men fought first, with the veterans coming in fresh on subsequent days. Each week was called a rotation. At the end of the seventh day, the survivors would draw lots to see which day of the next rotation they would fight. And so on, until the end of the season.

When you read this out of context, with no reason to care about the protagonist Caelan, much less worry whether he can survive the gladiatorial games, can you see how boring this is becoming?

Drill exercise 1:

Study your left shoe. Examine the details of its appearance and construction. Think about your feelings for it, whether you love it or hate it. Does it pinch your toes? Is it brand new or broken-in and worn? Remember what you expected from it when you bought it. Did you blow your budget or buy the cheaper pair that was your second choice?

Now, write a paragraph of objective, detailed description. Write vividly, using precise nouns and strong verbs, but omit your feelings and opinions. Describe the shoe as though you've never seen it before.

When you've finished, write a paragraph utilizing a dominant impression of the same shoe. What aspect do you most want to convey? Focus only on that. Go bold and be as subjective as you wish.

Compare the two versions. Which do you like best? Why? If you inserted one of these passages into a story, which one would convey the most entertaining and lasting impression on a reader? Why?

Drill exercise 2:

Imagine that you've received a mystery package in the mail. The box is narrow, long, and lightweight. There's no return address, no shop label to indicate where it came from. When you open it, you find that it contains a wooden wand. When you touch the wand and lift it from the box, it suddenly comes to life in your hand, spilling silver sparkles from the tip and making your palm tingle.

Write no more than a page of exposition regarding magic wands. Explain how they came about, what they're used for, what they're made of, and how they work.

Do not look up what anyone on the Internet has to say about them. Do not copy J. K. Rowling's version.

Invent your own facts, but make them plausible.

Drill exercise 3:

A wizard and his familiar are arguing over the best way to create an invisibility potion. You may name the characters, but do not describe them. Do not explain their positions or motivations through narrative. Do not use viewpoint, and do not employ internalizations. You may only use dialogue and minimal attributions, such as "A said," or "B asked."

Write a page of dialogue between them. Let their dialogue lines distinguish them. Let what they say and how they say it carry the scene.

Drill exercise 4:

Using the same scenario as Drill 3, expand the dialogue into a full-blown scene by adding dramatic action, viewpoint, A/R internalization, etc.

Drill exercise 5:

Read over what you wrote in Drill 4. Now compress the scene into a single paragraph of narrative summary.

16

Ending the story

Once you deliver the central story event or huge shocking plot twist in your book's middle, you've signaled that from now on everything else in the manuscript will be rushing toward its conclusion.

A novel is an intricate construction, requiring its first third to feature plot hooks, intriguing and flamboyant character introductions, plot complications, and a situation fraught with conflict. Its second third necessitates numerous plotting strategies, character development, surprises, and twists to keep the story from losing momentum and bogging down. Its final third should top everything with excitement, intensity, twists, and character change.

The story climax should deliver a finale that is psychologically fulfilling, dramatically thrilling, and emotionally satisfying. This conclusion must bring all the conflict to a big showdown, tie off the remaining subplots, lower the plates, resolve and answer the primary story question, prove the protagonist worthy of success and reward and the antagonist deserving of failure and defeat, and be worth both the reader's time and money.

That's quite a lot to do, isn't it?

And when you've put yourself through the fun, exciting, exhausting, and sometimes scary process of writing a novel, contemplating what remains to be done in the third act can be intimidating.

Don't let it discourage you.

We can cope with every responsibility and task at a time, just as we've done in the first two-thirds of the story.

Surviving the dark dismal middle is exhausting. A novel's third act can seem more difficult than it actually is simply because a writer is tired. But as you gain experience and practice, you'll build stamina. And as you grow to understand the elements that go into wrapping up a story—whether novel or short story—you'll know exactly how to do the job well.

The last section of a book is where the outcome looks its most uncertain. This adds suspense to the story no matter what its genre. And because the outcome is so uncertain, the suspense level should reach its highest level. In the third act, the story stakes should be raised as high as the plot will permit.

Here is where your protagonist will be facing the largest story challenges and the strongest measure of opposition. Here is where your protagonist will experience her greatest doubts.

The third act requires an ultimate showdown between the protagonist and his primary opponent. That's why Harry Potter only faces Voldemort at the climax of J. K. Rowling's books.

In the dismal middle, something terrible happens. Whether your characters are broadsided by an unexpected attack that kills off all the merry band of companions except the protagonist and a couple of sidekicks, or whether your protagonist and his friends venture into goblin territory in the London underground and barely make it out alive—they've hit disaster.

Whatever the disaster is, there must be sequels to it. The protagonist needs time to recover and regroup. He and his companions should reassess their situation.

But although the antagonist will have intended the central disaster to drive the protagonist away forever or to destroy the protagonist and his friends, this event is so shocking that it pulls the protagonist together. He's angry. He's had it. Psychologically and physically, he changes gears. Now he's determined to strike back, and he isn't going to be driven away.

He isn't going to accept defeat. He isn't going to stop until he's right in the antagonist's face and the matter is finished, once and for all.

This is why—in movies—you hear the music soundtrack change. This is why—in most stories—the pace picks up. New energy comes to the story because the protagonist is finished with caution and careful planning. She's going for broke, and there is no turning back from this point.

However, if you write the big event in the dismal middle and it doesn't pull the story together, or if—as you slog along—you find your story crumbling instead of coming together in a focused way, *something is very wrong with your plot structure.*

Should you push on?

No. It's like driving your car after the dashboard's engine lights flash a warning. You can keep going for a few more feet or a few more miles, but pretty soon smoke will start boiling from the engine. The car will stop running, stranding you completely.

If your book falls apart at the mid-point, it's because it lacks a clear, over-arching story question. Either your protagonist never formed a strongly focused story goal at the beginning or you lost sight of it somewhere in the dismal middle.

Remember that your story needs a main story question that can be answered at the end with a simple yes or no without muddled explanations or vague pointers toward possible conclusions.

Yes.

No.

Yes, Amanda will be able to escape the vampire's lair before she's turned into an undead. (Hurrah!)

No, Amanda will have all the blood sucked from her veins and she'll become a monster just like the others. (Bummer!)

If you've shrugged off my chapter about clear story goals and have been avoiding proper setup because—a) you're rebellious; b) you don't see the point of it; c) you have all your story events clearly imagined in your mind and don't care how you get from one to the next—then you're going to find yourself in a thorough mess by the time you reach the third act. You might be able to contrive your way to some sort of eventual stopping point, but you won't be delivering a well-written, exciting-to-read, satisfying-to-readers story climax.

The beginning and the ending of a book—or short story—are tied together. Writing fantasy according to the structure of elemental story design—which is what I've been defining for you all along—means the structure should fit together closely and link strongly together.

Stories where the protagonist fails to drive the story forward and instead simply reacts in a passive way to what the antagonist does or says will falter.

But if you can begin well with your protagonist establishing a proactive goal and going after it despite steady conflict ... if your scenes have ended with a progression of stronger setbacks ... if trouble has escalated and the stakes keep going up ... then you're in good shape. You may not know exactly how you'll accomplish everything you need to do in the ending, but elemental story design will always take you where you need to be if you'll just follow it.

Although I usually discourage students from stopping to revise while in rough draft, a missing story goal means you should halt. Backtrack through your manuscript to the point where you lost sight of the story goal or where your protagonist started eavesdropping and reacting passively to what other, stronger characters were doing. Fix it.

Will it mean a total rewrite of the scenes which follow? Yes, but you don't have to write them immediately. Instead, type up a new outline, scene by scene, to be done later. Or read through each scene that will be rewritten and attach a note of corrections to it.

When you have replotted, go back to the start of the third act, and write forward as though those corrections have been done.

It's a patch job, but it will hold the story together until you complete the rough draft and can turn your full attention to revision.

On the other hand, if you're writing a short story and it falls apart in the middle due to a muddled or missing story goal, go back to the beginning and rewrite it.

Testing the inner flaw

Memorable fantasy protagonists are opinionated, strong, and passionate, and they live by whatever set of principles they've carved out for themselves.

They're never content to sit on the sidelines and watch others. They take action. They may lead others or walk alone, but they don't sit around and hope for solutions. They go out and find them.

When they take action, they take risks. When they take risks, they get into trouble. And when they get into trouble, they keep on trying.

Such characters are inspiring to readers. They possess inner fire. Their opinions and beliefs may resonate with readers enough for readers to adopt them.

You don't want a perfect, well-behaved, prudent protagonist who never puts a foot wrong. Instead, you want one that tries hard, gives his all, stands by friends as well as strangers in need of help, takes chances, and is capable of making mistakes.

When you create your protagonist, your story ending is going to put him or her into the toughest ethical, emotional, psychological, and physical tests imaginable within your plot's parameters. You must test the deepest inner aspect of your protagonist. You must get at the fundamental inner flaw within this character and attack it, force it to the surface, and make it the key to whether the protagonist can solve the central story problem.

Some stories are just simple adventures, lacking characters that are truly dimensional. In them, the hero's sacrifice is minimal. Maybe he has to surrender his pride or drop his macho persona long enough to assure the heroine that he truly does love her—at least enough to say it aloud.

But if you can create a complex protagonist, and set up your plot so that your hero has to surrender something much more psychologically demanding than superficial pride, then you have a greater chance of writing a story that's compelling and rich.

When you examine the archetypal plot pattern of classic stories, a pattern I call elemental story design, you'll find that they usually devolve to a point where the protagonist is cornered and faced with a moral dilemma. All the options are poor, yet the protagonist must choose one and act on it according to his or her true nature.

Why do we test our protagonist so intensely at the end of the story? Because this last, toughest test is the story's final crisis. It shows readers what the protagonist really is made of. It demonstrates the protagonist's true worth as an individual, a leader, and a hero.

As writers, we face the task of showing readers whether our protagonist has learned anything during the course of the plot. Has the protagonist changed? Grown? Altered a perception? Developed an insight? Discovered the truth? Realized that any future happiness depends on changing past behavior?

Or has the protagonist stumbled along through the story, reacting to events as they occur, and gone on repeating the same errors from start to finish?

Have you ever had friends you needed to grow away from because you saw them indulging in self-destructive behavior, repeating mistakes, and refusing to face their situation or solve it?

We certainly don't want to abandon our friends when they're in trouble and need us. But when we've tried everything to help them, and they won't help themselves, do we continue to stand with them or do we draw back? If, for example, you can't stop a drunk friend from driving after a party, will you get in her car—choosing to let her risk *your* life—or do you opt to take a taxi home?

Your readers may begin a story feeling a sympathetic bond for your protagonist. But if your lead character makes too many mistakes, fails to learn from them, continues to repeat them, and becomes rather stupid by the end of the story, can you really expect readers to still be cheering him on?

Not likely.

We should instead show our protagonist learning from scene setbacks. Adapting. Changing. Becoming stronger, more determined, and more clever.

Elemental story design shows a steady progression in the lead character from start to finish. By the climax, when the biggest confrontation occurs, the protagonist can act from his inner truth, from the type of person he actually is. When written this way, the ending seems inevitable and natural.

By contrast, poorly written fiction either avoids the principle of character sacrifice or clumsily manipulates the protagonist to a contrived sort of conclusion. This kind of stumble indicates the writer's lack of understanding of how a climax is best constructed.

What readers want is to be brought to a deft, skilled finish that answers the story questions, resolves the story's issues, and brings them an emotional closure they can't forget.

Whether you're writing a short story or a novel, there are four elements—obligatory scenes, moral equations, climax construction, and resolution—necessary for a strong climax. In a short story, they're handled briefly. In a novel, they may be compressed into the final chapter or spread across the entire third act.

Obligatory scenes

This is the scene that must happen. According to whatever you've set up, whatever plates you've set spinning, whatever questions you've intrigued your readers with, you have to bring this confrontation about. If you skip it, then you cheat your readers and devalue your plot.

This scene should have power. It should be highly emotional and dramatic. It's designed and written to resolve, once and for all, the issue between the protagonist and antagonist.

The entire story has been pushing the protagonist and antagonist to this encounter from the beginning paragraphs.

A short story will have one obligatory scene. A novel—if it contains subplots or multiple viewpoints—will need a small obligatory, climatic scene to resolve each smaller plotline.

For example, from his first days at Hogwarts, Harry Potter has struggled to deal with Professor Snape. He's encountered trouble in Snape's classes. He doesn't like or trust Snape, and he knows Snape feels the same way about him.

This problem is a subplot, not the main story question spanning the entire series. But sooner or later, Rowling has to bring this issue between Harry and Snape out into the open. They must have a showdown, which Rowling does indeed provide.

In my novel, *The queen's knight*, the hero is a man named Talmor. He loves his queen very much, but his lineage is questionable and he possesses the ability to handle certain forms of magic. Both factors make him an unsuitable candidate to be her prince consort.

Talmor's chief rival is a knight named Perrell. This fellow is from an excellent noble family of impeccable background. He's also cold-hearted, self-righteous, and ambitious. Despite his pretense, he doesn't love the queen.

Despite his good looks and superb credentials, Perrell can't woo the queen's love away from Talmor. So he resolves to kill Talmor. The most efficient way is to order Talmor ambushed and assassinated. At the last moment, however, Perrell's conscience bothers him. He can't bring himself to issue such a dishonorable order. Instead, he challenges Talmor to a fight of single combat, one knight against another.

Why did he back from the easy way?

Because a fight was mandatory between these two warriors. Readers expect obligatory scenes to happen. As the writer, my job is to meet such expectations. Having set up two intense rivals—two strong men of action—vying for the hand of the woman they both want, I am required to provide this battle. The fight scene must take place.

Had I written that Perrell's men surrounded Talmor in the forest and slaughtered him, I would have been guilty of writing bad fiction. Not only would I have lost my story's hero, but it would have been a disappointing end to him—a flat, cheating plot twist for my readers.

Still, why would a man like Perrell choose not to have his rival taken out? It can't make sense on the surface. Consequently, unless I give him a good reason, such a decision looks contrived.

I provided Perrell with a personality that's torn consistently between ambitions and conscience. In other words, he always knows the right thing to do, but he's too weak to resist crooked shortcuts to achieving his dreams. (Such a man can never be happy, which works well in fiction.) He's also a knight, a man of action, so choosing combat seems plausible for him. And I gave him the petty but understandable desire to grind Talmor's face personally in the dirt. It never occurs to Perrell that Talmor might defeat him in combat. And that demonstrates his innate arrogance.

This example of an obligatory scene, incidentally, doesn't resolve the central story question. It's not the main climax of the entire novel. Instead, it deals with a subplot. Its outcome serves to further complicate story events and drive the book to its conclusion.

Drill exercise 1:

No doubt you've already spent a great deal of time designing your protagonist, but as you plan the ending of your story, consider the following questions and how you'll be answering them.

What is your protagonist's greatest flaw?

Maybe you didn't know earlier when you were creating a character dossier. Or perhaps that weakness has changed as your book has progressed. Before you attempt to write a story climax, know the answer to this question.

What does your protagonist fear most in this world—or any other?

This question is included in that lengthy questionnaire found in Chapter 2. Consider it anew. The ending of a novel is where your protagonist is obligated to confront that fear and deal with it.

What does your protagonist want more than anything else?

Yes, I've asked this question repeatedly. But do you remember your protagonist's story goal? Or have you forgotten it and left it behind somewhere in the dark dismal middle with several other elements you grew tired of managing?

Remember what the story goal is and why it matters so much, because in the climax your protagonist will be offered an easy way to achieve that goal. Does this sound too good to be true? It is! The easy shortcut must come with a price too high to pay. (I'll elaborate on this writing principle in Chapter 17.) ➡

Who stands in direct opposition to what your protagonist wants?

Why am I asking this question yet again? Because perhaps for the majority of your story, the true antagonist may have been hidden. In the third act, shadow villains must step forward and be revealed. That's where Voldemort always turns up, taking over from his chief minion to confront Harry Potter directly.

In other stories, however, perhaps the protagonist's best friend suddenly drops her mask and is revealed as a betrayer.

However it's done, the antagonist will now be playing a much more direct, openly confrontational role, bringing about what the protagonist most fears or dreads.

Drill exercise 2:

Read Jim Butcher's novel, *Grave peril* (2001), or choose one of your favorites in the series. Locate the obligatory scene between Harry and the antagonist in the climax.

Do you find additional obligatory scenes in any of the book's subplots?

For each such scene that you locate, think about how the book would have been affected by its deletion. List at least three ways the story would have been weakened.

17

Story climax

Ending a novel isn't about running your characters to the last story event in your plot outline and stopping.

It's about resolving the problems, challenges, and situations your characters have been dealing with for several hundred pages. And resolving them in a way that entertains and satisfies reader expectations.

Fantasy is about power struggles and heroism. This genre puts readers vicariously into dire situations that can't be solved in ordinary ways. And such quandaries require protagonists who are very special indeed—either because of their courage, willingness to take risks, magical powers, or a combination of all three.

Readers expect the protagonist to persevere against evil and eventually triumph.

Moral equations

This second factor in a well-written third act requires the protagonist to be cornered and forced to deal with some kind of inner dilemma. It may be the need to face a personality flaw. It may involve resolving some hang-up from the character's past. It may be a true moral dilemma where the hero must battle his own conscience.

Whatever the inner dilemma happens to be, passing this part of the final test requires the protagonist to reveal his true nature and face the internal problem squarely.

Self-revelation is where the protagonist stops denying the internal problem's existence, stops deferring dealing with it, stops ignoring it, etc. It's where the protagonist understands how she has been wrong—maybe about who or what she really is. More importantly, the protagonist realizes how she must change in her actions toward others.

In my novel, *The queen's gambit,* Sir Talmor is a man with a terrible secret. He lives in a country where magic is feared and avoided, yet—thanks to the legacy of his foreign mother—Talmor can throw magic fire. When he was a boy, he was subjected to a harsh program of training to enable him to control this ability and hide it. But whenever he's angry or upset, it tends to get away from him.

Because he lives with such a secret—one that would drive him out of the knighthood, society, the queen's service, and the royal court—he's a reserved, careful man. He hides his emotions and works twice as hard as other men at his duties.

When he becomes the queen's personal bodyguard, he falls in love with her. But that's forbidden, too. So he's a man of strong feelings and abilities that are bottled up. In the third act of the story, the queen flees her palace to avoid capture by invading enemies. Her realm is in chaos, teetering on the brink of civil war. She takes refuge in an adjoining land, one where magic is everywhere and demonic predators are common.

With such a set up, it's *obligatory* that she'll be attacked by a magical predator, one that can't be killed by ordinary swords.

When this happens, Talmor is forced to face his inner dilemma. Morally and ethically, he's caught in an impossible situation. Fighting a demon the ordinary way won't work. But if he uses his magic fire to destroy it and save the queen's life, his secret will be revealed. He'll be thrown out of the queen's service and made an outcast—if he's not executed for being a sorcerer.

At the end of a story, the character should not have any way to wiggle around the dilemma and escape it. That's what's meant by saying the protagonist should be boxed in.

The arc of change—a steady progression of small and larger character changes achieved via each scene and sequel—will culminate in the climax. The protagonist should realize what matters most and choose accordingly. Acting on this choice demonstrates once and for all who and what the protagonist really is.

My character Talmor faces the choice of letting the queen die while he preserves his secret, or saving her by using his magic in front of his fellow knights and the queen's officials. Will he change from someone concerned mainly with protecting himself, or will he drop his mask and reveal his true nature?

Ending your story with an inner dilemma or moral equation is emotionally and psychologically cathartic for readers. It's universal, and its appeal satisfies their instinctual story sense.

Think of the film, *The princess bride* (1987) and how—when it first appears that Princess Buttercup has agreed to marry Prince Humperdinck—the little boy grows so upset he stops the story and chastises his grandfather for messing up the plot. He even says, "Now get it right!"

Yes, the film's a parody, and the little boy's outrage is charming. But what's going on here from a writer's technical view is that the child's story sense has been offended. He knows instinctively that the plot shouldn't go in that direction. As indeed, when the grandfather resumes reading, it doesn't.

We read stories—and fantasy in particular—because we want to "get it right." We want to see characters cope with disasters and setbacks and eventually win—even if, in our real world, we can't ever seem to get the landlord to fix our leaking roof or dripping faucet. We want to experience settings more magical and enchanting than the mundane tedium of reality. We want to vicariously experience the power of possessing magical abilities because so many times in our actual lives, we can't do anything about what we see happening.

To achieve an arc of change, it's necessary to construct a character with flaws. Therefore, the protagonist can't be perfect. The protagonist needs a surface appearance different from who he is inside.

If you create a protagonist lacking any flaws, minus any internal conflict, a protagonist missing inner weaknesses, secrets, or problems, you cannot create an arc of change in him. If your protagonist is perfect and has nothing to learn, there's no dramatic worth in writing about him. There's nothing that can be tested.

Even Harry Potter—who's as fine a boy as ever devised in fiction's pages—has his inner problems to overcome.

Protagonists should be appealing to readers. They should have good qualities. They should share at least some reader values. But a well-designed protagonist always has something still to learn, or has yet to grow into her full potential, or needs to surrender whatever's been holding her back for a long time.

Keep in mind that your true story—the heart of any novel—lies inside your protagonist. All the outer events are happening to force your protagonist to confront the internal problem and fix it.

Perhaps you're thinking, *But if I put my protagonist in a really tough situation, he won't know how to do the right thing.*

That's okay. Often, protagonists are reluctant heroes—like Bilbo Baggins—or they're confused, or lost, or stuck. This makes them believable and endearing to readers, especially as they sort out their problems and overcome them.

It's also desirable to take some time at the climax to think through the quandary your protagonist is in. How will the inner dilemma be solved? If the difficulty is strong enough to temporarily perplex you, you can be sure you're on the right track. You'll be providing readers with excellent entertainment.

Climax length

Are you wondering how long the climax should be? The answer depends on story length, story complexity, and what's at stake.

If you're writing a short story or a simple quest adventure novel, the climax will occur in an obligatory Big Scene and its aftermath.

If you're writing a complex urban fantasy novel, with your protagonist caught in a moral dilemma, the climax may spread over several scenes spaced apart by intense, soul-searching sequels.

How important are the stakes? Exactly what is at stake? The higher the stakes, the more determined the villain will be. How far will the villain go to win? Probably all the way to eternal damnation. How will the protagonist counter that? How will the protagonist defeat that?

In some novels, especially those dealing with multiple viewpoints, numerous subplots, and stakes of Good versus Evil, the entire third act will comprise the climax.

Constructing the climax

This is one of my favorite parts of a book to write. I love to see the story coming together, and I'm always reassured by having an actual formula to use as a guide.

Step 1: the choice

In the first step of story climax, your protagonist should be cornered, with no way out.

There will be a confrontation between the protagonist and antagonist. The antagonist will be wily, clever, and devilish here by offering the hero a choice of two alternatives.

The choices will be specific and very clear. The threat is real and immediate—not some vague hint of retaliation later.

Your protagonist can pick one option or the other. There are only two choices. Neither of them should be attractive or easy.

I'll repeat the above point, because it's so critical to the climax's success: ***Neither choice should be attractive or easy.***

If you give your protagonist an easy solution here, you will destroy everything you've built from page one. You will lose all suspense as to the outcome. You will cheat your reader and prevent your story from reaching its full dramatic potential.

I realize that at this stage, you're likely fatigued and ready to just end the manuscript, but you must hang on and do your job as a writer properly to the very finish.

Step 2: the decision of sacrifice

Whenever facing an unpleasant or difficult decision, it's human nature to procrastinate as long as possible. Very few of us naturally spring forward eagerly, shouting, "Oh, that looks like a rotten situation from any angle. I can't wait to deal with it and choose a solution that's going to make me miserable!"

No, instead we'll dither. We'll defer. We'll go into denial. We'll "forget" about it. We'll hope it goes away.

Because all this hesitation can allow the story's natural build-up of suspense to dissipate, we have to keep events progressing.

Accordingly, the villain will start a ticking clock—a deadline by which an answer must be given.

Such deadlines help create suspense. Therefore, if you use a ticking clock in the climax, where suspense is already high, you can ratchet it up even more.

The ticking clock serves two functions: it adds to the suspense by drawing out the situation just a bit longer, and it creates a potential opportunity for escape or rescue.

If that opportunity closes without escape being achieved, the entertainment value rises. Do you see how disappointed readers will feel for the protagonist's sake, yet how enthralled they'll be? Because the stakes have nudged upward just a bit more. And the situation is even worse for the protagonist than before.

Now, let's look at the actual decision of Step 2. There's an important writing principle at work here that you need to understand.

Throughout the story, your protagonist has worked and struggled toward a goal that was specific, important, and of immense value to him or her. Despite every scene setback, the protagonist has persevered and found enough grit to keep going.

In Kim Harrison's novel, *Dead witch walking*, the protagonist changes herself into a mink in order to infiltrate the villain's base of operations. She's caught and held prisoner in a cage. Later she's put in a rat-fighting arena where fights are to the death. After she hangs on through that section of the story, do you think by the climax she's in a mood to tamely surrender and give up? Not at all.

In Step 2, the answer to the overall story goal appears to be "No." It appears that the protagonist is going to suffer defeat. The protagonist has done all she can. She's done her best. But she's outnumbered. She's trapped. She's alone. She's on her own. And now she's facing the worst choice of her life.

Step 2 is where the villain puts his finger on the inner weakness of the protagonist. And presses hard.

Whatever your protagonist's weakness, flaw, or area of emotional vulnerability, that's where the antagonist will strike.

Think about the real world for a moment. Let's say you have a dog that you've trained not to beg for food. Your parents come for a visit, and suddenly your dog is pestering everyone at the dinner table or is mooching in the kitchen while dinner is being prepared. Why? The dog has sensed the weakest human that will slip it treats and is seizing the opportunity.

Villains possess that same instinct in zeroing in on the hero's weak spot. They may have paid for the information. They may have cast a spell to learn it. Or they may have soul-gazed the hero and read his mind. But however they know, they'll use that knowledge against the protagonist.

Villains do not fight fair.

Let's back up a bit to the two choices presented to the protagonist. What are they?

Here's an example: *"If you will give me the Magic Sword of All-Encompassing Power, I will let your little sister live."*

This is a clear problem of two unwelcome choices. Putting a talisman of tremendous magical power in the hands of a villain is always a ***really bad idea***. On the other hand, letting the villain kill your little sister is unthinkable.

"Tell me the formula for the Potion of Eternal Life, or I will burn down the school."

These two examples of threats are straightforward, but can you tell which carries the most dramatic potential? Whether the sacrificed story goal will be the character's internal one or the external one depends on the type of story you're writing, but situations where the protagonist faces a moral quandary will always be dramatically stronger.

Remember that the decision should involve a sacrifice. One alternative must be chosen instead of the other. One must be sacrificed for the other.

The definition of hero is a willingness to sacrifice self for someone else.

Is your protagonist going to become heroic? In Step 2, we find out for certain.

Although the protagonist has pursued the story goal for good, possibly stubborn reasons, the cost of achieving it—in Step 2—will become too high because of the awful alternative choice.

Your protagonist should sacrifice the story goal in favor of principle, love, ethics, or morality. Yes, he really, really, really loves his sister but he can't let the villain destroy the world with the Magic Sword of All- Encompassing Power. *Or* he would like to help the world, but he feels his sister's life is more important. Yet, aside from his personal love for her, aren't the lives of many people more important than one?

How will your protagonist choose? What will he or she choose? That defines the character to readers once and for all.

The choice needs to be strong enough, unpleasant enough, and horrible enough to reveal the protagonist's true nature completely.

What's the character's inner code by which he lives? That's up to you and your character's design.

The protagonist can have been a gruff, cynical, grouchy old coot for most of the book, but when his back's to the wall, his true nature is really that of a hero who can't walk away from someone needing his help.

What does Harry Potter sacrifice in his ultimate stance against Voldemort?

In my novel, *The king betrayed*, the protagonist Dain chooses to sacrifice his life to spare his young daughter's. That choice is more of an external one, because of the plot's design. Still, survival is perhaps our most powerful instinct. To sacrifice it on behalf of another certainly demonstrates the depth of a father's love for his child.

Sometimes, the protagonist will be confused, so torn by these conflicting choices that he can't reach a decision. Or he may waver, almost ready to succumb to his flaw and back away from a sacrifice. In such instances, you will need to use a gimmick of principle to tip the character toward making the right choice.

The gimmick can be an object such as a gun or a crucifix or a broken doll—anything that will remind the protagonist of her priorities and principles. The gimmick can be a sound or a person in a crowd. Anything that serves to remind the protagonist of what matters most and helps her cross the final threshold of true change.

Step 3: taking action

So far, the story climax looks like a bummer for the protagonist, doesn't it? After a novel's worth of attempts and striving despite all those scene setbacks ... here we are at the finish, and the protagonist has just decided to sacrifice the story goal.

It seems like a lot of torment, angst, and trouble for nothing.

But the protagonist must do more. Making the right, difficult, selfless decision itself isn't enough.

Noble intentions mean nothing until they're acted upon.

New Year's resolutions have become a joke, haven't they? We earnestly write our list on January 1: I will lose weight; I will walk my dog every day; I will save ten percent of my paycheck every month; I will keep my kitchen cleaner; I will finish my novel.

And how long do we keep such good resolutions? A month? A few days? Do we even bother?

It's human nature to shy away from anything that requires effort, and good intentions often come to nothing.

If you're asking your protagonist to make a truly awful decision, he may want to do the right thing, but if given a chance to back out—will he really go through with the noble act?

Well, *duh*!

Remember we're writing fiction, which isn't real life. Writers can't afford to let their protagonists waffle and dither—much less back away from the chance to be heroic and sacrificial.

Therefore, we can't conclude the story with our protagonist making a noble decision about what he intends to do while he stares heroically into the sunset.

That's no place to stop!

We have to show readers that this character is truly a hero by having him act on his decision.

Taking action on the decision means burning all the bridges behind your protagonist. There can be no turning back. The protagonist is committed to a course of certain disaster and defeat.

In Step 3, by choosing to do the right or courageous thing—whatever that may be—instead of preserving personal survival or glory or success, the protagonist is forcing the villain to carry out—or initiate—whatever was threatened.

Step 4: the dark moment

This will be the lowest point of any story—whether short story or novel. Your protagonist is facing defeat. Worse, your protagonist is facing whatever unpleasant or horrific disaster the antagonist is about to unleash. There's no way out of it. Step 3 burned the bridge and cut off all lines of retreat.

So here, at this point in the climax, savvy writers put the story on pause. The protagonist is allowed to stop being heroic and instead can act human.

The dark moment is a sequel to the obligatory scene that has just played. Its emotional component should serve up the protagonist's strongest doubts and fears. This is where the protagonist has to face the crumbled disaster of everything she's striven for. This is where the story is at its bleakest, most dismal point.

Wise writers do not hurry the dark moment.

I'll repeat that because it's important: ***Wise writers do not hurry the dark moment.***

You may feel compelled to rescue your protagonist at this point. You don't want her to suffer. You do want to let him off the hook. You may feel the temptation to rush matters forward.

Don't.

Galloping heedlessly over what should be the very best part of the book is a sign of a clueless, inexperienced, and unsure amateur.

This is the place where your story contains more natural suspense than anywhere else. The entire story has been heading to this moment. The goal seems lost. The protagonist's happiness, survival, or emotional future looks well and truly doomed.

Again, you may feel compelled to skip Step 4 because you don't want to write about defeat and despair. Don't avoid it. Instead, embrace it and use it to touch the hearts of your readers.

A valuable dramatic principle is at work in Step 4. Letting the protagonist suffer has nothing to do with a writer being cruel and unfair to his creation. The dark moment is about finding the protagonist's true nature.

It is the ultimate test of a protagonist. It showcases the very worst scenario in a story world. Within the story's parameters, the protagonist needs to undergo what is the supreme, most difficult, test.

When readers enjoy vicariously experiencing the dark moment with the protagonist, they aren't cruel or twisted either.

Instinctively, readers know the dark moment is necessary to push the protagonist over the final difficult step of dropping his mask and genuinely changing.

As people, we all know how difficult it is for humans to change. Folk get into ruts. They form habits. They generally don't go through life analyzing themselves or their actions. Avoidance of change keeps them in circumstances they may not like much, but it's what they know and where they feel comfortable. It takes tremendous effort and determination to alter habitual actions.

Remember my discussion in Chapter 1 of how change should start a story? Remember how I stressed that change—whether good or bad—is perceived as threatening? And how far people will go to avoid it?

External change at the start of the story propelled your protagonist into adventure. Now, at the end of the story, internal change is needed in order to wrap up the adventure in a positive way. If your protagonist cannot change, cannot drop the mask, cannot move forward psychologically or emotionally, then your protagonist may indeed go down in defeat.

But that's not what readers want. They seek an affirmation that change is possible. They want to know that the protagonist they've bonded with for the duration of your story is someone who will succeed in spite of everything, and is a person courageous enough to actually change no matter how hard it is.

Step 4 provides readers with a necessary emotional catharsis because your story must hit bottom before it can achieve the next step of story climax.

Step 5: reversal

Elemental story design isn't about making the good guy lose. It isn't about jeering at readers for hoping the protagonist will prevail. It isn't about manipulating readers into caring about the story's outcome and then slapping them with loss and defeat just because you can.

Although in the dark moment, the protagonist seems defeated ... and although the protagonist has sacrificed a goal—the thing he thought he wanted most—instead of his conscience or his principles ... and although the story question appears to be answered with a no ... and although the antagonist seems to have won ... that's not the way the story's going to end.

In the story pattern that's been satisfying readers for thousands of years, elemental story design mandates that a worthy protagonist—someone who changes, who admits her true nature, who does her best, who doesn't toss aside morality for expediency—will win.

Therefore, in Step 5, a last-minute reversal takes place. Is this contrived, or what? Is this just too fake, too sentimental, too old-school?

Not necessarily. A plausible reversal depends on how you handle it.

The roots of reversal stretch back to antiquity. The ancient

Greeks and Romans would halt their plays and roll out a creaky cart with a statue of Zeus or Jupiter wobbling on it. *Deus ex machina* at work. Consider it early special effects. A lightning bolt would "blast" the bad guy, and the hero would win. Hurrah!

Consider some of the old movies from the 1930s and 1940s, when the Knights Templar would gallop up just in the nick of time. In films like *The adventures of Robin Hood* (1938) and *Ivanhoe* (1952), the day is saved by King Richard the Lionheart's arrival. All the beleaguered hero had to do in these plots was keep fighting with increasing desperation and loss of weapons, hanging on long enough for rescue to reach him.

Today, readers and film-goers are too sophisticated for rescue to serve as the reversal. They expect the protagonist to save herself. So the young, hipster witch may have to fight demons single-handedly in an alley while her pixie buddy flies for help. And usually she'll have just kicked the last demon butt and be staggering out on exhausted feet when help finally arrives.

Even so, the principle of reversal continues to work. Elemental story design rewards characters that do the right thing despite personal cost.

In the real world, good deeds aren't always noticed or rewarded. That's one reason why we turn to fiction for solace. Fiction ties up the loose ends, doesn't overlook a character's noble contributions—no matter how small—and dispenses reward or punishment according to what's fair. If you're cynical about Step 5 and if you punish your protagonist for growing into a better human being, for meeting a challenge, for making a noble sacrifice, for taking dangerous risks to help someone else—then you've affirmed nothing. You're saying to your readers that if a person does something good for someone else, she'll suffer for it.

A drop of cynicism lends urban fantasy a little edginess that modern readers relate to. Total cynicism that burns the protagonist at the climax has no place in commercial fiction.

In fiction, good deeds are rewarded. If your protagonist has done the right thing, he or she will not fail at the end.

Now, there are a few rules to follow in writing an effective, plausible reversal:

The reversal must be logical

Without giving it away, plant for it earlier in the story. Set up for it, so that it's possible, and then make sure that readers forget it's there.

The reversal must not happen from cheating with magic

Whatever rules of magic you set up for your story world, you must abide by them—even at the ending when you desperately need a way out for your hero. Paying a terrible price to use magic at the climax may well be the sacrificial act.

The reversal should come from the protagonist's own efforts

I've already explained this one, but if the Allied Ghost Protection Agency sends in operatives to the rescue, it's because the protagonist left a psychic channel open for the AGPA to listen in.

The reversal can occur from the protagonist appealing to the antagonist's sidekick

If a minion has demonstrated any unease at what's about to happen or shows even a scrap of decency or conscience, it's okay for the protagonist to ask for help.

Please keep in mind that the reversal will not work if your protagonist hasn't acted on a sacrificial decision. You can't skip some of the steps of story climax and use only the few that appeal to you. They are all designed to work together in the order I've discussed.

If there's no sacrifice, there's no need for a dark moment. If there's no dark moment or if it's rushed, the reversal will fall flat or feel contrived. If there's no sacrifice, what's the point of writing a reversal? Each step contributes to the next. And this entire structure is designed to take readers on a nail-biting, page-turning, emotionally harrowing, suspenseful reading experience.

Don't cheat through the steps of climax.

Step 6: reward and punishment

The final step of story climax construction depends on poetic justice. In other words, what does any character deserve at the end of the story? It doesn't matter what the societal rules and laws are. Instead, based on a character's actions, what does that individual deserve?

Rewards for the protagonist are usually some prize awarded on top of achieving the story goal. Rewards are more than the protagonist expected. Sometimes, the reward is an emotional one, through winning the love of another character.

As for the antagonist, what does this individual deserve besides losing the story goal? Punishment.

Let's reiterate how climax works: the protagonist is tested, but sticks with his personal code of honor or his ethics even when everything seems lost. By doing this, he proves himself worthy of success, plus a bounty, plus additional rewards, plus love.

The antagonist grows increasingly desperate and ruthless as the story progresses. She justifies doing anything to defeat the hero. She chooses expediency over ethics. The antagonist lies and cheats, and sacrifices others instead of herself. In doing this, she proves herself worthy of defeat, loses her goal, and is punished—even annihilated if necessary—according to what she's done. The more wicked and evil she is, the worse her punishment will be.

Those are the extremes. If you're writing more shaded fantasy, where the protagonist isn't all good and the antagonist isn't all bad, then the steps of climax remain the same. A character's choices and actions determine the prices that will be paid.

For example, if your protagonist makes some big mistakes along the course of the story, there won't be a complete reversal. Perhaps the main story goal will be achieved, but at the cost of a friend's life. Or the protagonist perhaps can't fully change or accept her true nature, and as a result she achieves the story goal but loses her lover. Or perhaps the protagonist can't sacrifice her magic for the sake of others, and as a result only part of the story goal is accomplished and the villain escapes—leaving the door open for a future return, to cause the community more trouble.

For example, in Joseph Delaney's book, *The curse of the bane* (2006), young Tom is ordered to abandon Alice—a young witch and his friend. Tom has been warned against Alice and taught not to trust her, yet Tom likes her. His personal code won't allow him to leave her behind, even when Alice's actions prove she's moving to the dark side of her true nature.

Tom is guided by his feelings, and he allows Alice to use him and manipulate him into making mistakes. He thinks he's following his personal code of honor, but actually he's endangering others. He's too immature to see the bigger picture, and he's too stubborn to listen to the older and wiser Spook. This flaw in Tom—this deliberate blind spot—keeps the door open for additional books in the series.

Conversely, the antagonist may have done wrong things, may have tried to steal the treasure, and still may not be an evil villain. This person may, in fact, be charming and likable to some degree. The antagonist may have performed acts of kindness occasionally, or shown mercy. Such an individual may lose her story goal, but may not be punished beyond that point. She may be allowed to escape by the protagonist.

Listen to your story. Observe your characters. What have the two primary characters done? What results do their actions dictate? Let your heart tell you what's fair, and stay true to that. Don't contrive the ending of your story to conform to anything that's phony or unjustified.

Never punish a character undeservedly just because you believe happy endings should be abolished.

Don't reward a character undeservedly just because you've been informed that happy or affirmative endings sell better. (They do, but only if the character deserves happiness.)

Please don't heed the cynics who are so jaded and filled with ennui that they think happy endings are old-fashioned, trite, and contrived. Because the public is not tired of well-written endings that serve poetic justice.

People do not read fantasy to spend time with boring, mundane, bland, stupid, dull, apathetic, discouraged characters. People read to be enchanted, to feel vicariously heroic, and to escape the boredom of reality. Give them that.

Climax example

[Pheresa—a young, as yet uncrowned, queen—and her personal entourage fled when invaders captured her capital city and burned her palace. In her absence, her husband and consort seized the throne for himself. Now Pheresa has returned, determined to stop Lervan's illegal coronation that will push her off the throne forever. Her friend Talmor has seen a vision that makes him believe he will—under evil magical influence—assassinate her on the cathedral steps. Although he's tried to talk her out of returning in order to thwart the prophecy, Pheresa is determined to have a showdown with her errant husband.]

Example from *The queen's gambit* by Deborah Chester

[The Choice] Lervan cocked his head to one side, and his mouth quirked in the little smile that had once charmed her. "Oh, you're angry with me. I can see that. Well, what if I lost my head for a while? I know I shouldn't have tried to be crowned without you, but it was all so tempting. I just could not bear to let the day of coronation go by without taking action. Mandria needs a crowned head of state, after all. I know I was wrong. Will you forgive me?"

She stared at him, saying nothing.

"I think, yes, I think we had better discuss everything," he said, glancing around for support. "Start anew, find the best solution. You are a lady both intelligent and reasonable. Will you not agree that I deserve some reward for my efforts to hold the realm together in your absence?" He smiled at her, so cocky, self-assured, and charming. "Come, my dear, let us make amends. We were meant to rule together, and that we shall."

With the crowd and army turning against him, Lervan has put a deal on the table in an effort to save himself. Now Pheresa must weigh her options.

[Decision of sacrifice] She saw what he was up to, and a part of her had to admire his audacity. Like the others around her, he had seen an opportunity to patch up this business to his advantage, and he had seized it. She realized that if she refused him, she would appear churlish and vindictive. Although support had moved to her side, she was by no means certain that she really had it. Perhaps negotiation was the best course. She would have to learn to stifle her hatred and resentment in order to deal with Lervan, but the damage to the realm could be repaired.

See how she's wobbling here? Lervan is a scoundrel, but he has charm. He's also made her remember her inmost doubts and insecurities.

[Gimmick of principle] But even as these thoughts ran through her mind, she found her gaze shifting past Lervan to where a tall, lean figure suddenly pushed his way free of the crowd and came up the steps toward her. The sight of Talmor, his bronzed face set and angry, his black curls atumble on his brow, filled her with a surge of love. How she adored this man, who was so noble and honorable, so courageous and truthful.

She knew then that she could never again be the weak,

uncertain Pheresa of old. She could not negotiate with Lervan, could not come to terms with his treason, could not forget all he had done against her. If she gave way now, she would despise herself forever.

Although Pheresa almost makes the wrong choice, notice how the sight of Talmor in the crowd enables her to remain strong rather than reverting back to her old habit of accepting political expediency instead of making policies of her own. Because of Talmor, Pheresa is able to regain her determination and demonstrate to herself—and to readers—that she has truly changed.

But intention is not enough in a story's climax. Pheresa must demonstrate what she's really capable of.

[Taking action] "Well, my dear?" Lervan asked, reaching out his hand in friendship. "Shall we go inside?"

Lifting her chin high, she stepped back from him with her eyes suddenly blazing. "No, Lervan," she said in a voice loud and firm. "You are a traitor. I trust you not, nor will I bargain with you."

"But—"

"No! I go alone to be crowned," she said. Turning her back on him, she gestured at the guards. "You men, see that the duc's way is barred."

When the protagonist acts on the decision, that action forces the antagonist in turn to carry out whatever has been threatened or—in this situation—strike back. The antagonist can see victory slipping from his grasp, and he will do anything to win.

[Dark moment] "Pheresa!"

It was Talmor's voice that shouted the warning.

At the same time, she heard a faint sound right behind her. Whirling around, Pheresa saw Lervan rushing at her, drawn dagger in hand. Cursing her name, he lunged.

There was no time to panic, no time to do anything but react exactly as Talmor had taught her. The long afternoons of drills on Thirst's wintry practice field came to her aid now. She dodged Lervan's strike instinctively and reached for the Saelutian dagger on her belt. Caught off balance when he missed her, Lervan stumbled on the steps and could not recover in time. She plunged her dagger deep into his side.

They froze there, glaring into each other's eyes. Lervan's gaze burned with hatred mingled with astonishment. Then the color drained from his face, and he sagged against her. She saw him try to lift his weapon, but it dropped from his fingers. He fell onto her, dragging her down. Pinned by his weight on the steps, she struggled to shove him off.

Lervan's body was yanked away, and Maltric stood over her with an upraised sword.

Because of lessons in fighting planted earlier in the story, Pheresa is no longer a helpless woman. She can defend herself successfully against Lervan's attack. However, Maltric is Lervan's bodyguard—a tough, highly trained knight. Maltric's attack raises the stakes one more notch because Pheresa's new fighting skills are no match for his.

[Reversal] Crying out, he swung at her, but Talmor came at him from behind and plunged his blade into Sir Maltric's back. The old protector fell, and Talmor stood there, grim and furious, his bloody weapon in his hand.

Although this reversal has a touch of the old cavalry-to-the-rescue motif in play, Pheresa has fought and acquitted herself well. She has also struggled long enough for her friend Talmor to reach her and provide assistance.

[Reward and punishment]

[for Lervan] His body lay sprawled at her feet, blood staining his gaudy robes.

[for Pheresa] "The queen!" Around her the cheers went up, louder than ever. "The queen! The queen!"

She faced her people with her head held high, her visage stern and regal, and knew at last what it meant to rule. This, she thought, was Verence's legacy. The people's trust resided in her hands once more, and she knew that she would not fail them again.

She started up the steps toward the cathedral, where her crown and scepter awaited her.

Drill exercise 1:

From your favorite novels, select one that ended in a way that satisfied you completely. Locate and mark the six steps of story climax, then study how the author has moved through a roller-coaster effect of suspense and emotion. Be aware that sometimes writers can include a step in a single sentence while a different step may take several pages. Then consider the following questions:

How clearly does the antagonist present the choice?

What sacrifice does the protagonist make?

Is there action taken, even if only verbal defiance?

How is the dark moment presented? (If you choose a children's book to study, be aware that stories aimed at young readers will feature a fairly short section of dark moment since children are inclined to be impatient with too much angst or introspection.)

What form does the reversal take? Is it plausible?

How is poetic justice served to the primary characters?

Is there any anti-climactic material? (If so, does it concern rewarding or punishing a character? Is it setting up for the next book? Or is it long-winded explanation? Does it make you impatient? How well do you think it works?)

How does the author raise a series question pointing to the next book?

Drill exercise 2:

Select a novel that you enjoyed very much until the end, when you felt somewhat let down or possibly disappointed in some way. Locate the steps of climax. Are any missing? Are too many questions left unanswered?

What does your examination tell you about how a book's ending can affect readers?

18

Writing the resolution

How did you plan to end your story when you began it? When was the last time you actually glanced at your story outline? What has changed? Have your characters taken over and moved the story far from what you originally intended? Has that improved it or put you at a dead end?

Go back to the two-sentence SPOOC equation I suggested in Chapter 1. Did you ever do that for your idea, or did you skip it? Try writing it now, when you're facing the story climax.

Has the climax you've written answered the central story question with a yes or no?

If you can't pull your third act into climax structure, think about the questions and issues you raised for your characters in the first act. Is your story completely off track, or can you deal with the issues to some degree without major rewrites?

Whether you write the climax as one large obligatory scene or as a scene cluster, remember that the ending is where you've been heading all along.

Once the six steps of story climax are written, you will have answered the main story question.

Are you done? Or do you still have dangling subplots, floating plates, and other unresolved questions? Try to deal with them before the climax.

Anti-climactic material is best avoided. If you must run a subplot's resolution past the main question, let it be only one subplot and let it be a resolution that will reward the protagonist.

In other words, avoid a huge epilogue or some long-winded

narrative about what the merry band of companions did thereafter for the rest of their lives.

If you're planning to write a series, then you're responsible for juggling a story question, answered at the book's conclusion, and a series question which will be left hanging for the next volume to pick up. Be sure that you resolve each volume's particular questions and subplots.

Getting back to climax, once the reversal and reward sections are written, the story is over. With the climax concluded, there's nothing more to include except the actual resolution. This is the final paragraph or page of the book. It's the close, the last punchline.

It's hard to describe because it's so esoteric. There are few rules here and next to no guidelines for you to follow. I find the closing paragraph to be possibly the hardest part of the book to write.

It's because I'm striving to end on just the right emotional note that will leave readers happy, satisfied, and fulfilled. Seek the turn of phrase that sums up where the protagonist and his friends are now psychologically and emotionally.

I wish we could still use the time-worn phrase, and they lived happily ever after, because it illustrates perfectly what a resolution is all about. But time has worn it too much.

Drill exercise:

Choose your five favorite fantasy novels. Turn to their last pages and type the closing paragraph of each book.

Are these resolutions funny, grim, or inspiring? When you re-read the passage, do you feel satisfied as a reader? Why?

Is there anything missing, anything you wish the author had included? If the resolution isn't there because the book is part of a continuing series, do you feel disappointed when you come to the last page? And how did the author compensate for its absence?

Select the best of your choices and rewrite that resolution in your own words. If there's anything you want to add or subtract, do so.

Compare your version with the author's. Look at the word choices and style. What's similar? What's different? Can you draw any useful conclusions?

19

Revision methods

When you've completed your rough draft, you are by no means finished. Depending on how rough your manuscript actually is, this third phase of the job may take a tremendous amount of work and effort. Face it. If you want to publish your fantasy work, the hard work is worth it.

I know writers who live only for the second phase of writing—the actual creative work of writing the action and dialogue, of seeing the story unspool before their mind's eye like a movie. Others enjoy the first phase—the planning—and they craft meticulous outlines, with every move and internalization considered in advance. Then there are the writers who can't wait to type "The End" so they can settle into the third phase—the revision. They love reworking dialogue and seeing their characters take final shape. Some writers enjoy all of it. Others swear they hate editing and would rather die than endure the tedium of rewriting.

No matter whether you enjoy revision or dislike it, there's no need to be confused about it, or feel lost, or dread it because you don't know what to do. Good revision can only improve your story. And if your manuscript is weak, you might as well face it and solve it.

You may be thinking that creating the story is a writer's sole task, that you're an artist and you can leave all the dull editing to others. Or you may believe that a fine editor will take you by the hand and guide your story to the next level.

Stop dreaming.

You have to be both writer and editor these days. Editors

would love to do nothing more than read manuscripts and pull them up to their full potential. But editors seldom have the time anymore. They're occupied with meetings or busy with numerous pre-production tasks that used to be handled by larger publishing staffs.

Therefore, a novelist needs to deliver manuscripts that are pretty much ready to go. This means it's time for you to hone your self-editing skills. Not only must you write your story with all the craftsmanship and passion you possess, but you should learn how to evaluate your story, size it up as to whether it's something that the public will buy, and fix its flaws. And if you become stuck at any point, you need to know how to repair whatever's wrong with your story and make it better.

Let's get started by first considering the terminology.

Revise means to look again, to see with fresh eyes.

Rewrite means to write a scene, chapter, dialogue, description, or a transition from a new angle, probably with a different outcome.

Polish means to spiff up your diction, punctuation, and grammar. It means to tighten, to rip out passive verbs and trim your reliance on adverbs and adjectives.

I could lead you step by step through a detailed, meticulous revision process, but my approach might not be the best one for you. Although you'll have to devise your own optimal working method—just as you will determine your best daily page quota or preferred writing time—there are a few key things to know that will help you stay on track, improve your manuscript, and avoid blunders.

My strongest recommendation is that you plan your story carefully at the onset, then write the first draft as quickly and with as much heart as you can pour into it without second-guessing yourself or re-doing sections as you go. Then cool off and revise as objectively as possible.

When you're writing short stories, try to write the first draft in one session. That will enable you to capture the verve and flavor of the story conflict with less chance of distraction.

Alas, if only a novel could be written as quickly. Instead, it's a long-term investment of time, effort, thought, and emotion. The rough draft is going to be very rough indeed, with ragged edges, gaps, soft spots, pacing sometimes spot-on or off-kilter, wobbly scenes, erratic viewpoint, and flat characters that simply refuse to come alive. Writing it takes so long that you'll have ample opportunities to doubt your story and feel tempted to throw the whole thing away.

Don't.

At least show your idea enough respect to write it to the end, no matter how rotten you fear it might be. Complete the first draft despite its imperfections. Then if you want to hide it in your attic, do so.

We writers are emotional, passionate, creative, and imaginative creatures. It's easy for us to get wound up about a project as complicated as a book. We start thinking the manuscript's worse than it actually is. Or we imagine that it's better than it will ever truly be.

The worst trap to fall into is the revise-as-you-go mentality, where you feel that each scene or chapter has to be perfected before you can go forward. That's foolish and counter-productive for about ninety percent of the writing population. Although occasionally a writer will claim to work that way, you're more likely to grind the life from your copy. And if you revise the first chapter again and again and again without ever getting to chapter two, how will you ever advance to the dark dismal middle or the climax?

Don't worry about the revision process until you've completed a rough draft.

Then, and only then, prepare yourself to tackle the third phase of producing a manuscript.

Take a reality check

If you've never attempted a novel before, don't set up impossible expectations for it. Your first book manuscript is probably going to be what we call a "learning novel."

That means that it's always going to be quirky and lopsided. Some of the plot holes will never be fixable, and the concept may be too derivative of every successful fantasy novel already published. Still, it's not wasted effort. Writing it will teach you a great deal and prepare you for tackling your second learning novel, which will train you to write your third.

How many learning novels must you write until you get the hang of things? I can't answer that question. It's up to you.

How much story sense do you have? How much talent do you possess? How willing are you to practice writing technique until you've mastered it? How far can you bring yourself to trust the techniques and writing formulas I've shared with you?

To paraphrase the old writing adage, you have to write about one million words of junk before you begin to produce stories that are any good.

Does that discourage you? (Then you may have talent but lack sufficient desire to be a writer.)

Does it fire you up to meet the challenge? (Then you have plenty of desire. Just make sure you master enough writing craft to harness it.)

Revision tips

Know what you're tackling

There are two general types of revision—writer revision and editorial revision. The first involves bringing the story as closely as possible to the writer's intended plan. The second deals with following an agent's or editor's instructions to improve the story and boost its chances of mass appeal.

You will have worked very hard to write and revise your novel. You may feel satisfied with it. However, perhaps the acquisitions editor of a publishing house expresses interest in your tome about magical eagles living in the Transylvanian Mountains but wants the length shortened, the characters developed more, events added to shore up the sagging mid-point, and two viewpoints eliminated. These can seem like contradictory instructions, when in fact they aren't. Writers and editors may share similar concepts, but they sometimes use different terminology. It's the writer's responsibility to interpret editorial instructions correctly in order to make acceptable changes.

Successful revisions are methodical

Don't run in all directions simultaneously. Maybe you can combine two or three tasks, or maybe you accomplish more when you perform only one revision task at a time. Maybe you'll decide you don't need to address certain issues in your manuscript. Maybe you'll go too far and throw out the best passages instead of what most needs cutting.

Don't assume that your flat characters will go unnoticed because you've written such terrific hooks in every chapter. When you know your story has a weak spot, fix it. Don't deny it.

Bite off what you can chew

Set yourself a checklist and work steadily. You're less likely to overlook details if you aren't scattered. Think about what needs to be done, and rank the tasks in order of priority. For example, don't bother with spelling and punctuation corrections until the middle scenes have been rewritten and a new climax is in place.

Don't experiment

The purpose of revision is to make a story better. If something doesn't need tweaking, leave it alone. If you're trying to prepare a manuscript for possible publication, don't tinker just for the sake of making changes.

Let your computer work for you

Although it seems very obvious, I frequently encounter amateur writers who ignore such common sense. Your word-processing software comes with spelling, punctuation, and grammar checks. Since you're writing fantasy, if you're using Word software, your manuscript will contain numerous red squiggles because Word doesn't recognize Bronikle, for instance, as a character name. It accepts lamias and elves, but it doesn't acknowledge the existence of whiffenpoofles or oolenghouls. It sternly rejects pseudo-Latin for spells, and balks at invented geographic locations such as Pecullan Falls.

With fantasy terms and exotic names sparking red on every page, it's immensely tempting to turn off the spell check function. That's fine, as long as you turn it on again for revision purposes. In this day and age, with all that computers do for us—I find few things as annoying as reading a sentence like this: *The small dark fox sliped on the ice befor vanishing into it's lair.*

The above sentence contains two typos and a punctuation error. My computer flagged the spelling mistakes in red, and the punctuation mistake (it's instead of its) in green.

When I encounter such a sloppy sentence it tells me 1) that the writer was too careless to read over his copy before submitting it; and 2) that the writer has turned off the computer functions that would have flagged these problems.

Do not sabotage your computer's capability to help you.

The computer cannot catch all the errors, of course. It can't distinguish whether you mean to, too, or two. It's confused by extremely long and complex sentence structure. And occasionally its suggested correction is wrong.

That doesn't mean it still can't be of invaluable service to you as you proof your manuscript. Put it to work. And if you can't tolerate all the red squiggles under your protagonist's noble name of Hermithrogarken, then add that to your computer's vocabulary list.

Revision phase 1

As soon as you type "The End" at the conclusion of your rough draft, save it to a thumb drive, save it to an external hard drive, email it to yourself, save it in Dropbox or elsewhere on The Cloud if you trust it, and print it out on paper. Lightning strikes, electricity spikes and surges, viruses attack—all sorts of horrors can befall computers and garble document files. Create insurance by not leaving your manuscript vulnerable to destruction or loss.

In the years before thumb drives were invented, I would store a paper copy of my manuscript-in-progress in my refrigerator. I lived in an old house with antiquated wiring, and I thought that in case of fire, the refrigerator would save my book. Then a friend who experienced a kitchen fire told me that the plastic insides of modern refrigerators melt and my manuscripts weren't safe there. I had to find other safeguards. Although I regret the demise of antiquated, porcelain-on-steel refrigerators, there are fireproof file cabinets, fire safes, and—as already mentioned—electronic copies. These days, I sometimes put a backup thumb drive in the bank just in case.

Even if you feel that your manuscript is safely under a charmed spell of protection, you will need backup copies of your original version for the revision process. Sometimes we rewrite scenes or several chapters, only to decide our first version was better. If you've edited your one and only copy, how do you undo it?

Revision phase 2

Your mind may be teeming with ideas of what you want to change, but resist the temptation to start revising immediately. Make notes of what you want to do. Maybe you didn't understand your protagonist's true nature until you wrote the climax. That's when you experienced an epiphany of brilliant insight. You see where you need to re-design her characterization. Wonderful! Make notes. Do not rely solely on your memory. Then put your manuscript aside for a month.

Yes, put it aside for four weeks. Leave it alone.

This rest period is necessary because of how the human brain works. Being a two-hemisphere organ, the brain operates in one hemisphere or the other but not simultaneously in both. Writing is directed by one hemisphere and editing by the other. That's why you shouldn't try to create and edit at the same time. Attempting it will very likely confuse and stress you.

If you've written a short story, you can set it aside for a week or two. But because you've spent months, perhaps even a year, writing your novel, the cool-down period will take longer. The purpose of the wait is to detach you from your emotional involvement with the story and characters so you can become an editor.

Objectivity takes separation, time, and distance. Treat yourself to a well-deserved break. Come out of your writing cave. Indulge in fun activities or go on a trip. Doing so might inspire your next plot. See movies. Visit museums or art galleries. Feed your imagination. Sit on a beach. Walk in the woods. Take up a new hobby or resume a neglected one. Clean out your closets. Play.

Revision phase 3

When it's time to commence work, go back through your notes and systematically tackle the small changes you've been wanting to make. Don't jump randomly from one thing to another. Organize the job and deal with one correction at a time through the entire manuscript. An example would be changing your antagonist's motivations. Or, if you're removing a viewpoint, make sure you comb carefully through every chapter to be sure you haven't overlooked any shifts to that character's perspective. Perhaps you've decided that your protagonist will be tall, with lavender eyes flecked with deepest purple. Find every descriptive reference and make it consistent. Or maybe you've chosen a ferret to be your villain's familiar. Introduce the creature vividly and add insertions where it's to appear each time.

If you're changing a character's motivations or goal, be aware that it will affect every scene which that character appears in. Don't rush the job. Take your time. Such rewriting isn't done quickly. Give it your full attention. If you're mending a plot hole, remember that you'll need to write a transition for the new material. There will be later consequences to include as well.

Warning—large rewrites and shifting of passages means there will be gaps in the manuscript. Worry about them later. Save major rewrites for Phase 6.

If you've decided to change a character's name, make the computer work for you by running its search-and-replace function.

Revision phase 4

Print out a paper copy of your manuscript if you don't have one already. Put it in a three-ring binder for ease of reference. You may want to attach tabs to mark pages that are chapter headings. Go through the manuscript, numbering each scene in the margin.

When you've done that, create a chart of all your significant plot developments. List them in the order they occur.

Are they in straight chronological order, start to finish? Or did you jump back and forth in story time, as events occurred to you?

If your chart is the former type, do you think your story might be dull, stodgy, and predictable?

If your chart is the latter, are you too random and chaotic to follow?

Now consider your scene order for best dramatic effect and for least amount of predictability. You want your story to make sense, but it should also be quick, exciting, and filled with unexpected twists. Modern readers are sometimes impatient with stories that follow a steady, linear, start-to-finish chronology. If they're "web thinkers," they'll like multiple viewpoints, judicious flashbacks, and jumps ahead in the story with brief, internalized summaries of what was skipped.

Now, take a pad of sticky notes—all in the same color, yellow for example—and write a brief descriptive sentence of each scene, one per note. Number them in the order on your chart, as they occur in your rough draft. If you have a long table, or a blank expanse of wall, arrange the scene notes across it in their charted order. Sticking them in place will keep them from being scattered by your cat or a breeze from the window.

Stand back and think about your story in general. What section of it feels dull and slow? If you put scene twenty, for instance, where scene eleven is, would that shake things up? Maybe doing so would create excitement in what's presently a slow spot. However, moving scene twenty will leave you without the Big Scene you need in your book's middle.

Fair enough. You'll have to write a new central story event for the spot that scene twenty formerly occupied. Make a note of it.

Maybe you decide to shift a subplot to a later section of the story. Find the scenes that belong to it, and move them on the wall.

Should you introduce a vivid sidekick in chapter two instead of chapter six? Move that scene accordingly.

Keep shifting until you have a story that makes sense but is more exciting. And if you need new material to fill in gaps that are created by this re-ordering, continue listing what you'll have to create.

Next, choose another color of sticky notes—pink, perhaps—and describe the sequel to each scene on your original chart. Number each sequel to correspond to the scene it should follow.

Look for scene one. Is it now in five's position? Stick sequel one to scene one. Have you created a scene cluster to create a big event? Maybe scenes six, seven, and eight are now jammed together. Stick sequels six, seven, and eight together and place them following scene eight. They will need to be rewritten into one big sequel to address the entire scene cluster. Make a note of that on your to-do list for new material.

Did you manage to write any Big Scenes? Do you have at least three in your story? Have they been moved in the shuffle? Even if they're still in their original positions, do they seem awkward or inadequate now that other scenes have moved?

Consider whether you need to rearrange the Big Scenes or whether you need to rethink them now. Note such decisions on your to-do list.

As you move scenes, remember that their new placement also will affect where viewpoint is shifted.

Think about how different scene placements will affect your subplots and their resolutions. Will they still make sense?

How will hidden story be affected?

If you grow confused, refer to your chart of the original scene/sequel order in your rough draft. You can always move scenes back to where they were, if necessary.

Revision phase 5

Ready to put on your rewriting hat and tackle your changes? Wait!

Think first about your settings, the culture your characters belong to, their species if they aren't human, their clothing and architecture, their climate, their money system, their weaponry, their religion or superstitions, and their sources of magic.

Have you included these details intrinsically in your story? Or have you been vague, glossing over information you never got around to inventing? Or—despite all my warnings—have you loaded chapters with immense info-dumps?

Perhaps your conception of how magic works in the story world has changed since you wrote the story's climax. Maybe the only way to achieve a reversal was to give your protagonist a special ability that now needs to be planted and demonstrated much earlier. Can you perhaps fit it into the character's introduction through action? Note it on your to-do list.

Maybe you meticulously designed the climate before you started writing the rough draft, but partway through you decided you wanted the story set in a desert instead of wooded mountains. Consider now how that change in terrain affects the culture, customs, clothing, and economy. What details need alteration? Where?

Examine hidden story. Have you allowed enough story time for your protagonist's brother to travel by magic carpet from one side of the world to the other? Even if events in the hidden story aren't going to be revealed to readers, check to be sure they could plausibly occur.

Revision phase 6

It's time to write a new draft. You aren't starting over from scratch. You aren't changing your original concept. You aren't selecting a different protagonist (unless you picked the wrong character in the first place).

Instead, you're following your notes, writing new transitions to weave shuffled scenes into the story's fabric. You're rewriting dialogue to include a new character. You're altering the A/R units in scene conflict because of changed character motivations. You're shortening some sequels and lengthening others.

You're moving blocks of copy here and there within your manuscript computer document. And you're running many search-and-replace changes.

Again, be systematic. Tackle all the sequels. Or make the viewpoint changes before you move to writing dialogue. Deal with the fact that your protagonist can now cast spells instead of simply foretelling the future.

As you rewrite a scene, for example, pull the corresponding sticky note off your wall. It will give you a psychological boost as you visibly make progress.

Revision phase 7

With the big changes in place, your plot reconstructed, and your characters more plausibly motivated, now you can shift your editorial attention to smaller details.

It's time to check your technique by considering the following questions.

- Are story goals clear?
- Do luck and coincidence play a part in any of your story events?

- Does every scene end in a setback?
- Is your protagonist happy with obvious solutions?
- Are conflict and opposition steadily becoming stronger?
- Could you make any of your Big Scenes bigger?
- Do your sequels show emotion before planning and decision?
- Are you protecting your protagonist?
- Are your characters appealing?
- Are your characters HUGELY exaggerated?
- Does each character—important or minor—have a set of tags to aid reader identification?
- Do you like your protagonist?
- Do you dislike your antagonist?
- Is there any character in your cast that you feel sorry for?
- Is there any character you feel indifferent about?
- Does each character speak in a distinct, individual way?
- Is your protagonist capable of surprising readers?
- Is there any sympathetic aspect to your villain?
- Have you remembered to set up at least one ticking clock?
- Are time pointers clearly indicating day or night, or the passage of time?
- If you're writing traditional fantasy based on a pseudo-medieval model, do you have

anachronisms of modern slang, time references based on clocks, showers, and poor understanding of blade weapons, combat tactics, or horses?

- Does the climax offer an obligatory scene?
- Have you skipped any steps in constructing your climax?
- Have you resolved all the questions?
- Is poetic justice served to all?

Revision phase 8

With rewrites and changes in place, print out another paper copy of your manuscript. Look at its physical appearance.

- Do all your chapters start on a new page? They should.
- Are all your chapter headings consistently capitalized or numbered? You have leeway in the style you choose. Just stick with the same one.
- Have you inadvertently mis-numbered your chapters? For example, do you have two Chapter 7s?
- Have you set up a header for your manuscript, one that states your last name, the manuscript's title, and the page number?
- Is your manuscript all in the same, consistent font?
- Is your manuscript double spaced?
- Look at how your chapters open. Do they all have identical beginnings? For example, do they all start with description? Or dialogue. Vary them.

- Look at how your chapters end. Do you ever end chapters with your protagonist falling asleep? Do you think that will keep readers turning pages? End chapters instead with strong hooks. Scene setbacks work very well. Decisions at the end of sequels that point to action ahead will also keep readers turning pages.
- Make sure your hooks vary. Avoid predictable patterns.
- Are all your paragraphs the same length?
- Are all your scenes the same length?
- Are all your chapters the same number of pages?

Readers are more interested in compelling characters and exciting story action than identical patterns of appearance.

Revision phase 9

Do you feel exhausted by the very prospect of so much work? The secret to whittling down this monumental revision task is to master writing technique.

In other words, if you've planned well, and your characters are vividly introduced in action, if they show powerful motivations and clear goals, if your scenes are centered on conflict and end in setbacks, and if your sequels supply emotion and logic, then you'll have less to do when it comes to revision.

Phase 9 is about polishing the manuscript, making it tidy and looking its professional best.

A sloppy manuscript shows no pride from the person that authored it. Doesn't your hard work deserve better? As a Tor editor once commented to me, "Why should I read someone's book if he doesn't take any pride in it?"

Polishing means tightening your sentences and eliminating the clutter of adjectives and adverbs in favor of strong nouns and verbs. It means paying attention to your word choices and syntax. It means using a style that's clear but appropriate to your book's setting.

Consider the following questions:

- Are your descriptions focused on dominant impressions?
- Have you eliminated massive information dumps?
- Are your sentences convoluted and awkward? Do they make sense?
- Have you run your computer's spell check program? And, more importantly, have you proofread every word?

Revision phase 10

Take another break. Set the manuscript aside for a couple of weeks and regain some of your objectivity. By now, you'll probably be sick of the story. You'll be exhausted from worrying over it, writing and rewriting, and second-guessing every decision you've made. You may be convinced that it's garbage, a total waste of effort.

Print out a fresh paper copy. Put it on your desk and leave it alone for at least two weeks.

I've always found this waiting to be the hardest part of revision. I'm very impatient, and I want the process to be finished.

But if you can, wait.

My writing teacher, Jack Bickham, recommended this last step; therefore, I'm passing it along to you.

Sit down in your usual comfortable reading chair with your manuscript and just read it as though it's a book you've taken off the shelf. If you notice a typo or something that doesn't make sense, turn down the page, but keep going. Don't start editing.

Read it for flow. Read it to enjoy the story. Read it to see if it makes sense. When you finish, think about any last minor changes you might want to make. Address the problems you found on the pages you tagged.

Now, at last, it's ready to send to publishers.

Dealing with editorial revisions

Let's say you receive an offer from a publisher who wants to launch your book, but this publishing house wants you to stay below 85,000 words. Currently your tome weighs in at a hefty 107,000 words.

After all your hard work, you have to cut it or the book deal's off the table. If you're unwise, you can protest, but an unproven writer is seldom published at excessive lengths. It has little to do with the quality of your story and a great deal to do with business economics.

It's best that you accept it and get the job done.

Now, you can cut a story and improve it far more than you may realize at the time. Or, you can cut a story and ruin it. It's all about what you remove and what you leave in.

Amateur cutting

Avoid foolish, ineffective tactics that waste your time or can potentially damage your story.

Don't key in only one space between sentences instead of two in hopes of making your manuscript shorter. Choose one or the other, but be consistent for stylistic reasons. It will not affect story length.

Don't reduce font size. Keep your manuscript easy to read.

Don't choose a peculiar, narrow font lacking serifs. Publishers generally accept Courier in 12 pitch or Times New Roman in 14 pitch. The objective is to attempt roughly 250 words per full page of manuscript.

Don't set your manuscript document to single spacing. Manuscripts are double spaced.

Don't eliminate or reduce margins. Never use less than an inch of space all around. Optimally margins should be one and one-fourth inches.

Don't start a new chapter on the same page as previous chapter text. Each new chapter starts on a new page.

Don't cut scenes to save your background information and description.

Don't preserve chapters of slow meandering through long forests or across desert wastelands.

Don't save conversations between characters that are recounting old stories, legends, and myths.

Don't keep a subplot centered around a minor character just because it's cute or your favorite cast member.

Professional cutting

The key to shortening your material without harming the story is to remove everything not needed to convey the main plotline, no matter how beautifully it's written. Still, how do you judge what's necessary? To you, everything may seem valid.

Don't rely on your subjective feelings. You can fall in love with a character that's adorable but doesn't really contribute to the story. You may have lavished hours or days writing a detailed tour of the Forbidden City of the Vampires, but although you love it and feel very proud of it, that chapter-long ramble might have to go.

So am I saying that you have to toss everything you love? Not always.

A good starting point for major cuts is within the modes

of discourse. Remember their effect on pacing? Let that guide you.

The slowest material—and therefore the least important—will be passages of exposition. Your history of the werewolf clans of Leeds doesn't have to go completely, but reduce those twenty-five pages to one. And make that one page count.

The next thing to go should be long descriptive passages. Use dominant impression. Hit your imagery quickly and move on.

In fantasy you shouldn't eliminate exposition and description completely. They're vital elements of the genre, but they must pull their weight and not bog down the story. Remember, if you have to choose between a vibrant, action-packed scene of conflict and your explanation of how magic first came to the land of Fairwater, keep the scene.

Next, if you need to cut more, look at the minor scenes. Can any of them be reduced to narrative summary?

Do all your sequels spread across several pages? Shorten some of them. Maybe you're relying too heavily on review and flashbacks in your sequels. If so, trim those.

If more cutting is necessary, move to the subplots. Can the least important of them be removed without hurting the story? If so, take it out. Sometimes the removal of a subplot will also necessitate the elimination of a secondary character or two. This is painful, but you can save the material for another story. Remember that just because you cut a character it doesn't mean you've killed her. Showcase her in a plot of her own.

Usually, such cuts will tighten your book nicely, and the focus will shine brighter on the central plotline.

When my first novel was accepted for publication, I had already cut it on my agent's recommendation. But one of the contract stipulations was that I reduce its length by half. I had to remove nearly 300 pages. So I understand precisely what it feels like to rip a carefully crafted manuscript apart and put it together again. The experience taught me an invaluable lesson in how to set priorities among the story elements, and how to be disciplined enough to keep the central plot focused and tight.

And should the cuts I've already suggested still not reduce your pages as much as the editor requests, then as a last resort—and with great care—reduce and shorten some of the main plot. Eliminate the least vital plot events or summarize them, and save your best, biggest, most conflictful scenes for the spotlight.

As always, whenever you cut your story's fabric, you'll have to mend it. This will require sentence-length transitions and tweaking here and there. Smooth over the patch jobs as best you can.

Critique groups

Do you belong to a writer's group? Are there professionals in the membership, or is everyone an amateur still trying to break in?

Personally, I've never relied on a group for feedback. Writers are often solitary creatures. We need to shut ourselves away where there are minimal distractions in order to concentrate on our writing.

I've found the biggest drawback to a writer's group to be the practice of someone reading his work aloud and then being lauded and praised, regardless of whether it's deserved. If you need that sort of encouragement and support and you don't intend to write for a living, then by all means enjoy the social fun of such gatherings. Sometimes, however, you can read your work aloud to a gathering of amateurs who don't understand what you're attempting. They may shoot down what's actually good in your writing while praising the story building you've done or your magic system. In such instances, they are inadvertently leading you astray and blunting your story instincts.

My suggestion is that you select one or two people you trust who read fantasy voraciously and have developed a very good sense of story as a result. They should not be writers. Let them read your manuscript—or certain chapters—for feedback on the story.

Does it flow? Did they understand the story action? Did they bond with the characters? Do they feel that something's implausible? Did the story drag? Was it too rushed? Were they confused at any point?

If they try to please you by praising everything, then they're worthless for feedback. Find someone else or rely on yourself.

If you have a group of friends who are really serious about writing and are all trying to break in, brainstorming sessions when you're trying to plot can be fun and useful. Just make sure these people really are your friends and they won't try to steal the best ideas for themselves.

If you belong to a writer's group that has published professionals among its members, try to acquire a mentor from their ranks. Don't pester this individual or expect her to read your work, but consult with her when you're stuck or can't figure out how to set up a certain kind of scene.

Check your favorite novelists' web sites to see if they write blogs or offer writing tips. If they're appearing on panels at fantasy conferences that you can attend, ask a technical question when the opportunity arises. Writers love to talk about the writing craft, and many will be delighted to share insights with you.

Keep in mind that the pros are usually busy trying to meet their own deadlines, and they won't read or critique unpublished manuscripts. Please don't ask.

20

The road to publication

The publishing industry rocked along fairly unchanged for perhaps a hundred and fifty years or so, but a major revolution occurred in the early twenty-first century that has been turning fiction publishing upside down. With the advent of electronic books and the invention of e-readers such as Kindle, Nook, and others, the age-old barrier to self-publication has largely been swept away.

In the past, self-publication was called vanity publishing, and it was considered a ghetto for the few pitiable souls that fell into its trap. People with insufficient talent or knowledge of the craft to achieve publication in any conventional way would shell out money and pay vanity presses to print their book. Their problem then became one of distribution. Other than peddling books from the back of their car or wheedling independent bookstores into letting them sit at a table near the cash register to try to sell a few copies, they had no means of putting their book into stores or the public's hands.

Distribution, however, is no longer a problem but a breeze. Best of all, it's worldwide.

Although traditional publishers are now putting out both physical copies and ebooks, and some ebooks are published first in digital format by their authors before being picked up by a traditional publisher, let's attempt to deal with the topic as simply as possible.

Generally, writers with manuscripts have two basic options. They can submit their work to the so-called legacy or traditional publishers, or they can upload their work to a digital platform and market it themselves through the Internet. Each approach has its advantages and disadvantages. You'll have to decide which one will fit you best.

Traditional publishing

If you choose to go this route, the first thing you should do is find a literary agent to represent you. Agents need clients and they're looking all the time for new talent. However, they need saleable clients who can write publishable manuscripts steadily and reliably. Agents don't have time for hobbyists who write sporadically as the muse strikes them.

Until you're proficient at writing novels—and you've gotten your million words of junk out of the way—you don't need an agent because you shouldn't be submitting your work.

If your aim is to write short stories, you don't need an agent to represent you, and you can market your stories directly to magazines and anthologies, whether in traditional print or online.

Agents are in the business to make money by representing clients with top-notch manuscripts. Publishers rely on agents these days to serve as a screen or filter against hobbyists, flakes, and promising unknown writers who are almost but not quite ready.

The agent serves two primary purposes: 1) to market a writer's novels to established, reputable publishers who will issue a book contract and an advance of money toward eventual royalties; 2) to negotiate and monitor a writer's publishing contracts.

Therefore, an agent is a deal maker, someone who can understand the terms of publishing contracts, who knows which rights you should sell and which you should withhold from the agreement, and who is authorized on your behalf to collect the money your book earns.

Having an agent doesn't automatically guarantee you

publication. The agent isn't obligated to hold your hand, or help you write your books, or loan you money.

The author–agent relationship is a business partnership. You should choose your agent carefully because this individual must be someone you can trust and rely on. The agent works for you, and as long as your work sells, making income that earns the agent his commission, the partnership will last. But if your sales diminish, or you start writing bad manuscripts that no one will buy, the agent will probably drop you from his client list. That's the way the business works.

You can find agents—as well as publishers—by consulting the annual *Writers' & artists' yearbook*, by attending writers' conferences, and through networking. Be aware that any individual that wants to be a literary agent can open an office. Check into how long the agent has been in business, what sorts of fiction the agent represents—and fantasy had better be on the list—how much experience the agent has had, whether she is accepting new clients, and how long she takes to decide whether she'll represent a manuscript, what her rate of commission is, and whether she requires a written agent–author contract.

An agent can be brand new, but perhaps she's worked as a book editor for the past twelve years at a major publishing house. She has contacts and experience. Because she's starting up a new venture, she'll be eager to build a client list of established writers and new unknowns.

Avoid agents who live far away from any major metropolitan publishing center, charge fees to read your manuscript, or will accept you as a client only if you'll pay them to help you edit your manuscript.

Look at a prospective agent's web site. If any submission guidelines are provided, follow them exactly. Most often you'll send the agent what's known as a "partial." This includes a brief letter of self-introduction that describes essentially what your book is about thematically. (Use the SPOOC to help you pitch succinctly.) If you've been published before, provide the particulars. Briefly mention whether you plan to write a series or what you're currently working on. Include a brief plot synopsis, summarizing what happens in the story from start to finish. The synopsis should be ten pages or less. And add the first three chapters of your novel.

Don't send a query of this kind to an agent—or directly to a publisher—if you don't have the entire novel completed, revised, and ready. So often, I talk to unpublished writers who meet an agent at a writer's conference, pitch their story, receive interest, and are then too eager and impatient to wait until they're done. If the manuscript's not ready, don't approach agents or editors until it is.

Although it may seem like agony to discipline yourself and wait, what happens if you submit a manuscript when it's rough and not fully polished? The rejection will feel doubly devastating, and chances are you'll be too discouraged to finish your project.

If an agent accepts you as a client, congratulations! You've crossed an important hurdle.

The standard rate for agent commissions is fifteen percent of your book's domestic earnings and twenty to twenty-five percent for book rights sold to foreign publishers or film options. Although some of the older agents operate on a handshake agreement with their clients, most representatives today insist on a contract of some kind. It's for their protection as well as yours. Read it carefully, especially the clauses regarding how you terminate representation if necessary. If there's anything you don't understand, ask questions.

Make sure your contract operates on a project-by-project basis and doesn't permit the agent to represent your entire literary output, which would prevent you from selling anything on your own. When you have a good agent, you will never want to cut him or her out of a deal, but sometimes novelists want to put something independently on Kindle or sell an article or short story to magazines. Such small projects don't require representation. Chances are they won't earn enough to justify the agent's time.

Once you have representation, the agent will select editors from the publishing houses she feels are the best fit for your manuscript. She'll prepare a pitch to the acquisitions editors, and she'll submit on your behalf.

Publishing moves at snail's pace. Be prepared to wait and wait and wait. Editors are busy people. They will read incoming manuscripts that are already under contract first. Your agent may have enough clout to get you a quicker reading than others. Certainly agent-represented manuscripts are read before unsolicited manuscripts arriving directly from hopeful writers.

Various publishing houses hold monthly acquisition meetings where each editor describes a handful of manuscripts that she likes and wants to buy. If your manuscript isn't discussed in that meeting, the editor may wait for a subsequent month to pitch it again.

You must be patient when dealing with publishers. You must remember that your manuscript isn't the only one under consideration.

If you're rejected, your agent will submit your work to the next publisher on her list. You'll wait again.

To keep from fretting yourself to pieces, write your next book. Stay busy, stay determined, and stay patient. If your book's good, it will sell.

Once you're offered a contract, your agent will advise you whether to accept it or negotiate for a better offer. Your agent will discuss the terms of the contract. Once you sign it you can celebrate.

Just don't run out and spend money. Payments are issued slowly. Checks are sent to your agent who will deduct her commission and forward the remainder to you. Royalties, if any, are tabulated twice a year. Meanwhile, you will have revisions to do and page proofs to check over. Production of a book takes approximately nine months to a year, depending on which month it's scheduled for release.

A cover artist will be commissioned to design your book's appearance, and the editor will write the blurb copy for the cover.

Will you have any input into the book cover? Probably not.

Will you get to choose the typeface or the swirling graphics around each chapter heading? No.

Can you stipulate that the print not be so tiny that your elderly grandmother can't read it? No.

By contract, these decisions are for the publishing house to make.

You may be asked to write a glossary of arcane terms, if your book is riddled with them. You may be asked to draw a map, although your sketch will probably be refined by a professional map artist.

It's rare these days that manuscripts and edits are shipped back and forth from your home to the editorial offices on paper—although each publisher uses different methods. One of my publishers always mailed a paper version of the copy edits for me to check over. Another publisher converted mid-contract from scanned paper pdfs to electronic tracking changes sent via email.

Even if your idea of technology is ye olde quill pen, you still have to keep abreast of new editing tools. Chances are, by the time my advice reaches your hands, technology will have changed again.

Book contracts

Whether you have a literary agent or choose to submit on your own, you should always read a contract carefully before you sign it, and ensure you understand what you've read. Once your signature inks the line, you are legally obligated to abide by the contract's stipulations.

Publishing contracts vary in length, but they all tend to have similar clauses. Some clauses can be negotiated by you or your literary representative for better terms, and some are iron-clad.

When you write a work of fiction, you are legally the "creator" of the work. You own all the rights to it. When you seek publication, you'll either sell a portion of your rights to the publisher, or you may sell all rights. The latter means you'll no longer control what happens to the story. Obviously you should retain as many rights as you can and sell as few as possible to any one market.

If you're selling a short story, for example, to a fantasy magazine, you want to sell First U.K. Serial Rights or First North American Serial Rights. In exchange for money, you're giving the magazine the right to publish your story for the first time in a serial publication. If you're selling a novel, you're relinquishing First U.K. Book Rights. Later, your agent will attempt to sell First North American Book Rights, and then to additional countries, one by one.

Short story contracts are usually very brief—only a page or two. Book contracts, however, can run to several pages.

The first portion of a book contract establishes that you're the author and that it's legal for you to sell publication rights. You're also indicating that you haven't plagiarized someone else's material—which means you haven't lifted entire passages verbatim from George R. R. Martin's *The game of thrones* and you haven't libeled someone. Libel, incidentally, means to defame someone in print. Although you're writing fiction, you can be sued if you inadvertently assign someone's real name to your villain and the real individual feels he's suffered as a result. Still, fantasy fiction is at less risk of being slapped with a defamation lawsuit than other genres, such as political thrillers. Furthermore, in case of a lawsuit, an author is responsible for his or her own legal fees. The publisher—if you get yourself into legal trouble—won't spend money to help you.

There's nothing in these clauses that you can change or negotiate. You needn't worry about them unless you have been copying chunks of a published writer's chapters. In which case, shame on you for thievery.

Also, the publisher takes on the responsibility for registering your book's copyright with the government in your name.

Your contract should contain a clause regarding what will happen if the publisher goes bankrupt before your book is published. A friend of mine spent a year researching a nonfiction book, only to see the company go under within days of his submitting the manuscript. His book—although promoted and scheduled—has never been published, and he can't get the rights back to sell it elsewhere.

A clause you can negotiate and should check very carefully is the delivery clause. This is the date by which you'll submit the completed manuscript, if you've made a sale based on a partial sample of the work. Or it can be the date when your revisions are due. Take this deadline very seriously. If you fail to meet it, you run the risk of seeing your deal crumble. If the agreement is terminated, you're required to repay any money the publisher has advanced to you.

I was taught that a professional always meets the deadline. Of course, editors aren't ogres. If you encounter a disaster and need two or three extra weeks, you can request an extension. But never rely on this. A manuscript under contract is a manuscript that has been scheduled and possibly advertised. I was unable to get a deadline extension when my entire house flooded from a broken hot water pipe in the dead of winter, and I spent months thereafter camped in a friend's house because my home was unlivable and under repairs. I was unable to get a deadline extension when I broke my knee and couldn't quite reach my desktop computer's keyboard because of the wheelchair. In both instances, my editor wasn't being unkind in denying me an extension. The books had been put into the scheduling pipeline already and had been advertised as coming out in a particular month. There was no leeway to grant me, which meant I had to get the job done. (I did.)

Another clause you should examine is the length of time between your delivery of the manuscript and when the book actually hits the shelves or online markets. Don't agree to a two-year or longer lag, especially if you're to be paid money on publication. Negotiate for no more than one year, which is plenty of time for a physical book to go through production.

The royalties and advance clause is very important. Books are sold for a certain retail price, and authors receive a percentage of that. It's usually ten percent of a hardback's price and six to eight percent of a paperback's. Publishers get a whopping share, don't they? But that's because they're taking on the huge costs of paper, ink, cover art, promotion, shipping, and the salaries of people to copy-edit your manuscript, design the font style and cover art, etc. They also sell books to bookstores at a discount, which whittles down their profit a bit more. Keep in mind that your contract will also contain clauses granting the traditional publisher your electronic rights.

It's common practice in the industry for publishers to advance a portion of the expected royalties to authors up front. Your agent will advise you on the amount and whether it's a good offer or just an acceptable one. Don't expect to be paid millions for a first novel. As long as you're an unknown, your advance will be in the four figures, or possibly very low five figures.

There will be a clause stipulating how many free author copies you'll be given. The contract may mention ten copies. Negotiate for twenty or thirty. When they arrive, don't hand them out gratis to all your friends or family. And don't sell them. Store them where they'll stay clean and in good condition. You'll need them someday when your agent is trying to market your work to foreign publishers. Years from now, you may have the only copy left in print when a movie deal or a new digital rights offer comes your way.

Should you want to sell copies yourself at book signings and family gatherings, you can purchase copies from the publisher at a sizable discount.

Most book contracts will contain what's known as an option clause. This gives your publisher the right to see your next work of fiction before any other competitor. Perhaps, by the time your first novel is published, you're disillusioned with Zombie Crawl Press and you'd like to submit your next book to Witchery Books, Ltd. instead. But the option clause will stipulate that you must show your new work to Zombie Crawl first, and you can't submit it elsewhere unless and until Zombie Crawl rejects it.

If Zombie Crawl's editors like your second book and make you an offer, you can turn it down and then submit elsewhere. However, it's possible that Zombie Crawl's editors don't care for your second book. They don't want to buy it but they don't want competitors like Witchery Books publishing it either. So they'll sit on your manuscript for months, holding you in limbo.

This practice is maddening, so in contract negotiations try to limit the option clause as much as possible. Instead of granting Zombie Crawl Press an option on your "next work of fiction," reword the sentence to read, "next novel of witchcraft for young adults," which Zombie Crawl is unlikely to publish. Also, make sure there's a time limit on how long Zombie Crawl can hold the option until a decision is reached. Three to six months to give you an answer isn't unreasonable.

Your contract should also give you the right of approval of any changes made to your manuscript. This means that the editors must send you the proofed and edited versions—which may come to you as paper or in an email attachment of track changes. You'll first receive the editor's marks and requests for changes, which you usually have a short time to address. Next, you'll be sent the copy edit, which is where your manuscript has been combed for fact and consistency errors, research problems, typos, or the manuscript has been altered to conform to the publishing house's particular grammatical style. You'll have about fourteen days to review the changes and deal with any corrections. After that, you'll receive page proofs whereby the manuscript has been converted to type and the page margins set up as they'll appear in the actual book.

Page proofs also have a short turnaround of about fourteen days. Don't assume that you've read over the story enough times by then. The type conversion can create new errors. Sometimes a sentence is left out, or words are transposed. Remember that readers find errors irritating, and they always blame the author. Why not? It's your name on the cover.

Although I've touched briefly on the most critical aspects of a book contract, there are many other clauses and issues you should prepare yourself to consider. Clauses regarding electronic rights are very important to examine carefully. Try to retain as many of them as you can.

For more information on deciphering book contracts, refer to *How to be your own literary agent* by Richard Curtis (2003). Mr. Curtis is an American literary agent with considerable experience. Despite the book's title, he's not advocating that authors represent themselves, but his thorough explanation of contracts is a valuable reference.

Online information is also available from sources such as www.authorsguild.org and www.writersdigest.com. If you join large writers' organizations, often they will provide information and tips on handling contracts.

Digital publishing

Perhaps you feel intimidated by the long, slow process of submitting your book to prospective agents and editors.

Or perhaps you're confident in your vision and your book, and you're too impatient to wait so long for conventional production methods.

Or possibly you've tried submitting your manuscript the conventional way and been rejected. Now you want to try a different route.

You can approach digital publishers such as Diversion Books, Lulu.com, BookBaby, and Booktango, who are hybrids between traditional publishing and self-publication. Some of these companies primarily seek the backlists of established authors, assisting them in the myriad tasks of readying their older books for digitized formats. Others are more focused on new work from unknown authors. A computer search will turn up several digital publishers for you to explore. Read contracts carefully and understand what rights you are possibly relinquishing and what their services, such as book cover design, will cost you.

However, if a company expects a hefty fee upfront simply for assistance in uploading your manuscript to a platform such as Kindle, be very cautious. The Internet can supply you with information on how to self-publish electronically, and here are a few pointers:

Start by selecting your platforms

Will you want to focus on just one, such as Amazon's Kindle? Or do you want to use numerous platforms, which will help your work reach a larger audience? Be advised that each platform requires its own format for your manuscript. For example, Kindle requires single-spaced copy set within specific margins. Paragraphs can't be indented with the Tab key on your computer's keyboard but instead are indented through how the margins are set in the top toolbar area of your document file.

Design your book cover

There are several options available for this task. If you know how to use Photoshop or can hire someone who does, you can make your own cover design using purchased images, photos, or copyright-free images. While your cover should pop, keep in mind that you want it to convey the essential concept of your story in a clear, easy-to-understand way. It should feature enough blank space to allow room for the book's title and your author name. And it should be eye-catching even when it appears as a postage-stamp sized icon on someone's computer screen or smartphone.

You can use the cover services provided by your platform. Just be aware that if you do, your cover will have a bland, generic look that won't stand out among your book's competitors.

You can hire a professional cover artist. Many of them are freelancers who work for both authors and publishing houses. Although some artists will agree to work for a royalty on each copy sold, you may not want to keep up with the necessary paperwork and accounting. Consider a deal where you pay the artist a flat fee of several hundred dollars up front.

Proofread your manuscript

Yes, you've done that already in revision. Proof it again. Get a friend to proof it also. Remember that if you're expecting the public to buy your book, it shouldn't be riddled with typos and misspellings.

Write the cover blurb

It should describe your story and entice readers to purchase it. (In traditional publishing, the editor does this for you.) Look at books on your shelves for ideas of how to strike the right tone in a hundred words or less.

Write an author bio and determine what price to charge

Regarding the latter, look at other fantasy e-books and see how they're priced. You shouldn't charge as much for a virtual book as you would for an actual paper copy.

Make your e-book available in print versions

Paperback editions require a different format for the manuscript and a separate upload. Pricing will also be somewhat higher than what you'll charge for an electronic version. Just don't overlook this potential slice of the market.

Prepare to promote your book

If you're shy, push past your comfort zones. Promote through every possible avenue. Make sure you take advantage of Author Profiles and Amazon's Author Pages. Goodreads allows you the opportunity to exchange Q & A with readers or to participate in Goodreads Giveaways—although the latter requires you to provide physical copies of your book. You can choose to launch your e-book as free for a limited time through Amazon in order to garner reader attention. If you belong to online groups, spread the news of your publication. If you attend events such as fantasy conferences or book signings of your favorite authors, publicize them in your blog or on Twitter and let readers know what you're doing.

Set up a web site or a blog site

Make sure it has Twitter/Facebook feeds at a minimum, and contribute to your site frequently. Look at what other fantasy authors are doing. Keep in mind, though, that well-known authors may have a large budget to support dazzling animated effects. Do your best, and don't over-spend your resources.

Once you have your site designed and up, consider whether you want to sell your work directly to readers in pdfs that they can download. As companies such as Amazon, Apple, and Barnes & Noble continue to jockey for bigger shares of author revenue, more writers are dispensing with these platforms altogether, to sell straight from their web sites and keep one-hundred percent of revenues instead of thirty-five percent, fifty percent, or possibly seventy percent.

The problem with selling straight from a web site, especially if you're an unknown writer without an established readership base, is how best to promote yourself and make the public aware of you and your work.

Determine your book's sales hook

What's unique about your story that makes it stand out? Can you tell someone what it's about in two sentences or less? (Refer to your SPOOC.)

Use a professional

If you can afford them, consider contacting professional public relations services that can promote you online.

Create a book video

Posted online via your web site or on YouTube.com, such a video—sometimes known as a book trailer—should be less than two minutes long. It should present your book's concept clearly and simply. Decide whether you want to generate a slideshow of still images or utilize actors. Music will have to be synced to the images, and may or may not be copyright free. You can hire a professional service to create the video for you. You're limited only by your skill set or your budget.

Network for online reviews

How far should you go in soliciting review quotes from published authors you don't know? A simple, single, straightforward request via email is all you can do. There should be no follow up. If the author ignores you, which is likely, leave him or her alone thereafter. I personally don't respond to such requests, especially for e-books. Some established authors will provide a review or cover quote only on request from their publisher or on a writer friend's behalf. You're better off sending a free e-book to review sources such as www.goodreads.com or the critic for your local newspaper.

21

Final suggestions

For every overnight success who is inspired by a dream, spends six weeks typing a novel, uploads it into an e-book, and is an immediate mega hit, there are the individuals who take the slow route of planning and outlining, practicing sound principles of the writer's craft, thinking through their story and their characters' personalities, and writing the very best book they can.

Whenever you hear a news splash about a Kindle author who's now being offered a mega-million deal by a traditional publisher, you may feel discouraged or left behind. Comfort yourself with Aesop's old parable of the tortoise and the hare.

Writers who are flukes burn across the media like comets and then they're gone. They may not know how they managed to slap their book together. They seldom know how to do it again.

You may be thinking that you don't care as long as you can be fabulously rich and successful.

Yes, but don't we write because we love it? And don't we enjoy doing what we're good at?

I challenge you to become good at the writer's craft. Understand the principles of elemental story design that lie beneath the rules. Practice diligently and work hard to constantly improve yourself. Author Ray Bradbury used to advise young writers to master the craft so that it becomes an intrinsic part of them, one they no longer have to think about consciously. Then you can concentrate fully on your story and characters without having to worry if you've fumbled a scene's A/R units.

Write about what moves you and what touches your heart. Put pieces of your vulnerability into your protagonists. Share your voice. Offer yourself to your readers.

And persist. Remember you can only truly fail if you give up.

Any performance art is incredibly difficult to master, much less catch the public's fickle eye. Writing is also a performing art. We authors don't have to stand on a stage and toss apples while jumping on one foot and reciting Keats, but even if we're fortunate enough to remain hidden behind the curtain, we juggle an intricate and complicated performance.

When you've written your first short story—or your eighth—and when you've written your first novel, be proud of what you've accomplished. Be proud of each story, whether it turns out the way you intended or not. Be glad you wrote it—not in false arrogance, believing you can do no wrong—but because of what you've learned as you crafted it and met the challenges it presented you.

Believe in yourself. Believe in your story, your dreams, and your ideas—even when others shoot them down. It can be very hard to keep going, but do it anyway.

And good luck!

THE END

Index

CPSIA information can be obtained
at www.ICGtesting.com
Printed in the USA
JSHW032358050522
25610JS00005B/96